I: AESTHETICS

ON ART

Literature

Painting

Architecture

Music

Contents

Music can say four or five different things at the same time, and can say them in such a way that the different things will combine into one thing. The nearest approach to a demonstration of the doctrine of the Trinity is a fugue or a good piece of counterpoint.

Painting too can exhibit the simultaneity of incompatibilities—serene composition along with agonized brushwork and the most passionate violence of color, as in so many of Van Gogh's landscapes; neurotically restless drapery, as in one of Cosimo Tura's saints or Virgins, combined with an image of beatitude or love; the final inwardness of mystical feeling expressed in the nonhuman otherness and outwardness of a Sung landscape.

We can see more than one thing at a time, and we can hear more than one thing at a time. But unfortunately we cannot read more than one thing at a time. In any good metaphor, it is true, there is a blending, almost at a point and almost in one instant, of differences harmonized into a single expressive whole. But metaphors cannot be drawn out, and there is no equivalent in literature of sustained counterpoint or the spatial unity of diverse elements brought together so that they can be perceived at one glance as a significant whole.

We are manifold amphibians falling perpetually between half a dozen stools, and so, to us, the co-existence of incompatibles is a commonplace of daily experience. But when a writer tries to render this experience of co-existing incompatibles, he is forced, by the very nature of language, to adopt a strategy, not of chords or of counterpoint, but of melodic modulation. Debarred from saying several different things at once, he must, willy-nilly, say them successively. The succession of his words and sentences may be ordered either in the obvious and sensible way—firstly, secondly, nthly; on the one hand *a* and on the other hand *b*; or else the order may be less mathematical and closer to actual experience, in which case the writer will rely on a kind of directional free association to produce a succession superficially random but subterraneously obedient to the inner logic of art. I myself have used both kinds of order. The first, I have found, makes for clarity, the second for depth and life. The first is relatively easy to achieve; the second (if the free associations are to lead to the desired goal and if the work is to be an artistic whole and not merely a specimen of automatic writing) is exceedingly difficult. I prefer the harder, second way of rendering the complexity of experience. Hence the essentially unsystematic nature of most of what I have written. In relation to the arts, for example, I have not aspired to be a methodical critic or an aesthetician with a full-blown philosophy. I have preferred to write of art without system and, so to say, tangentially. Sometimes the art is at the end of a tangent that glances off the surface of some other subject; sometimes the place of origin is a work of art and the tangents shoot out, north, south, east, and west, into other fields.

Thinking intently of the work in hand, one is apt to forget the work with which one is no longer concerned. (Hence a certain tendency on the part of writers to repeat themselves. What feels, at a given moment, like a brand-new inspiration may in fact be something written years ago, forgotten and now pushed up again into consciousness by the subliminal self.) For what he has done to remind me of my earlier reactions in a great variety of contexts to a great variety of works of art, I am grateful to Mr. Morris Philipson. Whether any gratitude will be felt by people who read these essays without having my own private reasons for gratitude, I cannot guess; I can only hope for the best.

INTRODUCTION *by Morris Philipson*

It appears to have been Aldous Huxley's intention to "know everything worth knowing," "see everything worth seeing," and "do everything worth doing"; a noble intention, but one rarely pursued in this life. Still, Huxley seems to have been more successful at it than most of his contemporaries. He has traveled through much of the world—to remote and nearly inaccessible places. His mind has traveled through time as his body in space: to the future as to the past, to the obscure, and unfashionable, or esoteric regions of thought as well as to the popular tourist centers.

If the *unexamined* life is not worth living, then Huxley's writings show us life as it is superbly worth living—performing the business and achieving the pleasure of *examining* experience, the variety and complexity of human experience; and, out of this performance, deriving the benefits of a civilized mind: comprehension without loss of comprehensiveness. For this is the overwhelming difficulty in fulfilling the demands of the "examined life": how to see experience both whole *and* clear.

More often than not, those who have the most comprehensive, diversified experiences comprehend them poorly or not at all. Whereas, those whose comprehension of one certain sphere of experience is profound have bought their speciality at the price of confined restrictions to their comprehensiveness. The distinguished *specialist*—particularly the research scientist, and the academic scholar—who is an emotional infant or a social adolescent, has been portrayed nowhere more knowingly, with both sympathy and satire, than in the novels of Aldous Huxley. Such a character may be a mature genius in his professional, impersonal life, but a terrified child in his subjective, personal life. Outside the precincts of his laboratory or study, the mind of the caricature professor is truly "absent." He is, of course, the exception and reverses the common situation. Most of us, who have developed some useful working knowledge of "the ways of the world,", are devoid of significant understanding in any specialized field of "the life of the mind." Inside a university department, a scholar's study, or a laboratory, the "common man" is a babbling and cooing baby. It seems to be an either/or condition: at best, one can see life whole *or* clear. Breadth at the price of depth; profundity at the cost of narrowness. We accept the spatial image: one cannot move in two directions at once. And we acquiesce in the prevailing attitude of our time, which sees the value of specialization—for society—as worth the price paid for it by the individual specialists.

Aldous Huxley's voice is one among those that speak against this lopsidedness in the individual, this imbalance, and insufficiency in thought; he speaks for the Good Life as a whole, the Whole Man, and the Whole of Life.

These expressions are, of course, metaphoric and cannot be taken literally. "The Whole" is not a quantity but the idea of unity, the image of fulfillment: experience fully comprehended. It is not a total to be grasped at the bottom of a column of addition, although quantities enter into it. The very idea of "Life" is an image, beginning with the biological, as the idea of "World" begins with the physical, and reaches out for a possible unity. One must begin with facts, but it is *values* that determine the relative importance of the various systems of facts to "the whole." The interpretation of "fact" is the business of the empirical sciences. And any science depends on specifying its subject matter as partial, limited; there is no "science of the whole of life." Clarity, thus, is achieved by giving up completeness; comprehension at the expense of comprehensiveness.

Nevertheless, Aldous Huxley has never betrayed the idea that the civilized mind must be as concerned with the one as with the other. The properly balanced comprehensiveness of "the whole" is as indispensable to the Good Life as is the accurately ascertained and acutely comprehended individual "part." The mind sacrifices something to both; it must give up prejudice and unjustifiable preconceptions. But it is totally passive to neither; any specific "part" being just as much a product of the imaginative intelligence as is any interpretation of "the whole."

Huxley is perfectly aware of the difficulties. They appear irresolubly paradoxical. This accounts for the extraordinary power of irony in Huxley's fiction. The "same" events or persons or situations viewed "clearly" from incompatible points of view produce the jarring juxtapositions of his points counter points. But beyond the shock of laughter, or hopelessness, or sardonic criticism which this yields— Huxley has gone on to pursue the idea that "incompatibility" is a product of the partial view, and that the possibility of reconciliation (in personal life as in the life of the mind) requires that bridges be built between the seemingly isolated, discrete categories of both behavior and thought. It is not that this intention is theoretically impossible, it is only because it demands so great an effort of intelligence and will that it has been passed up by most thinkers as a practical impossibility.

This intention alone would have been enough to characterize Huxley as a "mystic," had he not been so unfashionable as actually to study mysticism, and write about it explicitly. In much of his early writings on art, he is concerned with criticizing misleading arguments about the relations between art and other disciplines. But his purpose is corrective: to make way for such ultimate reconciliation as seems alone feasible to him. This whole development is foreshadowed in his early, and little-known, essay on Ben Jonson, where he writes: "the truth is that the greatest triumphs of art take place in a world that is not wholly of the intellect, but lies somewhere between it and the inenarrable, but, to those who have penetrated it, supremely real, world of the mystic."

The various, discrete and separable realms of art have been of as much importance to Huxley as have been the various sciences, the varieties of cultures, the different systems of social, religious, and political organizations. Opinions about artists and the arts are scattered throughout his fiction like so many polished shells along a beach. Surely, a substantial anthology could be arranged by culling these passages from Huxley's fiction, and stringing them together. But that might, in certain cases, be misleading. There he is not always speaking in his own voice. In fiction, an opinion often tells the reader more about the character than about the subject matter on which he opines. There, as often as not, Huxley has played the court jester who is allowed to say the outrageous because he does it so charmingly, and, since it is "only fiction," one need not take it "seriously." Therefore, the opinions that a fictional character expresses in one of Huxley's novels or stories cannot be compared with the reasoned positions Huxley takes, and for which he demonstrates his arguments, in his essays.

It is a typical consequence of this age of specialization that Aldous Huxley is generally thought of only as a novelist. That is his "speciality." Despite the fact that he has been writing essays in aesthetics and criticism for more than forty years, no collection of his writings on the arts alone has appeared prior to the publication of this volume.

Huxley's is a consistent mind, and the paradox of the "whole" and the "clear" informs his writings on the arts as persistently as it does his writings on philosophy, religion, social and political life. What he seeks is the clarity of appreciation of the *particular*, in the context of the unifying appreciation of the *universal*. Clarity is achieved by focus, by attention, by the principles of interpretation which yield specific meanings. Totality is aimed at by rejecting the limitations of preconceived rules, by absorbing as much as is genuine, regardless of prior theories; in sum, by the pragmatic test of what does something worthwhile for the appreciator. The two are complementary. Only by accepting the *particular* for what it is, can one develop a sense of what is appropriate and necessary to *general* understanding. Comprehension and comprehensiveness proceed reciprocally and rhythmically, to their mutual enrichment.

Huxley is not interested in taste or fashion in terms of restrictive principles that pre-limit experience. Throughout his writings one finds statements of his belief that there are "a great many kinds of merit and an infinite variety of human beings." How to do justice to it all? By being independent, open, responsive, and intellectually honest. By being willing to test ideas by experience as well as vice versa. By being as inclusive as your principles of what is genuine will allow you to absorb. What you exclude is only what is phony.

This general attitude of mind effects the structure of Huxley's essays as well as their contents. The individual study usually moves from a particular, often immediate, autobiographical instance to a significant generalization and back again; the abstract view illuminates the particular, the concrete supports the universal. Each essay has the literary suavity and polish of a single perfectly accomplished "period"; the sonata form.

This volume makes available a representative selection of Huxley's writings on art and artists. It is divided into two sections: (I) Aesthetics, and (II) Criticism. The section on Aesthetics, constituting Huxley's contributions to the theory of art, presents essays that seek to examine "bridges" between art in general and other specific activities or disciplines of thought. They are concerned with such questions as: What are the relations between art and religion? art and science? art and social, moral, or psychological values? What are the relations between individual talent and a school or tradition in a particular culture? What are the relations between art, sanity, and the preconceptions of one's *Weltanschauung?* In the Aesthetics section have been gathered together those essays that are most directly concerned with art as a "whole" in its relations with other general considerations.

In the section on Criticism, the essays and excerpted selections concentrate on particular works of art, or on individual artists, in the effort to see each separate work, or artist, as "clearly" as possible. There the subdivisions are by kinds of art, namely: Literature, Painting, Architecture, and Music. But there, as throughout the volume, specific knowledge established in one "part" only helps to make richer the understanding of another "part." This principle holds for all of Huxley's writings on art, as it does for the total body of his fiction and nonfiction. For, "ultimately," as Huxley says in "Adonis and the Alphabet," "nothing is irrelevant to anything else." Consequently, specific criticism is found in most of the pieces on Aesthetics, and principles concerning art-in-general are interfused in each article of Criticism.

The essays are gathered from a variety of books ranging in origin from the early 1920's to the late 1950's. The developments of subtlety and the expansion of power of

Huxley's mind become evident across the years. From the somewhat too facile and cynical judgments of youth, his ideas mature to exceptionally rich and firmly grounded positions. To take a small example: Van Gogh, whom he had described in a 1920's essay as possessed by a "queer pantheism," an "animistic superstition," is, in a 1950's essay, characterized as the creator of such "emblems" as are "sources of true knowledge about the Nature of Things."

The later writings of Huxley stand with one foot inside the realm of what he considers a rationally defensible mysticism. For him, the aim of seeing life "whole" as well as "clear" is achieved by accepting the conditions of such mysticism. In effect, the condition for ultimate comprehension requires recognizing the limits of rational thought only because one has used reason to its fullest. The rest may be silence (from the rationalist's point of view) but it is the singing, significant silence for one who has learned at last how to hear what does not speak to the mind.

It would not be amiss to end this Introduction with the same words of praise for Aldous Huxley as he had addressed to Piero della Francesca: "I am attracted to his character by his intellectual power; by his capacity for unaffectedly making the grand and noble gesture; by his pride in whatever is splendid in humanity." For in this, above all, Huxley is a great teacher, in enabling us to appreciate better *whatever is splendid in humanity.*

ON ART AND ARTISTS

1

On Tradition and Individual Style•

For an artist the material obstacles in the way of un-
restricted self-expression are easier to surmount than the
mental. Thus, the Maya sculptors had none but stone
implements; nevertheless, they were as highly accomplished, manually, as the best-equipped statuaries of the
age of steel. Skill and an inexhaustible patience had
taught them to transcend the limitations of their neolithic technique; they were free to do whatever they liked
with their material. "Whatever they liked. . . ." But
what did they like? The answer to that is that they liked
only what they could like, only what they were psychologically capable of liking, only what, in a word, they had
been conditioned to like. The *Zeitgeist* is just Professor
Pavlov on a cosmic scale.

People who are born into an isolated and homogeneous
community are liable to be conditioned much more strictly
than the members of a society composed of many diverse
elements and in contact with other societies, having traditions different from its own. An Eskimo never sees any
one but other Eskimos; and as Eskimo society is classless
and unspecialized, this means that he only sees people
who have been brought up in exactly the same way as
himself. Comparison is the beginning of criticism, and he

• From *Beyond the Mexique Bay* ("Quirigua"), 1934.

has nothing with which to compare the accepted conventions of his small world. With a contemporary European the case is different. He lives in a society divided into a great number of economic, professional, and denominational classes; two hours in an airplane will take him to places where people speak a different language, think different thoughts, obey other sexual taboos, and have unfamiliar table manners. The circumambient Pavlov rings a great diversity of bells; there is deconditioning and reconditioning; there are the conflicts that arise when loyalties are divided and of equal strength. Our minds, in consequence, are much less closely circumscribed than those of the Eskimos. Nevertheless, sooner or later even the most highly civilized and emancipated person comes to a mental frontier which he cannot pass—comes to it, of course, unaware, and does not realize his inability to go further; for it is of the essence of these inward barriers that they never reveal their presence, unless, as the result of some fortunate or unfortunate conjunction of circumstances, we are shaken out of our second nature and transported violently to the other side of what is thenceforward perceived to have been an arbitrary limitation of our freedom.

The Mayas occupied a position nearer to the Eskimos than to ourselves. The individual was born into a society not much differentiated (it was probably divided into only two classes, the ignorant laity and the learned priest-rulers) and in contact with other communities not very different from itself. Conditioning was not quite so strict as it is within the polar circle; but it was a good deal stricter than in modern Europe. Sculptors, as we have seen, could do what they liked with their materials. But there were certain things which they simply could not like. Perhaps the most conspicuous absence from Maya sculpture is that of the female form—*et tout ce qui s'ensuit.* True, there is, at the Peabody Museum, an incredibly beautiful terra-cotta figure from Campeche of a goddess with a worshipper resting like a tired child in her lap. It is a Maya version of the protective Madonna of Catholic Europe. Piero's at San Sepolcro is perhaps the finest example of the class—a monumental figure, spreading wide the folds of her cloak to give shelter to a group of poor mortals, whose helplessness and unhappiness have symbolically reduced their stature to that of children. This

Maya goddess is a strong mother, and the artist's treatment of the figure and the draperies beautifully expresses her character. There is no hint here of Mylitta or Diana of the Ephesians. The Maya pantheon included no goddess of love, and the heavenly person who looked after the fertility of Central American fields had none of the female —the all too female—attributes generally assigned to this deity, but was a man holding an axe—for he was the god of the thunderbolt as well as of rain—and grotesquely fitted with the snout of a tapir. The goddess represented in the Campeche statuette must have been one of the minor divinities, perhaps the object of a heretical cult.

No female principle was active in the Maya universe; and since Maya sculpture was a religious art, that concerned itself precisely with the divine Nature of Things, no representation of the female form appears among the ruins. I have seen a fair amount of Central American art and can recall only one reference to the act of generation. This was at Monte Alban, near Oaxaca, where there is a bas-relief of an ithyphallic man—the work, so far as I could make out, of the pre-Zapotec occupants of the site. There must, it is obvious, be other objects of the same kind; but they are certainly rare. Rare enough to justify us in saying that Maya sculptors were so conditioned by their environment that whatever might be their tastes in life, they found sex in art all but unthinkable.

Maya art is florid, but invariably austere; a more chaste luxuriance was never imagined. It is instructive, in this context, to compare the art of the Central Americans with that, no less richly ornamental, of the Indians. More than any other, Indian art is impregnated with sensuality. From Cape Comorin to the Himalayas, and for the last two thousand years, almost every Hindu artist seems to have been engaged in illustrating the works of Aretino. Even the most sacred persons tend to melt—and at the most solemn moment of their religious life—into suggestive postures. Buddha among the women of his father's court —here is a theme that calls for a sensual treatment. But Buddha taking leave of the world, Buddha resisting temptation, Buddha preaching—these are another story. Yet the renderings of these scenes in Indian art are of the same kind as the renderings of life in the harem. It is as though a Christian artist were to paint the Agony in the Garden in terms of Renoir's "Baigneuses," or Bronzino's "Love,

Folly, and Time." Indian art is the same outside the
Buddhist tradition as within it. The boneless limbs—dozens
of them, very often to a single personage—ooze about the
picture-space or the sculpture-volume like a voluptuous
ectoplasm. The haunches just to right or left; the waists
are tapered as though by a delicious process of suction;
even the men seem as though inflated about the chest; and
as for the women . . . But language fails. The very animals are symbols of sensuality. Elephants have the gracefully bulging appeal of Lakshmi or the girls in the seraglio
of Gotama's father; and I remember, in the Musée Guimet,
a fourth-century marble of the school of Amaravati sur-
mounted by a frieze of indeterminate quadrupeds, all
kneeling, all with their bodies bent in the shape of the
letter U, and the succession of their more than human
posteriors raised in curve after luscious curve towards the
sky. A very odd example of the pathetic fallacy.

Of all this treacly and ectoplasmic sensuality there is,
in Maya art, not the smallest trace. The female form, as
we have seen, never appears, and the male body, when
it is shown divested of its hieratic ornaments, is always
uncompromisingly male and never takes on those hermaph-
roditic attributes which distinguish gods and saviors in
Indian art. The nearest approach to the Indian spirit
is to be found in the few statues in the round which have
survived among the ruins of Copan. One of these—a beautiful head and torso of the maize god—may be studied in
the British Museum. It is a wonderfully graceful and
delicate piece of work: but its delicacy has none of the
equivocal, epicene quality of Indian elegance, and its
grace is wholly without lasciviousness.

In Indian art even the ornamental forms have a certain
sensual quality. Headdresses, bracelets, anklets tend to be
conceived as a series of rolls of flesh. A thigh with two
or three tourniquets round it—that is what the typical
Indian tiara looks like. All the lines in a passage of Indian decoration are curved, all surfaces gently swell and
retreat. The straight and the angular are of rare occurrence
in ornament, and even by the architects they are avoided
wherever possible. In such buildings as the Jambulinga
temple at Pattadkal, the Lingaraja temple at Bhuvanesvara,
or the later Kesava temple at Somnathpur (to name but a
few characteristic specimens), the Indians perfected a kind
of organic architecture, whose forms are those, not of

an abstract solid geometry, but of living tissue. Many of these temples are, in their own way, extraordinarily beautiful: but their way is an oppressive way: they give you a suffocating sense of animal heat, and their stone flesh seems as though turgid and pulsating with blood.

Maya decoration is luxuriant like a tropical forest; but it is a forest in which one can breathe freely of an air that is actually exhilarating. The life of the swarming ornaments—and they are all vehemently alive—is a life of the mind, of the imagination liberated from the obsessive warmth and heaviness of material bodies. Straight lines and angles, surfaces that are flat and perpendicular to one another—all the abstractions of pure geometry appear among the rich exuberance of the Mayas' symbolic decoration. Their sacred personages wear no Indian miters of tight-laced and bulging meat. No, their headdresses are sometimes pure geometrical abstractions, like those metal-smooth cones and cylinders worn by the people in Piero della Francesca's frescoes; sometimes, as on most of the stelae at Quirigua and Copan, they consist of fantastic combinations of decorative and symbolic motives; sometimes, best of all, they are representations of the feather tiaras worn by men of rank. These elaborate halos of feather fireworks are decorations that are at once gracefully naturalistic and as austerely abstract in their formal arrangement as the most mathematical of cubist designs.

Among the most extravagant of the Mayas' ornamental combinations are the hieroglyphs. The fantasies of Gothic decoration seem pedestrian by comparison. But however rich and strange, this extravagance is always rigidly disciplined. Each hieroglyph is contained by, and completely fills, its appointed square. The *mise en page* is almost always impeccable. These fantastic and often wildly grotesque symbols are subject to the severest intellectual discipline.

As for Maya architecture—its style is all that is most un-Indian, most abstractly inorganic. An affair of pyramids, of flat walls divided up into rectangular panels, of wide and regular flights of steps, it is an embodiment of man's most distinctively human, his most antinatural imaginings.

Indian artists, then, liked to use their skill to express sensuality through plastic symbols, to render the emotion accompanying the immediate contact of flesh with living flesh in terms of pictorial, sculptural, and even architectural forms. The Mayas, on the contrary, did not like to use their artistic skill in this way. Their decorative forms have no quality of sensuality, and they almost never made direct representations of erotic scenes or of what I may call erotically significant persons. There is no sex in the art of the Mayas; but, by way of compensation, what a lot of death! From ten onwards, all the glyphs representing numerals in their vigesimal system are variations on the theme of the death's-head. Nine faces, each with its distinguishing character and emblems, but all with the same big fleshless lower jaw. The inscriptions on the monuments are mainly concerned with the recording of dates, so that emblems of death are as common among the Central American ruins as numerals upon the stones of a modern cemetery. But death among the ruins is by no means exclusively a by-product of Maya arithmetic. Copan, for example, is full of skulls, or rather of those magnificent skull-symbols, more gruesome than any realistic imitation—those decorative abstractions in stone, by means of which the Maya sculptors expressed the idea of death with a penetrative force only surpassed, in all the history of art, by the Aztecs.

To compare two widely different artistic traditions is to find oneself, inevitably, confronted by a question. Why are the traditions different? Of two artists, both capable, so far as technique is concerned, of doing what they like, why should the one who lives in India like, and the one from Central America dislike, expressing sensuality? Why should one find in death a congenial and stimulating theme, while the other is best inspired by, indeed can hardly escape from, thoughts of sexual pleasure?

In either case, as I have already pointed out, the immediate causal agent is the Local Pavlov—the spirit pervading each particular extent of time and place. But why should the Local Pavlov have chosen to ring just those particular bells which happen to be rung, and no others? The people who believe in a determinism of Race will answer this question by saying that the Local Pavlov had to ring those particular bells, because every Local Pavlov is merely the expression of the fundamental character of the Local Race. Pavlov conditions, but has himself been conditioned by, his victims.

It is possible that there may be some small element of truth in this theory of racial determinism. Congenital differences in metabolism, nervous sensibility and, more doubtfully, intelligence have been observed as characteristic of the members of different races. Certain Melanesians, for example, seem to be, on the average, more sensitive to pain than we are; Bushmen, Australian Blackfellows, and perhaps some races of Negroes are perhaps a little less bright in the head than Europeans and Asiatics. But it must be remembered that over large areas of the earth's surface pure races are unknown. In Europe, for example, all talk about the congenital difference of one race from another (let alone its congenital superiority or inferiority) is perfectly irrelevant, for the simple reason that it is only in the remotest recesses and blind alleys of the Continent that anything like a pure race can be discovered: and even here the purity of blood is certainly not untainted. Moreover, even when pure, the race is not, biologically speaking, a true race, but only one of several variations on a single racial theme, the European. Some cultures are, in certain respects, superior to others, but the explanation of the fact must be sought in the nature of the cultural tradition, not in the congenital differences between the "races," brought up within these diverse traditions. We are back again with the Local Pavlov, and the question why one Local Pavlov should differ from another still remains unanswered.

It is possible that there are some slight congenital differences between Indians (whoever the Indians may be; for the geographical term connotes every possible combination of numerous races) and Central Americans. But I see no particular reason to suppose that the difference between the two artistic traditions is attributable to these congenital dissimilarities. Dr. Gann, it is true, has remarked several times on the apparent indifference to sexual matters displayed by the contemporary descendants of the Mayas. Can it be that the absence of all erotic themes from Maya art and its prevailing tone of austerity are due to the fact that the people were, as a whole, congenitally less interested in sex than the Indians or ourselves? It may be so, of course; but I think it improbable.

In his classical study of *The Sexual Life of Savages*

in North-Western Melanesia, Dr. Malinowski has recorded the fact that "the nervous excitability of the natives is much less than ours, and their sexual imagination is relatively very sluggish." So far as sex is concerned, the Trobriand Islanders are without faith: only unequivocal contact has power to rouse them to a state of erotic excitement. Compared with ourselves they are congenitally undersexed. And yet, as Dr. Malinowski has shown, the preoccupation of these people with sexual matters surpasses even that of the contemporary European.

In the case of the Mayas, it should be remembered that Dr. Gann's observations were made among the wretched inhabitants of the Central American lowlands. Malaria and hookworm, raw alcohol and malnutrition have reduced these people to a very low ebb of vitality. It is difficult to make love on an empty stomach, and still more difficult to make it on a duodenum that is full of *ankylostoma.* The Ancient Mayas were masters of the jungle and had all the land under intensive cultivation. Food, in their time, must have been abundant, and "full feasts," as the poet has remarked, are ever the "increasers of desire." Properly fed, the Mayas were probably as amorous as any other people; and even if their nervous excitability was not so great as ours, that would not, as Malinowski has shown, have prevented them from taking at least as much interest in sex as we do.

I think, then, that we must attribute the differences between the Maya and the Indian, artistic traditions entirely, or at least mainly, to culture rather than racial heredity. If the Local Pavlov behaves in one way rather than in another, it is not because the Local Race has such and such congenital idiosyncrasies; it is rather because a number of accidents have conspired to make him what he is. According to Marxian theory, the accidents which determine the nature of the Local Pavlov are all of an economic kind. But this hypothesis fails completely to account for the frequently observed fact that two peoples, whose economic development is fundamentally the same, have dissimilar cultures. That economics have some influence on culture is obvious; but it is surely no less obvious that their influence is not completely decisive.

It has been fashionable for some time past to attribute the formation and development of cultures exclusively to impersonal forces. Depersonalized, the story of mankind gains in majestic dignity of appearance, but loses, unfortunately, in scientific adequacy and veracity. This august astronomical kind of history just doesn't happen to be true. Direct observation shows that accidents of the most trivially personal kind may play a decisive part in modifying the thought and behavior of entire communities. For example, the death of a medicine man during the absence of his appointed successor has been observed, in one of the tribes of Pueblo Indians, to lead to a radical change in the religious ceremonial and beliefs of the entire community. Knowledge of the rites was a trade secret reserved to a single man. The man died without having been able to pass on his knowledge to his official heir; consequently the religion of a whole tribe was changed.

Socially important secrets are seldom in the hands of a single man; but there have been, there still are, very many communities in which knowledge and, in general, all the elements of higher culture have been the possession of a few. Consider the contemporary world. The very existence of an industrialized and urbanized society depends on the knowledge and skill of, at the most, one per cent of its members. A selective massacre of three or four hundred thousand technicians—perhaps of a much smaller number—would bring the whole economic and social life of England to a standstill. True, it would be possible for us to make good this catastrophic loss. But it takes a long time to form a good technician, and while the new men were being trained, most of the population would have died of hunger and disease. Unspecialized agricultural societies are not so abjectly dependent on a class of technicians as are we. Accidents among the guardians of culture do not lead to the physical destruction of the community, but only to a modification of its psychological life.

Maya society consisted, in all probability, of a small ruling class of learned priests and a large, subservient, and ignorant laity. In such a community (and even the most democratic and best-educated of modern societies are still fundamentally of this type) the fortuitous appearance among the rulers of an individual possessed of some special congenital ability, or preoccupied for whatever reason with one particular class of ideas, may lead to the formation of a certain tradition of culture that will canalize the thought and behavior of the whole people for generations. European history provides a striking example of this process. At the beginning of the seventeenth century European thought had broken the banks of its medieval conduits and was seething in confused and uncertain flood. The astonishing accident of Galileo reconverted this flood into a river. With ever-increasing impetus thought flowed along the new channels he had prepared for it.

Concernnng the history of the Mayas we have no documents beyond the ruins, the dates, and the traditions preserved by Landa and in the Popul Vuh and the books of Chilam Balam. One can only speculate about the causes which made their culture what it was. My own conviction is that its distinguishing peculiarities were due to such personal accidents as the birth, in a favored social position, of exceptional individuals. To what cause, for example, must we attribute that obsessive preoccupation with time, which is such a striking feature of Central American culture? Other agricultural communities have not found it necessary to work out elaborate calendars or to devise an intellectual instrument for thinking back into remotest antiquity. There was nothing, therefore, in their economic development that made it inevitable for the Mayas to invent the Great Cycle and establish dates many thousands of years removed from their own position in time. Personal accident offers the only plausible explanation of the fact. We must postulate the appearance among the Maya priesthood of one man, or a succession of men, haunted by the consciousness of the perpetual perishing of things and congenitally equipped to deal with this obsession in mathematical terms. (The god Itzamma is possibly the original inventor of the calendar, defied and worshipped by his compatriots.) Once the practice of calendar-making became established, it would be as "natural" for all succeeding Maya priests to bother their heads with problems of time as it was "natural" for the Greeks of Herodotus' day not to bother theirs.

A similar explanation may be suggested to account for the absence of the female element from Maya theology and of sensuality from Maya art. The pantheon of the codices and the monuments is an elaborate affair, which looks as though it were the product of a selection and crystallization from some more primitive folk religion. Significant in this context is the fact that, in the Archaic

Culture which preceded that of the Mayas, the principle of fertility is symbolized by a female figure. Why did the Mayas reject this symbol in favor of the less obviously appropriate man-with-a-nose-like-a-tapir's? The answer, I think, is that somebody, with an antiphallic turn of mind, rejected it for them. There was an editing of the old religion—*in usum serenissimi Delphini*. An edited cosmology must necessarily reflect the character of the editors, and this character will become, to a certain extent, the character of all those who accept the edited religion as their guide through life. Philosophy, according to Bradley, is the finding of bad reasons for what we believe by instinct. But most of what we believe by instinct turns out, on analysis, to be merely what we happen to have picked up in childhood. *Instinctively,* the Mayas believed that the god of fertility was a tapir-snouted man. Somebody had once said so and the assertion had been constantly repeated; therefore they "felt it in their bones." In *their* bones, on the contrary, the Indians felt that the principle of fertility was a Yoni-Lingam; and the Ephesians *knew* (and we may be sure that their intuition had a quality of irrefragable certainty) that the same deity was a woman with four rows of mango-shaped breasts and a swarm of miniature animals crawling up her arms.

The Mayas' preoccupation with the emblems of mortality may also have been due to an intellectual fashion set by a few people. Periods when death was all the rage recurred several times in European history. The fifteenth century, for example, was a time when corpses, skulls, and skeletons were extravagantly popular. Painted, sculptured, written about and dramatically represented, the Danse Macabre was everywhere. To the fifteenth-century artist a good death-appeal was as sure a key to popularity as a good sex-appeal is at the present time. The forties of the eighteenth century witnessed a revival of this fashionable interest in death. Blair and especially Young were instrumental in making the grave as popular, during a number of years, as the bed. The *Night Thoughts* had an international success comparable to that of *The Green Hat.* The Maya and the later Aztec preoccupation with the more gruesome aspects of death may have been the inevitable result of their economic development or of any other abstraction you like to mention.

But it may, even more probably, I think, have been the result of a tradition inaugurated by a few individuals of a peculiar turn of mind. Similarly, the unspeakable horrors of the Aztec sacrifices were a logical outcome of the cosmological speculations of a few philosophers. The sun was alive and required nourishment; if it were not properly nourished it might die or at least become angry; therefore, for the good of humanity at large, human victims had to be bent backwards over a stone and have their hearts ripped out with an obsidian knife. It is the sort of argument that a solitary theologian, brooding over the problems of the world, would first of all devise to account for the existence of sporadic sacrificial rites and then develop, abstractly, to the logical conclusion that, since the sun is large and more than human, solar appetite must be extraordinarily hearty and the supply of victims therefore never sufficiently copious.

We are now in a position to suggest an answer to our original question. Why is one artistic tradition different from another? Geographical, climatic, and economic factors play their part. So, perhaps, does racial idiosyncrasy. But the finally decisive element is accident—the accident of an unusual combination of chromosomes and the consequent birth of an unusually gifted person; the accident in an individual's peculiar upbringing or of his finding himself so favorably placed in society that he can exercise an influence on his fellows; the accident of the existence of royal or clerical patronage—and so on, indefinitely. If we care to risk a generalization, we may say that the main features of a culture are predictable by any one acquainted with the impersonal forces at work upon and within the community; but that the details are the result of accident and are therefore unpredictable. For example, we may predict that an agricultural people will have more highly developed arts than a hunting people. But we shall not be able to predict the nature of the traditional forms, nor their artistic quality. No amount of knowledge of the impersonal forces at work will allow us to prophesy that *this* agricultural people will represent the principle of fertility as a phallus or a yoni; *that,* as a man with an axe and the snout of a tapir. All the concrete peculiarities of a cultural tradition are the fruit of accident and cannot be foreseen.

Accident determines not only the traditional themes

and forms of a people's art, but also its quality. At first sight it might seem as though artistic ability were a matter of racial inheritance. But when we look more closely we find reason to doubt if this is so. There are no artistic or inartistic races; there are only, within each social group, certain sets of artistically fortunate or unfortunate accidents. Many facts point to this conclusion. Thus, in the course of its history, the same people may produce works of art of widely varying quality. Egyptian art was sometimes superb; but at other times (as the contents of Tutankhamen's tomb made only too clear) it could be deplorably cheap, theatrical, and vulgar. Italian painting was very nearly nonexistent after 1750. English music was once as fine as any in Europe; with the death of Purcell it evaporated. And yet the English were still the English and, so far from being a decadent race, were displaying immense energy and resourcefulness in almost every other field of human activity.

Again, it is often asserted that the different European races are distinguished by different artistic aptitudes: that the Italians excel in the plastic arts, the English in literature, the Germans in music, and so on. Now, first of all, none of these social entities is a race. The only objective test for difference of race is the Precipitin-Test. Applied to the so-called races of Europe, it shows that "Nordic," "Alpine," "Mediterranean" are the names of inconstant variations, and that all Europeans are fundamentally of the same stock. In the second place, such laudatory or disparaging epithets as "musical," "inartistic," and so on, do not apply permanently to any social group. The English have had their excellent composers and even one or two first-rate painters. For generations at a time, the Italians have been without decent literature or plastic arts. And so on. We are brought back once again to the accident.

Considered genetically, any given population is a vast roulette table. Every fertile conjunction of a man and a woman is a spin of the wheel. Sometimes there will be, so far as the arts are concerned, an extraordinary run of luck. The literary, or pictorial, or musical lucky number will turn up again and again; there will be a long succession of artists of genius, of patrons with good taste. Then, suddenly, the luck will turn, and for generations the winning color or number will obstinately refuse to come out.

These runs of luck and of mischance are enough to account for most of the differences in quality between one national art and another. But there is also another factor which must be taken into account. Once established (mainly as the result of personal accidents), an artistic tradition canalizes the activity of artists—and the more isolated and homogeneous the society, the more strict, as we have seen, is their conditioning. Now, it is possible that some traditions are more propitious to artists than others. An extreme case of the unpropitious tradition may be found in Mohammedan India. Here, all representations of human and even of animal forms are against the rules. There is, consequently, no sculpture worthy of the name, and such bootleg miniature painting as exists is on a miserably small scale and qualitatively poor and unsubstantial.

More subtly unpropitious are certain purely formal traditions, such as the Middle Minoan or the recent and very similar Barcelona *art nouveau* traditions. Perhaps a very great artist might be able to surmount the obstacles which these put in his way. I do not know. Anyhow, the difficulty of making something satisfactory out of forms that are a mixture of the naturalistic and the slimily decorative is obviously very great.

2

Art and Religion•

Does art hold up the mirror to its period? Or does every period hold up the mirror to its art? Does the artist follow or lead? Or does he walk alone, heeding only the categorical imperatives of his talent and the inner logic of the tradition within which he works? Is he the representative of his epoch? Or does he stand for a constituency no wider than that particular class of talented persons—his predecessors and successors—to which, by the predestination of his heredity, he happens to belong?

All these questions can be answered now in the affirmative, now in the negative, now with a simultaneous yes and no. There are no general rules; there are only particular cases, and most of these cases exist, so far as we are concerned, in a thick night of ignorance.

Let us consider, by way of example, a case that presents itself to every tourist who goes to Rome—the fascinating case of baroque art and seventeenth-century Catholicism. In what way were the two related? What was the nature of the connection between the aesthetic and the religious experiences of the age?

Three hundred years after the event all that we know for certain is that the personages represented in baroque religious art are all in a state of chronic emo-

• From *Themes and Variations*, 1950.

tional excitement. They wave their arms, they roll their eyes, they press their hands to palpitating bosoms, sometimes they swoon away into complete unconsciousness. We look at them with a mixture of aesthetic admiration and moral distaste, then start to wonder about the men and women who were contemporary with them. Was their religious life as wildly agitated as the life of these creatures of the imagination? And, if so, had the art been modeled on their agitation, or was their agitation due to familiarity with an art which had become agitated for purely aesthetic reasons, because baroque artists were tired of doing what their predecessors had done and were anxious to experiment with the emphatic and the inordinate? Or, finally, was there no agitation in the real world corresponding to the frenzies prevailing in the worlds of painting and sculpture? In spite of the frantically gesticulating images above the altars, did the religious life of the time go on very much as it had gone on when art was more restrained? Were there then, as always, a few ardent contemplatives and actives imperfectly leavening a great lump of the lukewarm, the fickle, the time-serving, and the indifferent?

I myself incline to the last alternative. Environment is never the sole determinant, and heredity is always at work, producing every variety of physique and temperament at every period of history. All the potentialities of human nature exist at all times, and at all times (in spite of an environment which may be unfavorable to some of them) practically all the potentialities are to some extent actualized. One has only to read Salimbene's *Chronicle* and Law's *Serious Call* in order to realize that there were as many irreligious people in the "ages of faith" as there were pietists in the "ages of reason." The Byzantines who went mad about trinitarian theology were the same Byzantines who went mad about the chariot races, and our own age of atomic physics is also an age of astrology and numerology. At every period there exists, not a synthesis, but a mere brute collocation of opposites and incompatibles. And yet at any given epoch there is only one prevailing style of art, in terms of which painters and sculptors treat of a strictly limited number of subjects. Art may be defined, in this context, as a process of selection and transformation, whereby an unmanageable multiplicity is reduced to a semblance of unity. For this reason we must never expect to find in art a reflection of reality as it is actually experienced by individual human beings in all their congenital and acquired variety. Thus, from a study of the restrained and formalized art of the Italian *trecento,* who could infer the experienced reality of those wild religious revivals, which were so characteristic a feature of the period? And, conversely, from the frenzies of the baroque who could infer the most important facts of sixteenth- and seventeenth-century mysticism? Who, looking at a Carlo Dolci *"Magdalen,"* could guess what St. John of the Cross had said about true Charity—that it is a matter, not of feeling, but of the will? Or who, with Bernini's *"St. Teresa"* or *"Blessed Ludovica"* before his eyes, would ever suspect that Bernini's contemporary, Charles de Condren, had deplored the weakness which caused ecstatics to receive God *"si animalement."* The truth would seem to be that while the great masses of the people remained, as ever, indifferent or fitfully superstitious, and while the masters of the spiritual life preached a worship of the Spirit in spirit and in truth, the artists chose to glorify a Christianity of thrills and visceral yearnings, now violent, now cloyingly sentimental. And they chose to do so for reasons connected, not with the problems of life, but with those of art. Their painting and sculpture did not, and indeed could not, reflect the manifold religious experience of the time; nor did the religious experience of most of their contemporaries reflect the prevailing art. Art and reality went their separate ways, the artists using religion as their opportunity for developing a baroque expressionism and the religious using that art as an instrument for achieving the various kinds of experiences for which their temperaments had fitted them. And precisely the same relations between religion and art had existed when the "Primitives" were using a multiform Catholicism as their opportunity for creating one particular kind of static composition, and when the religious were using these works as instruments for practicing now revivalism, now contemplation, now magic.

From Rome and the baroque, let us shift for a few moments to Tuscany and the rococo. A few miles from Siena there stands among the vineyards a large Carthusian monastery, called Pontignano. The habitations of the monks (now occupied by a score of peasant families) consist of three rooms apiece—a kitchen, a bedroom, and a tiny oratory. Their front doors give on to the arcaded cloisters, and at the back are little walled gardens, where a man could grow vegetables and dig his own grave. Each of the brethren lived independently of all the rest, a solitary in a community of solitaries, a mute among the silent. Most of the buildings at Pontignano date from the fourteenth century, but were refurbished by an interior decorator of the eighteenth. The church was adorned with an enormous high altar made of wood painted to look like marble, and the little oratories in which the monks said their private prayers were stuccoed over with rococo twiddles, till they looked like the boudoirs of so many provincial Pompadours. To us, with our incorrigible sense of history, this conjunction of St. Bruno and Louis XV seems grotesquely, impossibly inappropriate. But how did it strike the monks who actually prayed in those oratories? Did they suddenly start to think, feel, and behave like those libertine abbés whom we associate with rococo decoration? Surely not. "Never reformed, because never deformed," the Carthusian order held on its way regardless of changes in aesthetic fashion. In their newly plastered oratories the brethren continued to meditate on death, just as their predecessors had meditated when the decorations were baroque or Renaissance, Gothic or Romanesque. Styles change; but death remains itself, a brute fact of every individual's experience—a fact that has no history and to which, in consequence, the successive changes in the modes of artistic expression are completely irrelevant. The Pompadourish art in the Pontignano chapels tells us nothing whatever about contemporary Carthusian religion. All we learn from it is that, when eighteenth-century Carthusians felt the need of restoring ancient buildings, the only restorers available were, as we might have expected, men brought up in the current tradition of art.

In our own days the religious are worse off than were the monks of Pontignano. Not living rococo, but the sham antique or some atrocious piece of mass-produced *bondieuserie* is all that they can find for their purposes. And yet, in spite of the horrors of modern religious art, religion in all its aspects from the fetishistic to the contemplative continues to flourish and to produce its good or evil fruits. Man and society are, doubtless, wholes; but they are wholes divided, like ships, into watertight compartments. On one side of a bulkhead is art; on the other is religion. The level may be high in one compartment, low in the other. The connection between the two is not below the water line, but only from above, only for the overseeing intellect that looks down and can see both simultaneously and recognize them as belonging, by juxtaposition rather than by fusion, to the same individual or social whole.

Art and Religion: The View from India•

A visit to India makes one realize how fortunate, so far at any rate as the arts are concerned, our Europe has been in its religions. The Olympian religion of antiquity and, except occasionally, the Christianity which took its place, were both favorable to the production of works of art, and the art which they favored was, on the whole, a singularly reasonable and decent kind of art. Neither paganism nor Christianity imposed restrictions on what the artist might represent; nor did either demand of him that he should try to represent the unrepresentable. The Olympian deities were men made gods; the Savior of the Christians was God made man. An artist could work to the greater glory of Zeus or of Jesus without ever going beyond the boundaries of real and actual human life.

How different is the state of things in India. Here, one of the two predominant religions forbids absolutely the representation of the human form, and even, where Moslem orthodoxy is strict, of any living animal form whatever. It is only occasionally, and then in purely secular art and on the smallest of scales, that this religious injunction is disobeyed. Mohammedan art tends, in consequence, to be dry, empty, barren, and monotonous.

Hinduism, on the other hand, permits the representa-

• From *Jesting Pilate* ("Chitor"), 1926.

tion of things human, but adds that the human is not enough. It tells the artist that it is his business to express symbolically the superhuman, the spiritual, the pure metaphysical idea. The best is always the enemy of the good, and by trying to improve on sober human reality, the Hindus have evolved a system of art full of metaphysical monsters and grotesques that are none the less extravagant for being symbolical of the highest of "high" philosophies. (Too high, I may add parenthetically, for my taste. Philosophies, like pheasants, can be hung too long. Most of our highest systems have been pendant for at least two thousand years. I am plebeian enough to prefer my spiritual nourishment fresh. But let us return to Hindu art.)

Readers of the *Bhagavad Gita* will remember the passage in the Eleventh Discourse, where Krishna reveals himself to Arjuna in a form hitherto unbeheld by mortal eyes:

> With mouths, eyes, arms, breasts multitudinous . . .
> Long-armed, with thighs and feet innumerable,
> Vast-bosomed, set with many fearful teeth . . .

And further: "With many divine ornaments, with many upraised divine weapons, wearing divine necklaces and vestures, anointed with divine unguents, the God all-marvellous, boundless, with face turned every way." And so on. The catalogue of Krishna's members, features, and wardrobe covers several pages of Mrs. Besant's translation of the *Gita*. We recognize the necessarily inadequate embodiment of the description in innumerable Indian statues and paintings. And what is the significance of these grotesque and repulsive monsters? Krishna himself explains it. "Here today," he says to Arjuna, "behold the whole universe, movable and immovable, standing in one in my body." These many-limbed monsters are symbolic, then, of the cosmos. They are the One made manifest, the All in a nutshell. Hindu artists are trying to express in terms of form what can only be expressed—and not very clearly at that, for it is difficult to speak lucidly about things of which one knows nothing—in words. The Hindus are too much interested in metaphysics and ultimate Reality to make good artists. Art is not the discovery of Reality—whatever Reality may be, and no human being can possibly know. It is the organization of chaotic appearance into an orderly and human universe.

Among tall stories, surely one of the tallest is the history of Mormonism. A founder whose obviously homemade revelations were accepted as more-than-gospel truth by thousands of followers; a lieutenant and successor who was "for daring a Cromwell, for intrigue a Machiavelli, for executive force a Moses, and for utter lack of conscience a Bonaparte"; a body of doctrine combining the most penetrating psychological insights with preposterous history and absurd metaphysics; a society of puritanical but theater-going and music-loving polygamists; a church once condemned by the Supreme Court as an organized rebellion, but now a monolith of respectability; a passionately loyal membership distinguished, even in these middle years of the twentieth century, by the old-fashioned Protestant and pioneering virtues of self-reliance and mutual aid—together, these make up a tale which no self-respecting reader even of Spillane, even of science fiction, should be asked to swallow. And yet, in spite of its total lack of plausibility, the tale happens to be true.

My book knowledge of its truth had been acquired long since and intermittently kept up to date. It was not, however, until the spring of 1953 that I had occasion

• From *Tomorrow and Tomorrow and Tomorrow,* 1956.

actually to see and touch the concrete evidences of that strange history.

We had driven all day in torrential rain, sometimes even in untimely snow, across Nevada. Hour after hour in the vast blankness of desert plains, past black bald mountains that suddenly closed in through the driving rain, to recede again, after a score of wintry miles, into the gray distance.

At the state line the weather had cleared for a little, and there below us, unearthly in a momentary gleam of sunshine, lay the Great Salt Desert of Utah, snow-white between the nearer crags, with the line of blue or inky peaks rising, far off, from the opposite shore of that dry ghost of an inland sea.

There was another storm as we entered Salt Lake City, and it was through sheets of falling water that we caught our first glimpse, above the chestnut trees, of a floodlit object quite as difficult to believe in, despite the evidence of our senses, as the strange history it commemorates.

The improbability of this greatest of the Mormon Temples does not consist in its astounding ugliness. Most Victorian churches are astoundingly ugly. It consists in a certain combination of oddity, dullness, and monumentality unique, so far as I know, in the annals of architecture.

For the most part Victorian buildings are more or less learned pastiches of something else—something Gothic, something Greek or nobly Roman, something Elizabethan or Flamboyant Flemish or even vaguely Oriental. But this Temple looks like nothing on earth—looks like nothing on earth and yet contrives to be completely unoriginal, utterly and uniformly prosaic.

But whereas most of the churches built during the past century are gimcrack affairs of brick veneered with imitation stone, of latticework plastered to look like masonry, this vast essay in eccentric dreariness was realized, from crypt to capstone, in the solidest of granite. Its foundations are cyclopean, its walls are three yards thick. Like the Escorial, like the Great Pyramid, it was built to last indefinitely. Long after the rest of Victorian and twentieth-century architecture shall have crumbled back to dust, this thing will be standing in the Western desert, an object, to the neo-neolithic savages of post-atomic times, of uncomprehending reverence and superstitious alarm.

* From *Tomorrow and Tomorrow and Tomorrow,* 1956.

To what extent are the arts conditioned by, or indebted to, religion? And is there, at any given moment of history, a common socio-psychological source that gives to the various arts—music and painting, architecture and sculpture—some kind of common tendency? What I saw that night in Temple Square and what I heard next day during an organ recital in the Tabernacle, brought up the old problem in a new and, in many ways, enlightening context.

Here, in the floodlights, was the most grandiose by far of all Western cathedrals. This Chartres of the desert was begun and largely built under economic and social conditions hardly distinguishable from those prevailing in France or England in the tenth century. In 1853, when the Temple's foundation stone was laid, London could boast its Crystal Palace, could look back complacently on its Exhibition of the marvels of Early Victorian technology. But here in Utah men were still living in the Dark Ages—without roads, without towns, with no means of communication faster than the ox wagon or mule train, without industry, without machines, without tools more elaborate than saws and scythes and hammers—and with precious few even of those. The granite blocks of which the Temple is built were quarried by man power, dressed by man power, hauled over twenty miles of trackless desert by man power and ox power, hoisted into position by man power. Like the cathedrals of medieval Europe the Temple is a monument, among other things, to the strength and heroic endurance of striped muscle.

In the Spanish colonies, as in the American South, striped muscle was activated by the whip. But here in the West there were no African slaves and no local supply of domesticable aborigines. Whatever the settlers wanted to do had to be done by their own hands. The ordinary run of settlers wanted only houses and mills and mines and (if the nuggets were large enough) Paris fashions imported at immense expense around the Horn. But these Mormons wanted something more—a granite Temple of indestructible solidity. Within a few years of their arrival in Utah they set to work. There were no whips to stimulate their muscles, only faith—but in what abundance! It was the kind of mountain-moving faith that gives men power to achieve the impossible and bear the intolerable, the kind of faith for which men die and kill and work themselves beyond the limits of human capacity, the kind of faith that had launched the Crusades and raised the towers of Angkor-Vat. Once again it performed its historic miracle. Against enormous odds, a great cathedral was built in the wilderness. Alas, instead of Bourges or Canterbury, it was *This*.

Faith, it is evident, may be relied on to produce sustained action and, more rarely, sustained contemplation. There is, however, no guarantee that it will produce good art. Religion is always a patron of the arts, but its taste is by no means impeccable. Religious art is sometimes excellent, sometimes atrocious; and the excellence is not necessarily associated with fervor nor the atrocity with lukewarmness. Thus, at the turn of our era, Buddhism flourished in Northwestern India. Piety, to judge by the large number of surviving monuments, ran high; but artistic merit ran pretty low. Or consider Hindu art. For the last three centuries it has been astonishingly feeble. Have the many varieties of Hinduism been taken less seriously than in the times when Indian art was in its glory? There is not the slightest reason to believe it. Similarly there is not the slightest reason to believe that Catholic fervor was less intense in the age of the Mannerists than it had been three generations earlier. On the contrary, there is good reason to believe that, during the Counter Reformation, Catholicism was taken more seriously by more people than at any time since the fourteenth century. But the bad Catholicism of the High Renaissance produced superb religious art; the good Catholicism of the later sixteenth and seventeenth centuries produced a great deal of rather bad religious art. Turning now to the individual artist—and after all, there is no such thing as "Art," there are only men at work—we find that the creators of religious masterpieces are sometimes, like Fra Angelico, extremely devout, sometimes no more than conventionally orthodox, sometimes (like Perugino, the supreme exponent of pietism in art) active and open disbelievers.

For the artist in his professional capacity, religion is important because it offers him a wealth of interesting subject matter and many opportunities to exercise his skill. Upon the quality of his production it has little or no influence. The excellence of a work of religious art depends on two factors, neither of which has anything to do with religion. It depends primarily on the presence in the artist of certain tendencies, sensibilities, and talents; and, secondarily, it depends on the earlier history of his chosen art, and on what may be called the logic of its formal relations. At any given moment that internal logic points toward conclusions beyond those which have been reached by the majority of contemporary artists. A recognition of this fact may impel certain artists—especially young artists—to try to realize those possible conclusions in concrete actuality. Sometimes these attempts are fully successful; sometimes, in spite of their author's talents, they fail. In either case, the outcome does not depend on the nature of the artist's metaphysical beliefs, nor on the warmth with which he entertains them.

The Mormons had faith, and their faith enabled them to realize a prodigious ideal—the building of a Temple in the wilderness. But though faith can move mountains, it cannot of itself shape those mountains into cathedrals. It will activate muscle, but has no power to create architectural talent where none exists. Still less can it alter the facts of artistic history and the internal logic of forms.

For a great variety of reasons, some sociological and some intrinsically aesthetic, some easily discernible and others obscure, the traditions of the European arts and crafts had disintegrated, by the middle years of the nineteenth century, into a chaos of fertile bad taste and ubiquitous vulgarity. In their fervor, in the intensity of their concern with metaphysical problems, in their readiness to embrace the most eccentric beliefs and practices, the Mormons, like their contemporaries in a hundred Christian, Socialist, or Spiritualist communities, belonged to the Age of the Gnostics. In everything else they were typical products of rustic nineteenth-century America. And in the field of the plastic arts nineteenth-century America, especially rustic America, was worse off even than nineteenth-century Europe. Barry's Houses of Parliament were as much beyond these Temple-builders as Bourges or Canterbury.

Next morning, in the enormous wooden tabernacle, we listened to the daily organ recital. There was some Bach and a piece by César Franck and finally some improvised variations on a hymn tune. These last reminded one irresistibly of the good old days of the silent screen—

the days when, in a solemn hush and under spotlights, the tail-coated organist at the console of his Wurlitzer would rise majestically from the cellarage, would turn and bend his swanlike loins in ackowledgment of the applause, would resume his seat and slowly extend his white hands. Silence, and then boom! the picture palace was filled with the enormous snoring of thirty-two-foot contra trombones and bombardes. And after the snoring would come the "Londonderry Air" on the *vox humana,* "A Little Grey Home in the West" on the *vox angelica,* and perhaps (what bliss!) "The End of a Perfect Day" on the *vox treacliana,* the *vox bedroomica,* the *vox unmentionabilis.*

How strange, I found myself reflecting, as the glutinous tide washed over me, how strange that people should listen with apparently equal enjoyment to this kind of thing and the Prelude and Fugue in E-flat major. Or had I got hold of the wrong end of the stick? Perhaps mine was the strange, the essentially abnormal attitude. Perhaps there was something wrong with a listener who found it difficult to adore both these warblings around a hymn tune *and* the Prelude and Fugue.

From these unanswerable questions my mind wandered to others, hardly less puzzling, in the domain of history. Here was this huge instrument. In its original and already monumental state, it was a product of pioneering faith. An Australian musician and early Mormon convert, Joseph Ridges, had furnished the design and supervised the work. The timber used for making the pipes was hauled by oxen from forests three hundred miles to the south. The intricate machinery of a great organ was home-made by the local craftsmen. When the work was finished, what kind of music, one wonders, was played to the Latter-day Saints assembled in the tabernacle? Hymns, of course, in profusion. But also Handel, also Haydn and Mozart, also Mendelssohn and perhaps even a few pieces by that queer old fellow whom Mendelssohn had resurrected, John Sebastian Bach.

It is one of the paradoxes of history that the people who built the monstrosities of the Victorian epoch should have been the same as the people who applauded, in their hideous halls and churches, such masterpieces of orderliness and unaffected grandeur as the *Messiah,* and who preferred to all his contemporaries that most elegantly classical of the moderns, Felix Mendelssohn. Popular taste in one field may be more or less completely at variance with popular taste outside that field. Still more surprisingly, the fundamental tendencies of professionals in one of the arts may be at variance with the fundamental tendencies of professionals in other arts.

Until very recently the music of the fifteenth, sixteenth, and early seventeenth centuries was, to all but learned specialists, almost completely unknown. Now, thanks to long-playing phonograph records, more and more of this buried treasure is coming to the surface. The interested amateur is at last in a position to hear for himself what, before, he could only read about. He knows, for example, what people were singing when Botticelli was painting "Venus and Mars"; what Van Eyck might have heard in the way of love songs and polyphonic masses; what kind of music was being sung or played in St. Mark's while Tintoretto and Veronese were at work, next door, in the Doge's Palace; what developments were taking place in the sister art during the more than sixty years of Bernini's career as sculptor and architect.

Dunstable and Dufay, Ockeghem and Josquin, Lassus, Palestrina, Victoria—their overlapping lives cover the whole of the fifteen and sixteenth centuries. Music, in those two centuries, underwent momentous changes. The dissonances of the earlier, Gothic polyphony were reduced to universal consonance; the various artifices—imitation, diminution, augmentation and the rest—were perfected and, by the greater masters, used to create rhythmical patterns of incredible subtlety and richness. But through the whole period virtually all serious music retained those open-ended, free-floating forms which it had inherited from the Gregorian Chant and, more remotely, from some Oriental ancestor. European folk music was symmetrical, foursquare, with regular returns to the same starting point and balanced phrases, as in metrical poetry, of pre-established and foreseeable length. Based upon plain chant and written, for the most part, as a setting to the liturgical texts, learned music was analogous, not to scanned verse, but to prose. It was a music without bars—that is to say, with no regularity of emphasis. Its component elements were of different lengths, there were no returns to recognizable starting points, and its geometrical analogue was not some closed figure like the square or circle, but an open curve undulating away to infinity. That such a music ever reached a close was due, not to the internal logic of its forms, but solely to the fact that even the longest texts come at last to their Amen. Some attempt to supply a purely musical reason for not going on forever was made by those composers who wrote their masses around a *cantus firmus*—a melody borrowed, almost invariably, from the closed, symmetrical music of popular songs. Sung or played in very slow time, and hidden in the tenor, sometimes even in the bass, the *cantus firmus* was, for all practical purposes, inaudible. It existed for the benefit, not of listeners, but of the composer; not to remind bored church-goers of what they had heard last night in the tavern, but to serve a strictly artistic purpose. Even when the *cantus firmus* was present, the general effect of unconditioned, free-floating continuousness persisted. But, for the composer, the task of organization had been made easier; for, buried within the fluid heart of the music, was the unbending armature of a fully metrical song.

While Dufay was still a choir boy at Cambrai, Ghiberti was at work on the bronze doors of Santa Maria del Fiore, the young Donatello had been given his first commissions. And when Victoria, the last and greatest of the Roman masters, died in 1613, Lorenzo Bernini was already a full-blown infant prodigy. From Early Renaissance to baroque, the fundamental tendency of the plastic arts was through symmetry and beyond it, away from closed forms toward unbalanced openness and the implication of infinity. In music, during this same period, the fundamental tendency was through openness and beyond it, away from floating continuousness toward meter, toward foursquare symmetry, toward regular and foreseeable recurrence. It was in Venice that the two opposite tendencies, of painting and of music, first became conspicuous. While Tintoretto and Veronese moved toward openness and the asymmetrical, the two Gabrielis moved, in their motets and their instrumental music, toward harmony, toward regular scansion and the closed form. In Rome, Palestrina and Victoria continued to work in the old free-floating style. At St. Mark's, the music of the future—the music which in due course was to develop into the music of Purcell and Couperin, of Bach and Handel—was in process of being born. By the sixteen-thirties, when even sculpture had taken wing for the infinite, Bernini's older contemporary, Heinrich Schuetz, the pupil of Giovanni Gabrieli, was writing (not always, but every now and then) symmetrical music that sounds almost like Bach.

For some odd reason this kind of music has recently been labeled "baroque." The choice of this nickname is surely unfortunate. If Bernini and his Italian, German, and Austrian followers are baroque artists (and they have been so designated for many years), then there is no justification, except in the fact that they happened to be living at the same time, for applying the same epithet to composers, whose fundamental tendencies in regard to form were radically different from theirs.

About the only seventeenth-century composer to whom the term "baroque" can be applied in the same sense as we apply it to Bernini, is Claudio Monteverdi. In his operas and his religious music, there are passages in which Monteverdi combines the openness and boundlessness of the older polyphony with a new expressiveness. The feat is achieved by setting an unconditionally soaring melody to an accompaniment, not of other voices, but of variously colored chords. The so-called baroque composers are baroque (in the established sense of the word) only in their desire for a more direct and dramatic expression of feeling. To realize this desire, they developed modulation within a fully tonal system, they exchanged polyphony for harmony, they varied the tempo of their music and the volume of its sound, and they invented modern orchestration. In this concern with expressiveness they were akin to their contemporaries in the fields of painting and sculpture. But in their desire for squareness, closedness, and symmetry they were poles apart from men whose first wish was to overthrow the tyranny of centrality, to break out of the cramping frame or niche, to transcend the merely finite and the all too human.

Between 1598 and 1680—the years of Bernini's birth and death—baroque painting and sculpture moved in one direction, baroque music, as it is miscalled, moved in another, almost opposite direction. The only conclusion we can draw is that the internal logic and the recent history of the art in which a man is working exercise a more powerful influence upon him than do the social, religious, and political events of the time in which he lives. Fifteenth-century sculptors and painters inherited a tradition of symmetry and closedness. Fifteenth-century composers inherited a tradition of openness and symmetry. On either side the intrinsic logic of the forms was worked out to its ultimate conclusion. By the end of the sixteenth century neither the musical nor the plastic artists could go any further along the roads they had been following. Going beyond themselves, the painters and sculptors pursued the path of open-ended asymmetry, the free-floating musicians turned to the exploration of regular recurrence and the closed form. Meanwhile the usual wars and persecutions and sectarian throat-cuttings were in full swing; there were economic revolutions, political and social revolutions, revolutions in science and technology. But these merely historical events seem to have affected artists only materially—by ruining them or making their fortunes, by giving or withholding the opportunity to display their skill, by changing the social or religious status of potential patrons. Their thought and feeling, their fundamental artistic tendencies were reactions to events of a totally different order—events not in the social world, but in the special universe of each man's chosen art.

Take Schuetz, for example. Most of his adult life was spent in running away from the recurrent horrors of the Thirty Years' War. But the changes and chances of a discontinuous existence left no corresponding traces upon his work. Whether at Dresden or in Italy, in Denmark or at Dresden again, he went on drawing the artistically logical conclusions from the premises formulated under Gabrieli at Venice and gradually modified, through the years, by his own successive achievements and the achievements of his contemporaries and juniors.

Man is a whole, but a whole with an astounding capacity for living, simultaneously or successively, in watertight compartments. What happens here has little or no effect on what happens there. The seventeenth-century taste for closed forms in music was inconsistent with the seventeenth century taste for asymmetry and openness in the plastic arts. The Victorian taste for Mendelssohn and Handel was inconsistent with the Victorian taste for Mormon Temples, Albert Halls, and St. Pancras Railway Stations. But in fact these mutually exclusive tastes coexisted and had no perceptible effect on one another.

Consistency is a verbal criterion, which cannot be applied to the phenomena of life. Taken together, the various activities of a single individual may "make no sense," and yet be perfectly compatible with biological survival, social success, and personal happiness.

Objective time is the same for every member of a human group and, within each individual, for each inhabitant of a watertight compartment. But the self in one compartment does not necessarily have the same *Zeitgeist* as the selves in other compartments or as the selves in whom other individuals do their equally inconsistent living. When the stresses of history are at a maximum, men and women tend to react to them in the same way. For example, if their country is involved in war, most individuals become heroic and self-sacrificing. And if the war produces famine and pestilence, most of them die. But where the historical pressures are more moderate, individuals are at liberty, within rather wide limits, to react to them in different ways. We are always synchronous with ourselves and others; but it often happens that we are not contemporary with either.

At Logan, for example, in the shadow of another Temple, whose battlemented turrets gave it the air of an Early Victorian "folly," of a backdrop to Edmund Kean in *Richard III*, we got into conversation with a charming contemporary, not of Harry Emerson Fosdick or Bishop Barnes, but of Brother Juniper—a Mormon whose faith had all the fervor, all the unqualified literalness, of peasant faith in the thirteenth century. He talked to us at length about the weekly baptisms of the dead. Fifteen hundred of them baptized by proxy every Saturday evening and thus, at long last, admitted to that heaven where all the family ties persist throughout the aeons. To a member of a generation brought up on Freud, these posthumous prospects seemed a bit forbidding. Not so to Brother Juniper. He spoke of them with a kind of quiet rapture. And how celestially beautiful, in his eyes, was this cyclopean gazebo! How inestimable the privilege, which he had earned, of being allowed to pass through its doors! Doors forever closed to all Gentiles and even to a moiety of the Latter-day Saints. Around that heavenly Temple the lilac trees were in full scent and the mountains that ringed the fertile valley were white with the snowy symbol of divine purity. But time pressed. We left Brother Juniper to his paradise and drove on.

That evening, in the tiny Natural History Museum at Idaho Falls, we found ourselves talking to two people from a far remoter past—a fascinating couple straight out of a cave. Not one of your fancy Magdalenian caves with all that modernistic art work on the walls. No, no—a good old-fashioned, down-to-earth cave belonging to nice ordinary people three thousand generations before the invention of painting. These were Australopiths, whose reaction to the stuffed grizzly was a remark about sizzling steaks of bear meat; these were early Neanderthalers who could not see a fish or bird or four-footed beast without immediately dreaming of slaughter and a guzzle.

"Boy!" said the cave lady, as we stood with them before the solemn, clergyman-like head of an enormous moose. "Would *he* be good with onions!"

It was fortunate, I reflected, that we were so very thin, they so remarkably well fed and therefore, for the moment, so amiable.

5

Sincerity in Art •

In a recently published volume on the commercial side of literature, Mr. Michael Joseph, the literary agent, discussed the Best Seller. What are the qualities that cause a book to sell like soap or breakfast food or Ford cars? It is a question the answer to which we should all like to know. Armed with that precious recipe, we should go to the nearest stationer's shop, buy a hundred sheets of paper for sixpence, blacken them with magical scribbles, and sell them again for six thousand pounds. There is no raw material so richly amenable to treatment as paper. A pound of iron turned into watch springs is worth several hundreds or even thousands of times its original value; but a pound of paper turned into popular literature may be sold at a profit of literally millions per cent. If only we knew the secret of the process by which paper is turned into popular literature! But we don't. Even Mr. Joseph is ignorant. Otherwise, it is obvious, he would be writing Best Sellers, an occupation more profitable even than his present profession, which is selling them.

The only thing Mr. Joseph can tell us is this: the Best Seller must be sincere. The information is quite true— so manifestly true, indeed, that it is not particularly useful. All literature, all art, best seller or worst, must be

• From *Essays New and Old*, 1927

sincere, if it is to be successful. The deliberate pastiche,
be it of Charles Garvice or of Shelley, can never take in
any considerable number of people over any considerable
period of time. A man cannot successfully be anything
but himself. It is obvious. Only a person with a Best
Seller mind can write Best Sellers; and only someone
with a mind like Shelley's can write *Prometheus Unbound*.
The deliberate forger has little chance with his contemporaries and none at all with posterity.

In the annals of literary history, however, there have
been but few deliberate forgers. There was the Elizabethan Greene, for example, who pastiched *Euphues* and
forged the poetical style of Marlowe, in the hope of securing for himself some of the popular applause which greeted
the appearance of Lyly's novels and Marlowe's plays.
His own style, when he wrote in it, was an agreeable
and charming one. His borrowed plumes are a manifest
misfit and can never have impressed anyone.

Another and more recent literary man who attained a
considerable celebrity by forging and pastiching was the
Frenchman, Catulle Mendès. Reading his horribly clever
second-hand works one is astonished now that they took
in as many people as they did. His gold is so obviously
pinchbeck, his jewels such palpable stage copies of the
real gems. It is difficult to be interested in such people.
Their work has little or nothing to do with art, and their
unmysterious personality raises no curious or subtle problems of psychology. They are the literary counterpart of
the people who fake Sienese primitives or Chippendale
chairs for profit; that is all. The only kind of insincere art
that is worthy of the psychologist's attention is that
which is insincere, not deliberately, but unwittingly and
in spite of the efforts of the artist to be sincere.

In the affairs of ordinary life sincerity is a matter of
will. We can be sincere or insincere at choice. It may
seem, therefore, a paradox when I talk of works of art
that are insincere in spite of their author's desires and
efforts to make them sincere. If he wants to be sincere,
it may be argued, he can be; there us nothing to prevent
him but his own lack of good will. But this is not true.
Sincerity in art depends on other things besides the mere
desire to be sincere.

It would be easy to adduce many examples of artists
whose works have been insincere, in spite of the fact that

they themselves have been, in life, perfect models of sincerity. There is, for instance, the case of Benjamin Robert Haydon, the friend of Keats and Shelley, the painter of some of the largest and most pretentious religious pictures ever executed. His autobiography—one of the best books of its kind, which the stupidity of publishers has permitted to remain out of print for the last fifty years—exists to testify to the man's sincerity in life, to his spontaneous ardors, his genuinely noble idealism, his numerous and not unlovable failings. But look at his pictures—the pictures to which he devoted a lifetime of passionate endeavor. Look at them—that is, if you can find any to look at; for they are mostly in the cellars beneath our galleries, not on the walls. They are full of stage grandeur, the cold convention of passion, the rhetorical parody of emotion. They are "insincere"—the word comes inevitably to the lips.

The same dramatic contrast between the man and his works can be found in the Belgian painter Wiertz, whose studio at Brussels draws more visitors than does the city's picture gallery—but draws, not because the painter's pictures are moving works of art, but because they are monstrosities of size and melodramatic horror. This dreamer of Michelangelesque dreams survives as a sort of pictorial Barnum; his museum has the popularity of a Chamber of Horrors.

Alfieri was another of these sincere and thoroughly genuine human beings who produce an art that is insincere and stagy. It is difficult to believe that the *Autobiography* and the wooden, stilted, conventional tragedies were written by the same man.

The truth is that sincerity in art is not an affair of will, of a moral choice between honesty and dishonesty. It is mainly an affair of talent. A man may desire with all his soul to write a sincere, a genuine book and yet lack the talent to do it. In spite of his sincere intentions, the book turns out to be unreal, false, and conventional; the emotions are stagily expressed, the tragedies are pretentious and lying shams and what was meant to be dramatic is baldly melodramatic. Reading, the critic is chilled and disgusted. He pronounces the book to be "insincere." The author, conscious of the purity of his intentions when he wrote it, is outraged by an epithet which seems to impugn his honor and his sense of moral values, but which, in reality, stigmatizes only his intellectual capacities. For in matters of art "being sincere" is synonymous with "possessing the gifts of psychological understanding and expression."

All human beings feel very much the same emotions; but few know exactly what they feel or can divine the feelings of others. Psychological insight is a special faculty, like the faculty for understanding mathematics or music. And of the few who possess that faculty only two or three in every hundred are born with the talent of expressing their knowledge in artistic form. Let us take an obvious example. Many people—most people, perhaps —have been at one time or another violently in love. But few have known how to analyze their feelings, and fewer still have been able to express them. The love letters that are read aloud in the divorce courts and at the inquests on romantic suicides prove how pathetically inept as literary artists most men and women are. They feel, they suffer, they are inspired by a sincere emotion; but they cannot write. Stilted, conventional, full of stock phrases and timeworn rhetorical tropes, the average love letter of real life would be condemned, if read in a book, as being in the last degree "insincere." I have read genuine letters written by suicides just before their death, which I should, as a reviewer, have pilloried for their manifest "insincerity." And yet, after all, it would be difficult to demand of a man a higher proof of the sincerity of his emotions than that which he furnishes by killing himself because of them. Only suicides of talent write letters that are artistically "sincere." The rest, incapable of expressing what they feel, are compelled to fall back on the trite, "insincere" rhetoric of the second-rate novel.

It is the same with love letters. We read the love letters of Keats with a passionate interest; they describe in the freshest and most powerful language the torments of a soul that is conscious of every detail of its agony. Their "sincerity" (the fruit of their author's genius) renders them as interesting, as artistically important as Keats's poems; more important even, I sometimes think. Imagine, now, the love letters of any other young apothecary's assistant of the same epoch! He might have been as hopelessly in love as was Keats with Fanny Brawne. But his letters would be worthless, uninteresting, painfully "insincere." We should find their slightly superior counterpart in any of the long-forgotten sentimental novels of the period.

We should, therefore, be very chary of applying the epithet "insincere" to a work of art. Only those works are insincere in the true, the ethical sense of the word, which are—like Greene's, like Catulle Mendès's—deliberate forgeries and conscious pastiches. Most of the works which we label as "insincere" are in reality only incompetent, the product of minds lacking in the (for the artist) indispensable gifts of psychological understanding and expression.

6

*On the Experience of Nature and Literary Expression**

"Poetry," said Mallarmé, "is not written with ideas; it is written with words." Hence, if you are a man of letters, those tears; and hence, when the words have fallen of their own free will or been laboriously bullied into the proper, the inevitable pattern, hence also those triumphant elations. Cholula, for example—how find the words to render the magnificence, the queerness, the general improbability of Cholula? Happy Prescott! He, it is evident, had no difficulties with the place. "Nothing," he writes, and writes it obviously without a qualm, "nothing could be more grand than the view which met the eye from the area on the truncated summit of the pyramid. Towards the north stretched that bold barrier of porphyritic rock which Nature had reared around the Valley of Mexico, etc. . . . At the foot of the spectator lay the sacred city of Cholula, with its bright towers and pinnacles sparkling in the sun, reposing amidst gardens and verdant groves, which then thickly studded the cultivated environs of the capital. Such was the magnificent prospect which met the gaze of the conquerors, and may still, with a slight change, meet that of the modern traveller, as from the platform of the great pyramid his eye wanders over the very nice too! But, alas, the days when verdant groves

* From *Beyond the Mexique Bay* ("Cholula"), 1934.

fairest portion of the beautiful plateau of Puebla." And studded the environs are over. We are expected to use words that will give the reader an illusion of being close to the physical and psychological reality they express. Prescott had never been in Mexico. But for one who wrote in terms of verdant groves and sparkling pinnacles, this was no handicap, was actually an advantage. For, even if he had visited Cholula, his words would have been carefully chosen so as to conceal this somewhat compromising fact. Not having visited Cholula, he had nothing to conceal, but could devote himself wholeheartedly and without an afterthought to the description of the magnificent prospect. With us, the case is altered. The sort of words we use are meant to prove to the reader that we have been there, quiveringly in the flesh, even when in fact we haven't. Badly used, such words are much worse than Prescott's rhetorical proofs of a personal, an emotional alibi. They are worse, because they protest too much, whereas Prescott's words, for all their absurd pomposity, protest very little. A "word picture" (the very name makes one feel slightly sick) by a fluent contemporary journalist has a poignant vulgarity unknown in earlier days. It is the old story of opportunity making the thief. During the last century certain prose stylists made possible the arranging of words so as to produce in the reader an imaginative conviction of personal intimacy with the reality that they were artistically rendering. By their technical discoveries they enlarged the kingdom of literary art, conquered new provinces of the inexpressible. Now, the better a man's tools, the more effectively will he be able to stamp his personality upon the raw material of his chosen art—the more easily will he be able to "express himself." If the self he has to express is of poor aesthetic quality (as it generally is), the possession of better tools will merely result in the production of more vulgar art. In the course of the last ninety years, good writers have provided the "word-painter" with a great number of technical resources entirely unknown to Prescott. He was content to stud the environs with groves and leave his pinnacles to sparkle in the sun; was content because, in the last resort, he could do nothing else. Which was perhaps fortunate. For when one *can* do something else, something more, this is the sort of thing one does: "The temple tapered above the soft bronze of the river, above the dimmed green of the palms, the

spire of its tallest pagoda stained with the drench of sunset. Its beauty was the brutal beauty of blood-dark steel."
(The quotation is from a novel which I found in the smoking-room of a hotel.)

Its bright towers and pinnacles sparkling in the sun . . .
Its tallest pagoda stained with the drench of sunset . . .

Between those two phrases lie ninety years of stylistic experiment. Prescott, in 1843, simply could not have written the second of them. Pater, Rimbaud, Conrad, D'Annunzio—these and a score of others had to live and work before such stuff became writable.

"And lead us not into temptation, but deliver us from evil." With this prayer on my lips, let me return to Cholula, to the platform of that mountainous pyramid of Quetzalcoatl from which Cortes looked down on the holy city, "*y certifico a Vuestra Alteza que yo conté quatro-cientas y tantas Torres en la dicha Ciudad, y todas son de Mezquitas.*" Even today one can still see almost as many "towers of mosques." But the mosques are no longer mosques of Quetzalcoatl and Tonantzin and Huitzilo-pochtli. They are the mosques of St. Joseph and St. James, of St. Francis and St. Dominick, of the Holy Trinity and Our Lady of Guadalupe. The Spaniards, it is evident, must have built a church, or at least a chapel, on the site of every pagan temple in Cholula. It was a sanitary precaution, a process of magical disinfection.

I did not bother to count the churches visible from the top of the great pyramid. But one did not have to invoke the aid of arithmetic to perceive that the town at one's feet was fairly bubbling with round domes, that all the plain for miles around was strewn with the fossil remains of ecclesiastical life. The religious emotions rank, with sunlight, hunger, and falling water, as one of the great natural sources of energy. Harness this Niagara, and at once millions of horsepower are at your disposal. There are enough bricks in the Cholula pyramid to cover an area twice as large as the Place de la Concorde to a depth equal to twice the height of the Louvre. And when Quetzalcoatl had gone, the missionaries recanalized the old energies in the imported name of Jesus; the towers of the new *mezquitas* sprouted everywhere like mushrooms on an autumn morning. It was the decay of faith that made it necessary to invent the steam engine.

Humboldt, in his *Essai politique sur la Nouvelle Espagne*, makes a remark which every enthusiastic pyramid-climber should strictly meditate. "If," he says, "we analyze the mechanism of the Peruvian theocracy, generally so much over-praised in Europe, we observe that, wherever nations are divided into castes, and wherever men do not enjoy the right to private property and work solely for the profit of the community, we shall find canals, roads, aqueducts, pyramids, huge constructions of every kind. But we shall also find that these people, though for thousands of years they may preserve the air of external prosperity, will make practically no advance in moral culture, which is the result of individual liberty."

Pyramids on the one hand; personal liberty on the other. We have an ever-increasing number of pyramids, or their modern equivalents; an ever-diminishing amount of personal liberty. Is this merely a historical accident? Or are these two goods essentially incompatible? If they turn out to be essentially incompatible, then, one day, we shall have to ask ourselves very seriously which is better worth having—pyramids and a perfectly efficient, perfectly stable community; or personal liberty with instability, but the possibility, at least, of a progress, measurable in terms of spiritual values.

Descending from Quetzalcoatl's mountain of petrified energy, we set out to explore the Christian monuments. The most remarkable of these are San Francisco Acatepec and Santa Maria Tonantzintla. San Francisco, which stands on a little hill, quite alone in the rolling, campagnalike country, some three miles out of Cholula, is just the typical Pueblan church, raised, so to speak, to the nth power. In the city of Puebla all the churches have blue or yellow glazed cupolas; and some have panels of the same bright tiles on their façades. San Francisco Acatepec is tiled from top to bottom. Dome, belfry, pillars, cornices—every inch is covered with blue and yellow *azulejos*. One would expect the church to glow like a flock of parrots. But, oddly enough, the total effect is drab. "Jazzed up" to the extreme limit of variegated brilliancy, San Francisco is like one of those ships one used to see during the war; it has been dazzle-painted into indistinctness, almost into invisibility. Within, the wealth of molded plaster and carved wood is astonishing. There is hardly a blank space in the whole church. The effect is queer, but not extraordinary. For the designs are all relatively orthodox—Spanish baroque only slighly Indian-ized. To see how far Indianization can be carried, one must go to Santa Maria Tonantzintla. From the outside the church looks like any other Mexican church—the usual dome, the usual pleasantly picturesque but ill-propor-tioned façade and, since it stands near Puebla, the usual Pueblan *azulejos*. But enter; you find yourself in what is probably the oddest church in Christendom. The whole of the interior is fairly crawling with stuccowork, brilliantly gilt and painted in red, green, blue, and pink, on a spot-less white ground. And what stuccowork! Cherubs, with Aztec feathers stuck in their back hair, peer out at you from the walls. On the vaulting, overhead, a group of Indian angels are playing the cello (the tom-tom I suppose was too closely related to the old religion to be tolerated in a nominally Christian church). It is, as everywhere in Central America, a baroque theme interpreted by neo-lithically-minded craftsmen—but interpreted far more freely (and also with greater artistic power) than in any of the other churches I saw in Mexico or Guatemala.

Four or five Indians, all men, were busy, when we entered, decorating the church for Easter with palm branches and pieces of gold and silver foil. There was certainly no resident priest in the place; perhaps no mass would be said even on Easter Day. But I doubt if the Indians minded. Since the Revolution, the church is wholly theirs; they can do what they like in it, practice whatever queer blend of Catholicism and Quetzalcoatlism pleases them best. The priests, it is true, could make strong magic; but since their departure experience has doubtless proved to the Indians that, magic for magic, their own is just as effective as any one else's. There is not any less rain since the *padres* were turned out, nor any more disease. And there is certainly less to pay. We asked permission to take some snapshots. The Indians had no objection—were indeed delighted that we should find their church so interesting. But would we send them the photographs when they were developed? We certainly would. The two most important members of the group wrote down their names and addresses for us. One was called Lorenzo Pancoatl, the other Encarnación Azcoatl. Merely from the names of the vergers one could have deduced the nature of the church.

7

Tragedy and the Whole Truth*

There were six of them, the best and bravest of the hero's companions. Turning back from his post in the bows, Odysseus was in time to see them lifted, struggling, into the air, to hear their screams, the desperate repetition of his own name. The survivors could only look on, helplessly, while Scylla "at the mouth of her cave devoured them, still screaming, still stretching out their hands to me in the frightful struggle." And Odysseus adds that it was the most dreadful and lamentable sight he ever saw in all his "explorings of the passes of the sea." We can believe it; Homer's brief description (the too poetical simile is a later interpolation) convinces us.

Later, the danger passed, Odysseus and his men went ashore for the night, and, on the Sicilian beach, prepared their supper—prepared it, says Homer, "expertly." The Twelfth Book of the *Odyssey* concludes with these words: "When they had satisfied their thirst and hunger, they thought of their dear companions and wept, and in the midst of their tears sleep came gently upon them."

The truth, the whole truth, and nothing but the truth—how rarely the older literatures ever told it! Bits of the truth, yes; every good book gives us bits of the truth, would not be a good book if it did not. But the whole

* From *Music at Night*, 1931.

truth, no. Of the great writers of the past incredibly few have given us that. Homer—the Homer of the *Odyssey* —is one of those few.

"Truth?" you question. "For example, $2 + 2 = 4$? Or Queen Victoria came to the throne in 1837? Or light travels at the rate of 187,000 miles a second?" No, obviously, you won't find much of that sort of thing in literature. The "truth" of which I was speaking just now is in fact no more than an acceptable verisimilitude. When the experiences recorded in a piece of literature correspond fairly closely with our own actual experiences, or with what I may call our potential experiences—experiences, that is to say, which we feel (as the result of a more or less explicit process of inference from known facts) that we might have had—we say, inaccurately no doubt: "This piece of writing is true." But this, of course, is not the whole story. The record of a case in a textbook of psychology is scientifically true, in so far as it is an accurate account of particular events. But it might also strike the reader as being "true" with regard to himself —that is to say, acceptable, probable, having a correspondence with his own actual or potential experiences. But a textbook of psychology is not a work of art—or only secondarily and incidentally a work of art. Mere verisimilitude, mere correspondence of experience recorded by the writer with experience remembered or imaginable by the reader, is not enough to make a work of art seem "true." Good art possesses a kind of supertruth—is more probable, more acceptable, more convincing than fact itself. Naturally; for the artist is endowed with a sensibility and a power of communication, a capacity to "put things across," which events and the majority of people to whom events happen, do not possess. Experience teaches only the teachable, who are by no means as numerous as Mrs. Micawber's papa's favourite proverb would lead us to suppose. Artists are eminently teachable and also eminently teachers. They receive from events much more than most men receive, and they can transmit what they have received with a peculiar penetrative force, which drives their communication deep into the reader's mind. One of our most ordinary reactions to a good piece of literary art is expressed in the formula: "This is what I have always felt and thought, but have never been able to put clearly into words, even for myself."

We are now in a position to explain what we mean when we say that Homer is a writer who tells the Whole Truth. We mean that the experiences he records correspond fairly closely with our own actual or potential experiences—and correspond with our experiences not on a single limited sector, but all along the line of our physical and spiritual being. And we also mean that Homer records these experiences with a penetrative artistic force that makes them seem peculiarly acceptable and convincing.

So much, then, for truth in literature. Homer's, I repeat, is the Whole Truth. Consider how almost any other of the great poets would have concluded the story of Scylla's attack on the passing ship. Six men, remember, have been taken and devoured before the eyes of their friends. In any other poem but the *Odyssey*, what would the survivors have done? They would, of course, have wept, even as Homer made them weep. But would they previously have cooked their supper, and cooked it, what's more, in a masterly fashion? Would they previously have drunk and eaten to satiety? And after weeping, or actually while weeping, would they have dropped quietly off to sleep? No, they most certainly would not have done any of these things. They would simply have wept, lamenting their own misfortune and the horrible fate of their companions, and the canto would have ended tragically on their tears.

Homer, however, preferred to tell the Whole Truth. He knew that even the most cruelly bereaved must eat; that hunger is stronger than sorrow and that its satisfaction takes precedence even of tears. He knew that experts continue to act expertly and to find satisfaction in their accomplishment, even when friends have just been eaten, even when the accomplishment is only cooking the supper. He knew that, when the belly is full (and only when the belly is full) men can afford to grieve, and that sorrow after supper is almost a luxury. And finally he knew that, even as hunger takes precedence of grief, so fatigue, supervening, cuts short its career and drowns it in a sleep all the sweeter for bringing forgetfulness of bereavement. In a word, Homer refused to treat the theme tragically. He preferred to tell the Whole Truth.

Another author who preferred to tell the Whole Truth was Fielding. *Tom Jones* is one of the very few Odyssean

books written in Europe between the time of Aeschylus
and the present age; Odyssean, because never tragical;
never—even when painful and disastrous, even when pathetic and beautiful things are happening. For they do
happen; Fielding, like Homer, admits all the facts, shirks
nothing. Indeed, it is precisely because these authors shirk
nothing that their books are not tragical. For among the
things they don't shirk are the irrelevancies which, in
actual life, always temper the situations and characters
that writers of tragedy insist on keeping chemically pure.
Consider, for example, the case of Sophy Western, that
most charming, most nearly perfect of young women.
Fielding, it is obvious, adored her (she is said to have
been created in the image of his first, much-loved wife).
But in spite of his adoration, he refused to turn her into
one of those chemically pure and, as it were, focused
beings who do and suffer in the world of tragedy. That
innkeeper who lifted the weary Sophia from her horse—
what need had he to fall? In no tragedy would he (nay,
could he) have collapsed beneath her weight. For, to
begin with, in the tragical context weight is an irrelevance; heroines should be above the law of gravitation.
But that is not all; let the reader now remember what
were the results of his fall. Tumbling flat on his back, he
pulled Sophia down on top of him—his belly was a
cushion, so that happily she came to no bodily harm—
pulled her down head first. But head first is necessarily
legs last; there was a momentary display of the most
ravishing charms; the bumpkins at the inn door grinned or
guffawed; poor Sophia, when they picked her up, was
blushing in an agony of embarrassment and wounded
modesty. There is nothing intrinsically improbable about
this incident, which is stamped, indeed, with all the marks
of literary truth. But however true, it is an incident which
could never, never have happened to a heroine of tragedy.
It would never have been allowed to happen. But Fielding
refused to impose the tragedian's veto; he shirked nothing—neither the intrusion of irrelevant absurdities into the
midst of romance or disaster, nor any of life's no less
irrelevantly painful interruptions of the course of happiness. He did not want to be a tragedian. And, sure
enough, that brief and pearly gleam of Sophia's charming
posterior was sufficient to scare the Muse of Tragedy out
of *Tom Jones* just as, more than five and twenty centuries

before, the sight of stricken men first eating, then remembering to weep, then forgetting their tears in slumber
had scared her out of the *Odyssey*.

In his *Principles of Literary Criticism* Mr. I. A.
Richards affirms that good tragedy is proof against irony
and irrelevance—that it can absorb anything into itself
and still remain tragedy. Indeed, he seems to make of this
capacity to absorb the untragical and the anti-tragical
a touchstone of tragic merit. Thus tried, practically all
Greek, all French, and most Elizabethan tragedies are
found wanting. Only the best of Shakespeare can stand
the test. So, at least, says Mr. Richards. Is he right? I
have often had my doubts. The tragedies of Shakespeare
are veined, it is true, with irony and an often terrifying
cynicism; but the cynicism is always heroic idealism turned
neatly inside out, the irony is a kind of photographic
negative of heroic romance. Turn Troilus's white into black
and all his blacks into white and you have Thersites.
Reversed, Othello and Desdemona become Iago. White
Ophelia's negative is the irony of Hamlet, is the ingenuous
bawdry of her own mad songs; just as the cynicism of
mad King Lear is the black shadow-replica of Cordelia.
Now, the shadow, the photographic negative of a thing,
is in no sense irrelevant to it. Shakespeare's ironies and
cynicisms serve to deepen his tragic world, but not to
widen it. If they had widened it, as the Homeric irrelevancies widened out the universe of the *Odyssey*—why,
then, the world of Shakespearean tragedy would automatically have ceased to exist. For example, a scene
showing the bereaved Macduff eating his supper, growing melancholy, over the whisky with thoughts of his murdered wife and children, and then, with lashes still wet,
dropping off to sleep, would be true enough to life; but
it would not be true to tragic art. The introduction of such
a scene would change the whole quality of the play;
treated in this Odyssean style, *Macbeth* would cease to
be a tragedy. Or take the case of Desdemona. Iago's
bestially cynical remarks about her character are in no
sense, as we have seen, irrelevant to the tragedy. They
present us with negative images of her real nature and of
the feelings she has for Othello. These negative images
are always *hers*, are always recognizably the property of
the heroine-victim of a tragedy. Whereas, if, springing
ashore at Cyprus, she had tumbled, as the no less ex-

quisite Sophia was to tumble, and revealed the inadequacies of sixteenth-century underclothing, the play would no longer be the *Othello* we know. Iago might breed a family of little cynics and the existing dose of bitterness and savage negation be doubled and trebled; *Othello* would still remain fundamentally *Othello*. But a few Fieldingesque irrelevancies would destroy it—destroy it, that is to say, as a tragedy; for there would be nothing to prevent it from becoming a magnificent drama of some other kind. For the fact is that tragedy and what I have called the Whole Truth are not compatible; where one is, the other is not. There are certain things which even the best, even Shakespearean tragedy, cannot absorb into itself.

To make a tragedy the artsit must isolate a single element out of the totality of human experience and use that exclusively as his material. Tragedy is something that is separated out from the Whole Truth, distilled from it, so to speak, as an essence is distilled from the living flower. Tragedy is chemically pure. Hence its power to act quickly and intensely on our feelings. All chemically pure art has this power to act upon us quickly and intensely. Thus, chemically pure pornography (on the rare occasions when it happens to be written convincingly, by some one who has the gift of "putting things across") is a quick-acting emotional drug of incomparably greater power than the Whole Truth about sensuality, or even (for many people) than the tangible and carnal reality itself. It is because of its chemical purity that tragedy so effectively performs its function of catharsis. It refines and corrects and gives a style to our emotional life, and does so swiftly, with power. Brought into contact with tragedy, the elements of our being fall, for the moment at any rate, into an ordered and beautiful pattern, as the iron filings arrange themselves under the influence of the magnet. Through all its individual variations, this pattern is always fundamentally of the same kind. From the reading or the hearing of a tragedy we rise with the feeling that

> Our friends are exultations, agonies,
> And love, and man's unconquerable mind;

with the heroic conviction that we too would be unconquerable if subjected to the agonies, that in the midst of the agonies we too should continue to love, might even learn to exult. It is because it does these things to us that tragedy is felt to be so valuable. What are the values of Wholly-Truthful art? What does it do to us that seems worth doing? Let us try to discover.

Wholly-Truthful art overflows the limits of tragedy and shows us, if only by hints and implications, what happened before the tragic story began, what will happen after it is over, what is happening simultaneously elsewhere (and "elsewhere" includes all those parts of the minds and bodies of the protagonists not immediately engaged in the tragic struggle). Tragedy is an arbitrarily isolated eddy on the surface of a vast river that flows on majestically, irresistibly, around, beneath, and to either side of it. Wholly-Truthful art contrives to imply the existence of the entire river as well as of the eddy. It is quite different from tragedy, even though it may contain, among other constituents, all the elements from which tragedy is made. (The "same thing" placed in different contexts, loses its identity and becomes, for the perceiving mind, a succession of different things.) In Wholly-Truthful art the agonies may be just as real, love and the unconquerable mind just as admirable, just as important, as in tragedy. Thus, Scylla's victims suffer as painfully as the monster-devoured Hippolytus in *Phèdre;* the mental anguish of Tom Jones when he thinks he has lost his Sophia, and lost her by his own fault, is hardly less than that of Othello after Desdemona's murder. (The fact that Fielding's power of "putting things across" is by no means equal to Shakespeare's is, of course, merely an accident.) But the agonies and indomitabilities are placed by the Wholly-Truthful writer in another, wider context, with the result that they cease to be the same as the intrinsically identical agonies and indomitabilities of tragedy. Consequently, Wholly-Truthful art produces in us an effect quite different from that produced by tragedy. Our mood when we have read a Wholly-Truthful book is never one of heroic exultation; it is one of resignation, of acceptance. (Acceptance can also be heroic.) Being chemically impure, Wholly-Truthful literature cannot move us as quickly and intensely as tragedy or any other kind of chemically pure art. But I believe that its effects are more lasting. The exultations that follow the reading or hearing of a tragedy are in the nature of temporary inebriations. Our being cannot long hold the pattern imposed by tragedy. Remove the magnet and the filings tend to fall back into confusion. But the pattern of acceptance and resignation imposed upon us by Wholly-Truthful literature, though perhaps less unexpectedly beautiful in design, is (for that very reason perhaps) more stable. The catharsis of tragedy is violent and apocalyptic; but the milder catharsis of Wholly-Truthful literature is lasting.

In recent times literature has become more and more acutely conscious of the Whole Truth—of the great oceans of irrelevant things, events, and thoughts stretching endlessly away in every direction from whatever island point (a character, a story) the author may choose to contemplate. To impose the kind of arbitrary limitations, which must be imposed by anyone who wants to write a tragedy, has become more and more difficult—is now indeed, for those who are at all sensitive to contemporaneity, almost impossible. This does not mean, of course, that the modern writer must confine himself to a merely naturalistic manner. One can imply the existence of the Whole Truth without laboriously cataloguing every object within sight. A book can be written in terms of pure fantasy and yet, by implication, tell the Whole Truth. Of all the important works of contemporary literature not one is a pure tragedy. There is no contemporary writer of significance who does not prefer to state or imply the Whole Truth. However different one from another in style, in ethical, philosophical, and artistic intention, in the scales of values accepted, contemporary writers have this in common, that they are interested in the Whole Truth. Proust, D. H. Lawrence, André Gide, Kafka, Hemingway —here are five obviously significant and important contemporary writers. Five authors as remarkably unlike one another as they could well be. They are at one only in this: that none of them has written a pure tragedy, that all are concerned with the Whole Truth.

I have sometimes wondered whether tragedy, as a form of art, may not be doomed. But the fact that we are still profoundly moved by the tragic masterpieces of the past —that we can be moved, against our better judgment, even by the bad tragedies of the contemporary stage and film—makes me think that the day of chemically pure art is not over. Tragedy happens to be passing through a period of eclipse, because all the significant writers of our age are too busy exploring the newly discovered, or re-discovered, world of the Whole Truth to be able to pay any attention to it. But there is no good reason to believe that this state of things will last forever. Tragedy is too valuable to be allowed to die. There is no reason, after all, why the two kinds of literature—the Chemically Impure and the Chemically Pure, the literature of the Whole Truth and the literature of Partial Truth—should not exist simultaneously, each in its separate sphere. The human spirit has need of both.

8

To the Puritan All Things Are Impure[*]

Mrs. Grundy resembles the King and that infernal worm of the Bible—she cannot die. *La Grundy est morte. Vive la Grundy!* There is no getting rid of her; she is immortal and succumbs only to be reborn. Disguised as Sir William Joynson-Hicks (for she frequently wears trousers), the old lady has been very active in England during the last few years. When the General Election put an end to Jix and his party, the optimists hoped that an end had been put to Mrs. Grundy. But the optimists, as usual, were wrong. In the sphere of sexual behavior the new government is as rigidly orthodox as the old, and as actively intolerant. Among the last acts of the departing Home Secretary were the banning of D. H. Lawrence's novel, *Lady Chatterley's Lover,* and the confiscation of the registered letter containing the manuscript of his "Pansies." One of the first acts of his Laborite successor was to set the police on to D. H. Lawrence's exhibition of paintings. *La Grundy est morte. Vive la Grundy!*

Sexual orthodoxy preserves not only its Athanasian Creed, but also its Grand Inquisitor. "I believe in one heterosexual Love, monogamous and indissoluble. And I believe in Respectability. And above all in Silence." Against the heretics who will not accept this profession

[*] From *Music at Night,* 1931.

of sexual faith, the Grand Inquisitors are permanently at war. At the beginning of last century, English Catholics and Jews had no political rights; atheists were expelled from English universities; blasphemers were severely punished. Today a man is free to have any or no religion; about the Established Church and its divinities he can say almost anything he likes. But woe to him if he deviates from the narrow path of sexual orthodoxy! Penal servitude awaits those who act on their disbelief in the exclusive sanctity of heterosexuality; and for sexual blasphemy —that is to say, the writing of certain forbidden words and the frank description or representation of certain acts which every one performs—the penalty ranges from confiscation of the offending picture or writing to a fine and, possibly, in certain cases, imprisonment. It will thus be seen that, as things stand at present, any member of the Holy Trinity may be insulted with almost perfect impunity. But do, or say, or draw anything to offend Mrs. Grundy, and the avenging Inquisitor will immediately swoop down on you. Mrs. Grundy, in a word, is the only deity officially recognized by the English State. Men are free not to worship the God of Anglicanism; but the law compels them to bow down before the divine Grundy.

To argue the case against Grundyism would be easy, but wholly unprofitable. For in these matters, it is obvious, argument is perfectly useless. Argument appeals to reason, and there is no reason in Grundyism. There are at best only rationalizations of prejudices—prejudices that, in most individual Grundyites, date back to the teaching received in childhood. Those who accept the creed of sexual orthodoxy do so because, in Pavlov's phrase, their reflexes have been conditioned at an impressionable period. It would be absurd to doubt the sincerity of people like Mr. Sumner of the New York Vice Society, and the right honorable gentlemen who have filled the post of Home Secretary in England. They are obviously quite genuinely shocked by such things as *Lady Chatterley's Lover* and Lawrence's paintings. Such things *really* disgust and outrage them. Given their upbringing, it is inevitable; just as it is inevitable that Pavlov's dogs, after having been regularly fed to the sound of a bell, should start to dribble with hungry anticipation each time, in the future, that the bell is rung. Our vice crusaders and home secretaries were doubtless brought up in surroundings where an improper word, and overfrank reference in Saxon phrases to the processes of reproduction and evacuation (notice how perfectly respectable these homely acts become when shrouded in the decent obscurity of a learned language!), was accompanied, not by anything so mild as the tinkling of a bell, but by appalling silences, by the blushing or swooning away of maiden aunts, by the sadly pious horror or Jehovahistic indignation of clergymen and schoolmasters. So that to this day they cannot hear these words or read these descriptions without at once recapturing (the process is as automatic as the salivation of Pavlov's dogs) the painful emotions aroused in them during childhood by the portentous accompaniments and consequences of what I have called sexual blasphemy. At present, most of those old enough to be occupying positions of power and responsibility were brought up in environments which conditioned their reflexes into the form of Grundyism. A time may come, perhaps, when these posts will be filled by men whose reflexes have not been so conditioned. When the contemporary child takes a normal, healthy interest in sex and scatology, the majority of young parents do not weep over him, or beat him, or tell him that his soul will roast in hell-fire. It follows, therefore, that his future reactions to sex will be less violently painful than the reactions of those who were children in the high old days of Podsnapian respectability. We are therefore justified in cherishing a mild hope for the future. For when I said that Mrs. Grundy was immortal, I was exaggerating. She may, old cat that she is, possess nine lives; but she is not everlasting. That a time may come when she will be, if not stone dead, at least enfeebled, chronically moribund, is, as we have seen, quite possible. Moreover, it is perfectly certain that during long periods of history she hardly existed at all. If we throw our eyes over the whole expanse of historical time, we perceive that active Grundyism is not a normal phenomenon. During the longest periods of recorded history Puritanism has been, if not absolutely inexistent, at least without significance or power. The epochs of higher civilization have been conspicuously unpuritanical. It was to the naked Aphrodite that the Greeks of the fifth and sixth centuries B.C. made sacrifice, not to the much-petticoated divinity worshipped by the Pilgrim Fathers, by the later Podsnap and our contemporary vice crusaders and Home secretaries. Seen through the eyes of the philosophic historian, the Puritan reveals himself as the most abnormal sexual pervert of whom we have record, while Grundyism stands out as the supremely unnatural vice.

It was against this unnatural vice and the perverts who practice it that D. H. Lawrence waged almost his latest battle. A militant, crusading moralist, he hurled himself on what he regarded as the evil thing, the wicked people. But unfortunately the evil thing is sacred in our modern world, and the wicked people are precisely those Good Citizens who wield the powers of the State. Lawrence was often discomfited. The giant Grundy popped her huge crinoline over him and extinguished him by force. But not for long; his courage and his energy were inextinguishable and, in spite of the Home secretaries, the bright dangerous flame of his art broke out again, the warning, denouncing, persuading voice was heard once more—up to the very end.

Cultured and tolerant people often ask: What is the point of this crusading? What is the point of shocking the Jixes into legal retaliation? What is the point of using the brief Saxon words that people shudder at, when you can express the same meaning, more or less, by means of circumlocutions and Graeco-Roman polysyllables? Might not Grundyism be attacked without ringing those particular alarm bells which cause the mouths of the smuthounds, not indeed to water, like those of Pavlov's dogs, but to foam with righteous indignation? In a word, might not as good or even better results be obtained if the crusade were conducted with tact and circumspection?

The answer to all these questions is: No. What Lawrence was crusading for was the admission by the conscious spirit of the right of the body and the instincts, not merely to be a begrudged existence, but to an equal honor with itself. Man is an animal that thinks. To be a first-rate human being, a man must be both a first-rate animal and a first-rate thinker. (And, incidentally, he cannot be a first-rate thinker, at any rate about human affairs, unless he is also a first-rate animal.) From the time of Plato onwards there has been a tendency to exalt the thinking, spiritual man at the expense of the animal. Christianity confirmed Platonism; and now, in its turn, what I may call Fordism, or the philosophy of industrialism, confirms, though with important modifications, the spiritualizing doctrines of Christianity. Fordism demands that we should sacrifice the animal man (and along with the animal large portions of the thinking, spiritual man) not indeed to God, but to the Machine. There is no place in the factory, or in that larger factory which is the modern industrialized world, for animals on the one hand, or for artists, mystics, or even, finally, individuals on the other. Of all the ascetic religions Fordism is that which demands the cruelest mutilations of the human psyche—demands the cruelest mutilations and offers the smallest spiritual returns. Rigorously practiced for a few generations, this dreadful religion of the machine will end by destroying the human race.

If humanity is to be saved there must be reforms, not merely in the social and economic spheres, but also within the individual psyche. Lawrence concerned himself primarily with these psychological reforms. The problem, for him, was to bring the animal and the thinker together again, was to make them co-operate in the building up of consummate manhood. In order to effect this bringing together certain barriers must be broken down. They are strong barriers; for the conscious mind has taken extraordinary precautions to keep itself out of contact with the body and its instincts. The spirit refuses to be livingly aware of the animal man. Very significant in this context are the tabooed words which describe in the directest possible manner the characteristic functions of bodily life. Early training has so conditioned the reflexes of the normal bourgeois and his wife that they shudder whenever one of these words is pronounced. For these words bring the mind into direct contact with the physical reality which it is so desperately anxious to ignore. The circumlocutions and the scientific polysyllables do not bring the mind into this direct contact. They are mere algebraical symbols, almost empty of living, physical significance—a fact which must somewhat diminish the hope for the future which I expressed just now. Brought up in a world that is learning to treat sexual matters only too scientifically, the future Jixes and Sumners will be quite undisturbed by literary references to micturition fantasies, autoerotism, and the like. But if the same phenomena are described in plain Saxon words, they will

probably be just as painfully shocked as the present inquisitors. For when these Saxon words are pronounced,
the mind suddenly finds itself in actual touch with that
physical reality which Platonism, Christianity, and Fordism
have one after another insisted on its ignoring. It shrinks
with horror. But it ought not to shrink with horror. Lawrence set out to overcome this shrinking. The methods
he used were drastic—too drastic for many even of those
who, in principle, were on his side. "More tact, more circumspection!" they implored. But the use of forbidden
words, the describing and portraying of things ordinarily
veiled were absolutely essential tactics in the crusade.
The mind had to be made conscious of the physical
reality from which it was accustomed to shrink. This
was the only way of doing it. The fact that people are
shocked is the best proof that they need shocking. Their
reflexes have been wrongly conditioned; they should be
given a course of shocks until the conditioning is undone.
The theory, I am sure, is psychologically sound. But
to put it into practice is difficult. At every ringing of
their familiar "pornographic" bell, the right-thinkingly
conditioned smut-hounds foam at the mouth. And unfortunately they are in a position to do more than foam;
they are in a position to open our letters, confiscate our
books, and burn our pictures. What's to be done about
it? Perhaps Professor Pavlov might be able to tell us.

DOCUMENT

From the reports of a debate on the censorship of obscene
literature in the United States Senate, March 1930. Senator Smoot of Utah: "I did not believe there were such
books printed in the world." (Senator Smoot had
brought, as exhibits, Robert Burns's *Poems* (unexpurgated
edition), Balzac's *Contes Drolatiques*, Casanova's *Memoirs*,
George Moore's *Story Teller's Holiday*, D. H. Lawrence's
Lady Chatterley's Lover, *My Life and Loves*, by Frank
Harris, and that Mrs. Beeton's cookery book of love-
making, the *Kama Sutra*.) "They are lower than the
beasts. . . . If I were a Customs Inspector, this obscene
literature would only be admitted over my dead body.
. . . I'd rather have a child of mine use opium than
read these books." (Compare with this the yet more

heroic declaration of our own Mr. James Douglas. Mr. Douglas would rather give a child prussic acid than allow it to read *The Well of Loneliness*. In an article written at the time I offered to provide Mr. Douglas with a child, a bottle of prussic acid, a copy of *The Well of Loneliness*, and (if he kept his word and chose to administer the acid) a handsome memorial in marble to be erected wherever he might appoint, after his execution. The offer, I regret to say, was not accepted.)

Senator Blease of South Carolina was more eloquent even than Senator Smoot. True, he was not prepared to give children opium and prussic acid in preference to improper literature, but he was quite ready to "see the democratic and republican form of government for ever destroyed, if necessary to protect the virtue of the womanhood of America. . . . The virtue of one little sixteen-year-old girl is worth more to America than every book that ever came into it from any other country. . . . I love womanhood. Take from a government the purity of its womanhood and that government will be destroyed."

9

Art and the Obvious•

All great truths are obvious truths. But not all obvious truths are great truths. Thus, it is to the last degree obvious that life is short and destiny uncertain. It is obvious that, to a great extent, happiness depends on one-self and not on external circumstances. It is obvious that parents generally love their children and that men and women are attracted one to another in a variety of ways. It is obvious that many people enjoy the country and are moved by the varying aspects of nature to feel elation, awe, tenderness, gaiety, melancholy. It is obvious that most men and women are attached to their homes and countries, to the beliefs which they were taught in child-hood and the moral code of their tribe. All these, I repeat, are obvious truths and all are great truths, because they are universally significant, because they refer to funda-mental characteristics of human nature.

But there is another class of obvious truths—the obvious truths which, lacking eternal significance and having no reference to the fundamentals of human nature, cannot be called great truths. Thus, it is obvious to any one who has ever been there or even remotely heard of the place, that there are a great many automobiles in New York and a number of very lofty buildings. It is obvious that

• From *Music at Night*, 1931.

evening frocks are longer this year and that very few men wear top hats or high starched collars. It is obvious that you can fly from London to Paris in two and a half hours, that there is a periodical called the *Saturday Evening Post*, that the earth is round and that Mr. Wrigley makes chewing-gum. In spite of their obviousness, at any rate at the present time—for a time may come when evening frocks, whether long or short, will not be worn at all and when the motor car will be a museum curiosity, like the machines in *Erewhon*—these truths are not great truths. They might cease to be true without human nature being in the least changed in any of its fundamentals.

Popular art makes use, at the present time, of both classes of obvious truths—of the little obviousnesses as well as of the great. Little obviousnesses fill (at a moderate computation) quite half of the great majority of contemporary novels, stories, and films. The great public derives an extraordinary pleasure from the mere recognition of familiar objects and circumstances. It tends to be somewhat disquieted by works of pure fantasy, whose subject matter is drawn from other worlds than that in which it lives, moves, and has its daily being. Films must have plenty of real Ford cars and genuine policemen and indubitable trains. Novels must contain long descriptions of exactly those rooms, those streets, those restaurants and shops and offices with which the average man and woman are most familiar. Each reader, each member of the audience must be able to say—with what a solid satisfaction! —"Ah, there's a real Ford, there's a policeman, that's a drawing room exactly like the Brown's drawing room." Recognizableness is an artistic quality which most people find profoundly thrilling.

Nor are small obvious truths the only obviousnesses appreciated by the public at large. It also demands the great obvious truths. It demands from the purveyors of art the most definite statements as to the love of mothers for children, the goodness of honesty as a policy, the uplifting effects produced by the picturesque beauties of nature on tourists from large cities, the superiority of marriages of affection to marriages of interest, the brevity of human existence, the beauty of first love, and so forth. It requires a constantly repeated assurance of the validity of these great obvious truths. And the purveyors of popular art do what is asked of them. They state the great, obvious, unchanging truths of human nature—but state them, alas, in most cases with an emphatic incompetence, which, to the sensitive reader, makes their affirmations exceedingly distasteful and even painful. Thus, the fact that mothers love their children is, as I have pointed out, one of the great obvious truths. But when this great obvious truth is affirmed in a nauseatingly treacly mammy-song, in a series of soulful close-ups, in a post-Wilcoxian lyric or a page of magazine-story prose, the sensitive can only wince and avert their faces, blushing with a kind of vicarious shame for the whole of humanity.

The great obvious truths have often, in the past, been stated with a repellent emphasis, in tones that made them seem—for such is the almost magical power of artistic incompetence—not great truths, but great and frightful lies. But never in the past have these artistic outrages been so numerous as at present. This is due to several causes. To begin with, the spread of education, of leisure, of economic well-being has created an unprecedented demand for popular art. As the number of good artists is always strictly limited, it follows that this demand has been in the main supplied by bad artists. Hence the affirmations of the great obvious truths have been in general incompetent and therefore odious. It is possible, also, that the breakup of all the old traditions, the mechanization of work and leisure (from both of which creative effort has now, for the vast majority of civilized men and women, been banished), have had a bad effect on popular taste and popular emotional sensibility. But in any case, whatever the causes, the fact remains that the present age has produced a hitherto unprecedented quantity of popular art (popular in the sense that it is made *for* the people, but not—and this is the modern tragedy—*by* the people), and that this popular art is composed half of the little obvious truths, stated generally with a careful and painstaking realism, half of the great obvious truths, stated for the most part (since it is very hard to give them satisfactory expression) with an incompetence which makes them seem false and repellent.

On some of the most sensitive and self-conscious artists of our age, this state of affairs has had a curious and, I believe, unprecedented effect. They have become afraid of all obviousness, the great as well as the little. At every period, it is true, many artists have been afraid—or, perhaps it would be more accurate to say, have been contemptuous—of the little obvious truths. In the history of the arts naturalism is a relatively rare phenomenon; judged by any standard of statistical normality, Caravaggio and the Victorian academician were artistic freaks. The unprecedented fact is this: some of the most sensitive artists of our age have rejected not merely external realism (for which we may be rather thankful), but even what I may call internal realism; they refuse to take cognizance in their art of most of the most significant facts of human nature. The excesses of popular art have filled them with a terror of the obvious—even of the obvious sublimities and beauties and marvels. Now, about nine tenths of life are made up precisely of the obvious. Which means that there are sensitive modern artists who are compelled, by their disgust and fear, to confine themselves to the exploitation of only a tiny fraction of existence.

The most self-conscious of contemporary artistic centers is Paris, and it is, as we should expect, in Paris that this strange new fear of the obvious has borne the most striking fruits. But what is true of Paris is also true of the other artistic capitals of the world. Either because they are deliberately imitating French models, or else because they have been driven by similar circumstances to make a similar reaction. The advanced art of other countries differs from the advanced art of France only in being rather less deliberate and less thoroughgoing. In every country, but in France a little more clearly than elsewhere, we see how the same fear of the obvious has produced the same effects. We see the plastic arts stripped of all their "literary" qualities, pictures and statues reduced to their strictly formal elements. We listen to a music from which almost every expression of a tragical, a mournful, a tender sentiment has been excluded—a music that has deliberately confined itself to the expression of physical energy, of the lyricism of speed and mechanical motion. Both music and the visual arts are impregnated to a greater or less extent with that new topsy-turvy romanticism, which exalts the machine, the crowd, the merely muscular body, and despises the soul and solitude and nature. Advanced literature is full of the same reversed romanticism. Its subject matter is arbitrarily simplified by the exclusion of all the great eternal obviousnesses of human nature. This process is justified theoretically by a kind of philosophy of history which affirms—quite gratuitously and, I am convinced, quite falsely—that human nature has radically changed in the last few years and that the modern man is, or at least ought to be, radically different from his ancestors. Nor is it only in regard to subject matter that the writer's fear of the obvious manifests itself. He has a terror of the obvious in his artistic medium—a terror which leads him to make laborious efforts to destroy the gradually perfected instrument of language. Those who are completely and ruthlessly logical parade a total nihilism and would like to see the abolition of all art, all science, and all organized society whatsoever. It is extraordinary to what lengths a panic fear can drive its victims.

Almost all that is most daring in contemporary art is thus seen to be the fruit of terror—the terror, in an age of unprecedented vulgarity, of the obvious. The spectacle of so much fear-inspired boldness is one which I find rather depressing. If young artists really desire to offer proof of their courage they should attack the monster of obviousness and try to conquer it, try to reduce it to a state of artistic domestication, not timorously run away from it. For the great obvious truths are there—facts. Those who deny their existence, those who proclaim that human nature has changed since August 4, 1914, are merely rationalizing their terrors and disgusts. Popular art gives a deplorably beastly expression to the obvious; sensitive men and women hate this beastly expression; therefore, by a natural but highly unscientific process, they affirm that the things so hatefully expressed do not exist. But they do exist, as any dispassionate survey of the facts makes clear. And since they exist, they should be faced, fought with, and reduced to artistic order. By pretending that certain things are not there, which in fact *are* there, much of the most accomplished modern art is condemning itself to incompleteness, to sterility, to premature decrepitude and death.

10

"And Wanton Optics Roll the Melting Eye"●

The sunrise was magnificent. The luminary of day,
like a disc of metal gilded by the Ruolz process, came
up from the Ocean, as from an immense voltaic bath.

JULES VERNE

Poetry and Science: a marriage has been arranged—again
and again, in the minds of how many ambitious young
men of letters! But either the engagement was broken off;
or else, if consummated, the marriage was fertile only of
abortions. *Education, The Sugar Cane, The Loves
of the Plants, Cyder, The Fleece*—their forgotten names
are legion.

On what conditions is the marriage possible? Let Wordsworth answer. "The remotest discoveries of the chemist,
the botanist, or the mineralogist, will be as proper objects
of the poet's art as any upon which he is now employed,
if the time should ever come when these things shall be
manifestly and palpably material to us as enjoying and
suffering beings." Poetry can be made out of science, but
only when the contemplation of scientific facts has modified the pattern, not only of the poet's intellectual beliefs,
but of his spiritual existence as a whole—his "inscape,"
as Father Hopkins calls it. Information which has modi-

● From *Music at Night,* 1931.

fied the poet's existence-pattern may be expected (when skillfully "put across" in terms of art) to modify the existence-pattern of his reader. In good scientific poetry the science is there, not primarily for its own sake, but because it is a modifier of existence-patterns. Bad scientific poetry is of two kinds: that in which the science is meant to be a modifier of existence-patterns, but owing to the poet's incompetence as a communicator, fails to do what it was meant to do; and that in which the science is there primarily for its own sake, and not to produce an effect on existence-patterns. Most professedly didactic poems are of this type.

> Gnomes, as you now dissect with hammers fine
> The granite rock, the noduled flint calcine;
> Grind with strong arm, the circling Chertz betwixt,
> Your pure Kaolin and Petuntses mixt.

The scientific information contained by implication in these lines would be much more effectively communicated in the prose of a geological textbook. Textbook prose exists for the purpose of imparting information as accurately as possible. To inform is only a secondary function of poetical language, which exists primarily as an instrument for the modification of existence-patterns.

Information about kaolin is not likely to modify the existence-pattern of any normally constituted human being, however learned in geology—though of course a lyrical poet who happened to be so learned might use a fact about kaolin to illuminate a wholly nongeological theme. The universally knowledgeable Donne made use of the most "remote discoveries" of the scientists of his time as illustrations and enrichments. Kaolin, or its equivalents, helped him to "put across" what he felt about love, God, death, and many other pattern modifying matters. It was as a suffering and enjoying man that he made use of his knowledge. The didactic poets, on the contrary, were, in almost all cases, primarily students. *The Botanic Garden* and *The Economy of Vegetation* provide no internal evidence to show that Erasmus Darwin's general "inscape" was modified by what he had learned about kaolin and the like.

There is much rhymed astronomy in the *Divine Comedy*; but it is never, like Erasmus Darwin's rhymed botany and rhymed geology, ridiculous. Why is this? In the first place, Dante had an incomparable capacity for "putting things across." And in the second place, that which he put across was not merely scientific information; it was always scientific information that had modified the pattern of Dante's whole existence. "And infidel astronomer is mad." For Dante, it is evident, the heavens (the Ptolemaic heavens in all their intricate detail of sphere and epicycle) proclaimed the glory of God. The most unlikely piece of information about the sun or the stars was never merely a piece of out-of-the-way information; it was indissolubly a part of that religious system which patterned the whole of Dante's existence. Most of us are ignorant where Dante was learned and sceptical about what he believed. Consequently, in such lines as—

> *Surge ai mortali per diverse foci*
> *la lucerna del mondo; ma da quella,*
> *che quattro cerchi giunge con tre croci,*

> *con miglior corso e con migliore stella*
> *esce congiunta.*

we are struck only by the musically perfect language and a certain oracular obscurity of utterance, intrinsically poetical (for the musically incomprehensible is always charged with a certain magical power). But this abracadabra of circles and crosses has a scientific meaning, this riddle is a statement of fact. Dante evidently liked conveying information in terms of riddles. Where, as in the present case, the riddling formation is about the "remotest discoveries" of astronomy, no one who does not know it in advance can possibly guess the answer to the enigma. Most of the *Divine Comedy* cannot be fully understood except by those who have a special culture. (The same is true of more or less considerable parts of many other poems.)

Solving riddles is an occupation that appeals to almost all of us. All poetry consists, to a greater or less extent, of riddles, to which the answers are occasionally, as in Dante's case, scientific or metaphysical. One of the pleasures we derive from poetry is precisely the crossword puzzler's delight in working out a problem. For certain people this pleasure is peculiarly intense. Nature's puzzle solvers, they tend to value poetry in proportion as it is obscure. I have known such people who, too highbrow to

indulge in the arduous imbecilities of crossword and acros-
tic, sought satisfaction for an imperious yearning in the
sonnets of Mallarmé and the more eccentric verses of
Gerard Hopkins.

To return to our circles and crosses: when you have
sufficiently mugged up the notes to your *Paradiso* you
realize that, when he wrote those lines, Dante was saying
something extremely definite, and that he must have had
before his inward eye a very precise and (what is poeti-
cally more important) a grandiose, a deeply impressive
picture of the entire Ptolemaic universe. Six centuries have
made of Dante's science (even as Chaucer foresaw that
they would make of his own fourteenth-century language)
something "wonder nice and strange." Past literature is a
charnel house of dead words, past philosophy a mine of
fossil facts and theories.

> And yet they spake them so,
> And sped as well in love as men now do.

Chaucer protested in advance against oblivion. In vain.
His speech and Dante's science are dead, forgotten. What
readers has the *Divine Comedy* now? A few poets, a few
lovers of poetry, a few strayed crossword puzzlers, and,
for the rest, a diminishing band of culture-fans and erudi-
tion-snobs. These last feel as triumphantly superior in their
exclusive learning as would the social snob if, alone of all
his acquaintance, he had met the Prince of Wales, or could
speak of Mr. Michael Arlen by his pet name. Even in
Dante's day the cultured few who knew offhand that
"da quella, che giunge quattro cerchi con tre croci" was
the esoteric pet name of sunrise at the equinox must have
felt a certain glow of conscious superiority. Now, six centuries later, these knowledgeable ones are justified in going
off into positive raptures of self-satisfaction. Deathless
verse dies like all the rest. A good dose of science can be
relied on, as we see in Dante's case, to abbreviate its immortality.

An infidel astronomer is mad; but even madder is a
believing and practicing one. So, at any rate, Lucretius
thought. That was why he wanted to convert everyone
to science. For most men are sane; convert them, and
they will automatically cease to be pious. The spectacle
of human life lying "foully prostrate upon earth, crushed
down by the weight of religion" was something that

moved Lucretius to righteous anger. His aim was to destroy the tyrant, to see that religion was "put under foot and trampled on in turn." For Dante, the heavens in all their intricacy of detail movingly proclaimed the glory of God; for Lucretius they no less movingly proclaimed God's impersonality, almost His nonexistence. To both poets "the remotest discoveries" of the scientists were profoundly and humanly important. The centuries have passed and the science of Lucretius and Dante is mostly obsolete and untrue. In spite of the ardor and enthusiasm with which they wrote, in spite of their prodigious powers of communication, it is as students primarily, as archaeologists, that we now read what they composed as suffering and enjoying beings. Leaving out of account the nonscientific, "human" parts of the two poems, the only passages in *De Rerum Natura* and the *Divine Comedy* which still move us as their authors meant them to move are those in which the poets generalize—those in which, by statement or implication, they set forth the hypothesis which their information about "remote discoveries" is supposed to prove, and proceed to show how this hypothesis, if accepted, must affect our attitude towards the world, modify the pattern of our being. Lucretius's statements of the materialist and Dante's of the spiritualist philosophy still have power to modify our existence-pattern, even though most of the "facts" on which they based their respective philosophies are now no more than archaeological specimens.

The facts and even the peculiar jargon of science can be of great service to the writer whose intention is mainly ironical. Juxtapose two accounts of the same human event, one in terms of pure science, the other in terms of religion, aesthetics, passion, even common sense: their discord will set up the most disquieting reverberations in the mind. Juxtapose, for example, physiology and mysticism (Mme Guyon's ecstasies were most frequent and most spiritually significant in the fourth month of her pregnancies); juxtapose acoustics and the music of Bach (perhaps I may be permitted to refer to the simultaneously scientific and aesthetic account of a concert in my novel, *Point Counter Point*); juxtapose chemistry and the soul (the ductless glands secrete among other things our moods, our aspirations, our philosophy of life). This list of linked incompatibles might be indefinitely prolonged. We live in a world of *non sequiturs*. Or rather, we would live in such a world, if we were always conscious of all the aspects under which any event can be considered. But in practice we are almost never aware of more than one aspect of each event at a time. Our life is spent first in one watertight compartment of experience, then in another. The artist can, if he so desires, break down the bulkheads between the compartments and so give us a simultaneous view of two or more of them at a time. So seen, reality looks exceedingly queer. Which is how the ironist and the perplexed questioner desire it to look. Laforgue constantly makes use of this device. All his poetry is a mixture of remote discovery with near sentiment. Hence its pervading quality of irony. In the remote future, when a science infinitely better informed than ours shall have bridged the now enormous gulf between immediately apprehended qualities, in terms of which we *live,* and the merely measurable, ponderable quantities in terms of which we do our scientific thinking, the Laforguian method will cease to be ironical. For the juxtaposition will then be a juxtaposition of compatibles, not of incompatibles. There will be no curious discord, but a perfectly plain and simple harmony. But all this is for the future. So far as we are concerned, the bringing together of remote discoveries and near feelings is productive of literary effects which we recognize as ironical.

11

On Handicraft

Poetry, *sarape* weaving, leatherwork, the ornamental plaiting of string, and the making of *machetes* and swords—these are the principal local handicrafts. The last seems to be mainly a white man's and mestizo's industry. The other crafts are purely Indian and are practiced in the outlying villages as well as in the town itself. The leatherwork is poor; but the pots are pleasant and the gaily colored string bags and haversacks very pretty, in a rather childish way. Of the *sarapes,* some are quietly unpretentious—dark blankets with a minimum of pattern in gray or white on a black ground. But there are also more ambitious designs. One finds, for example, a lamb or a Mexican eagle, carried out in white, black, and gray, with touches of red and green. Sometimes letters will be woven into the picture—a *Viva Mexico,* for example. A few of these blankets are excellent; the rest are dull and sometimes downright ugly. This is only to be expected; for the more ambitious the design, the greater scope for individual talent and the more narrowly restricted the influence of tradition. But individual talent is rare; correspondingly rare, it follows, must be the designs whose excellence depends upon it.

Much nonsense has recently been talked about Indian

• From *Beyond the Mexique Bay* ("Oaxaca"), 1934.

handicrafts. Fleeing from the slump and with the hideous vision of Zenith and Middletown still painfully fresh in their memories, the new William Morrises from the United States have come to Mexico and, confronted by its peasant arts, have broken out into an intemperate and hysterical enthusiasm. Middletown and Zenith are nightmarish; but this is no reason for asserting that the pretty little peasantries of the Mexican Indians are intrinsically significant works of art. Peasant art is hardly ever intrinsically significant as art; its value is social and psychological, not aesthetic. Mr. Chase says of a well-known arts-and-crafts shop in Mexico City that it is "as exciting to him as any art museum." If that is so, then either Mr. Chase is wholly without a feeling for aesthetic values, or else he is mistaking for aesthetic excitement the pleasure which he derives, as a sociologist, from the mere idea of craftsmanship. The wage-slaves of Middletown spend their days alternately working at machines and being passively amused by machines. The craftsmen of Mexico simultaneously work and play at making pots and blankets, lacquer bowls and the like. The wage-slave's life is restless and unsatisfying; the craftsman's life (at any rate in many cases) is serene and satisfying. Moreover, the craftsman is unaffected by slumps; the wage-slave periodically starves. Pots, blankets, lacquer, are the symbols of the Mexican craftsman's safer and more wholesome life. In the presence of these symbols, Mr. Chase, the sociologist, feels excited, and, through a roseate fog of mental confusion, the excitement communicates itself to Mr. Chase, the aesthete. This is, I think, the most plausible, as it is certainly the most charitable, explanation of Mr. Chase's remark. For, if he really finds a collection of peasant bric-a-brac as exciting as an art museum—*any* art museum, mark you: the Prado, for example, the National Gallery —well, then, heaven help him! For he is a man to whom nature has denied all sense of the qualitative difference between things.

The whole subject of folk art is in a state of great confusion and urgently demands to be clarified. Like Mr. Chase, most enthusiasts for handicrafts tend to attribute too much aesthetic merit to the result of activities whose real value is psychological, social, and economic. It is good that large numbers of people should be craftsmen, not because there is the smallest prospect of their producing a correspondingly large number of good works of art, but because craftsmanship is something which most men and women find psychologically satisfying. I myself, for example, spend much of my spare time painting pictures. The exercise of this manual skill gives me extraordinary pleasure; but I do not for that reason imagine that I am producing masterpieces. So far as the ordinary untalented, or slightly talented, individual is concerned, craftsmanship is its own reward. And because it is its own reward, it is also socially useful. Craftsmanship brings psychological fulfillment; a society of craftsmen is a society of satisfied individuals; and a society of satisfied individuals tends to be a stable society. Craftsmanship has a further social utility, inasmuch as an economy based upon handwork is less alarmingly liable to fluctuation than one whose foundation is mass production. Thus we see that, even if all craftwork and peasant art were uniformly hideous, craftsmanship would still be of the highest value. In point of fact, craftwork is never uniformly hideous. In their own way, the productions of a people of handicraftsmen are often excellent; but the nature of this excellence is essentially inferior to that of the excellence we find in the work of a great artist.

The life of an epoch is expressed by, and at the same time is itself an expression of, the art of that epoch. Where popular art is vulgar, there the life of the people is also essentially vulgar in its emotional quality. The popular arts in our industrialized communities are of an unprecedented vulgarity. Why should this be? And what is the precise nature of this vulgarity? What, again, is the nature of the relative refinement of the popular folk arts of peasants and craftsmen?

The nature of contemporary vulgarity has been well illustrated and analyzed by Mr. Leavis and Mr. Denys Thompson in their book *Culture and Environment*. So far as it goes, it is an excellent little book. Its great defect is that it does not go far enough. For its authors are content merely to describe the symptoms of the disease and to suggest an educational treatment to combat them. But it is not by palliating symptoms that you can effect a real cure. Rational treatment must be based on a knowledge of the deep-rooted causes of the disease. Mr. Leavis and Mr. Thompson are like clinicians who should carefully describe the fever and the pustules, without ever mentioning the virus which is the cause of these symptoms of smallpox. This is the principal defect of their book. Another, less serious, but still grave, is their extremely uncritical assumption that the arts of preindustrial civilization were not merely relatively refined, but always absolutely excellent. At the end of the book we find a series of questions, intended for the use of teachers. One of these is worded as follows: "Do you know of any ugly building, furniture, tools, etc., before 1820? Account, as far as you can, for your findings." The context makes it clear that one is supposed to answer this question in the negative. One is supposed never to have been any ugly building, furniture, or tools of a date anterior to 1820. And, of course, if one is an uncritical archaeolater, one never does see any ugliness in the productions of earlier civilizations. But for any sensitive and unprejudiced person, a walk through any museum of decorative art, through any old town, brings instant proof that the preindustrial age was rich in all manner of ugliness and ineptitude.

The truth is, of course, that most art has always been either bad or indifferent. This is inevitable. Artistic talent is an extremely rare phenomenon; therefore good art is extremely uncommon. The only substitute—and it is at best a partial substitute—for personal talent is a good artistic tradition. This enables people with little talent to produce good work because it relieves them of the necessity for using their own second-rate, or tenth-rate, imaginations. A good tradition may be defined as the ghosts of good dead artists dictating to bad living artists. So long as the bad artists listen to the dictations, and so long as they make no attempt to launch out on their own account, they will produce derivative work. But an artistic tradition need not necessarily be good. For generations the ghosts of bad artists may dictate to other bad artists; the results, when that happens, are deplorable. But even at its worst the bad art of preindustrial times is seldom quite so depressing and never so painfully vulgar as modern bad art.

The badness and vulgarity of modern popular art are the result of a number of interlocking causes. The most important of these are the increase of population; the improvement of old techniques for treating raw materials and the invention of new ones; the rise of the standard of living; and finally, the development within the arts themselves of new and more powerful modes of expression. Let us deal with these in order.

The enormous increase of population during the last century is due to several causes. The cultivation of virgin soil in the New World and the introduction of Chilean nitrates into the Old suddenly quintupled the world's available food supply. Power production made it possible to provide clothing and shelter for indefinite millions of new people. At the same time public hygiene reduced infantile mortality and raised the average age of death. Most of the new millions thus called into being collected in the towns, which were thus swollen to unprecedented dimensions. Now, it seems to me very doubtful whether it is mechanically possible for a very large city to be anything but ugly and depressing. Give to London all the town planning, all the civic centers, all the garden suburbs that the ingenuity of man can devise; it will still remain an assemblage of a million houses sprawling over five or six hundred square miles of ground. And even if every one of these million houses were a masterpiece of architecture (which is humanly impossible), the total effect of their agglomeration would still be profoundly depressing. Avila is a city of extraordinary beauty; but magnify it five or six hundred times, so as to make it as large as London, and Avila will be hideous, a place of interminable monotonies, of hopeless dreariness and suffocating oppression. All our great cities could do with an immense amount of improvement. But we must not flatter ourselves with the belief that these improvements will transform them into things of beauty. Only a ninety per cent destruction can accomplish that miracle.

Undue increase of city population has a psychological effect which I can best sum up by saying that all urbanization, pushed beyond a certain point, automatically becomes suburbanization. The inhabitants of a small city can take part in all its activities; they are able to experience their native place as a single living unit. A large city cannot be experientially known; its life is too manifold for any individual to be able to participate in it. Every great city is just a collection of suburbs. Its inhabitants have lost the advantages of living in the country without acquiring the compensating advantages of living in a town. For they do not *live* in their city; they merely inhabit it. Their minds are neither rustic nor urban, but suburban; and experience seems to show that a suburban mind is not a soil in which good traditions of art easily flourish.

The mechanization of industry has deprived millions of people of the opportunity to practice a handicraft, and by so doing has destroyed many excellent traditions of applied art. Mr. Leavis and Mr. Thompson have expatiated at some length of this obvious point. But mechanization has had another and no less disastrous effect on the popular arts. The general improvement of technical processes has helped to bring about the general deterioration of taste. We pray that we may not be led into temptation; and with good reason. For it is opportunity that makes most of the murderers, the thieves, the adulterers. Opportunity, too, that makes most of the vulgarians. One fact emerges clearly from the history of art: that whenever men have had the means to be vulgar, they have generally succumbed to the temptation and made use of them.

Vulgarity is always the result of some excess; and the means to vulgarity are therefore means to the realization in practice of an inward tendency toward the excessive. These means to vulgarity are of two kinds, economic and technical. You cannot achieve excess, and therefore vulgarity, unless, first, you have enough money to undertake personally, or to buy from others, works of art on a considerable scale, and, second, unless you or your employees are equipped with enough technical ability to make possible the artistic expression of your inward urge towards excess.

Before discussing the technical means to vulgarity, it will be as well to say a few words about the economic conditions for its realization in terms of art. "It pays to advertise" is a maxim as old as civilization. The rich and eminent members of every society have always spent a certain proportion of their incomes on display. They have paid copy writers and poster designers to "put them across" in nationwide publicity drives. Sometimes these copy writers were called Vergil or Spenser, these poster designers, Holbein or Velasquez or Tiepolo. But often the ruler's or the rich man's desire for publicity has been gratified by artists of inferior quality. Hence from the tomb of Tutankhamen to the Queen Victoria Memorial, those innumerable monuments of vulgarity which constitute, in such large measure, what is beautifully called the World's Artistic Heritage.

Folk art is often dull or insignificant; never vulgar, and for an obvious reason. Peasants lack, first, the money, and, second, the technical skill to achieve those excesses which are the essence of vulgarity. Vulgarity has always been the privilege of the prosperous and the highly educated. The general rise in the standard of living has meant a general increase in vulgarity. For the first time in the world's history the small bourgeoisie and even a part of the proletariat have been able to treat themselves to the luxuries previously reserved to members of the ruling class. Conspicuous among these luxuries is artistic vulgarity.

So much for the economic means to vulgarity. The technical means are of two kinds—those concerned primarily with the treatment of matter and those concerned primarily with the treatment of the invisible entities in a work of art: ideas and emotions.

Wherever artists find much technical difficulty in imposing form on brute matter, art tends to be simple, severe, and chaste. It cannot be anything else. Luxuriance, unchastity, and consequent vulgarity become possible only when men have acquired almost complete mastery over matter. It is when they can express themselves freely that artists begin to reveal their true character. The man of delicate and noble talent will express freely his delicacy and nobility; the man whose talent is coarse and vulgar will be able at last to give free rein to his coarseness and vulgarity. This is why any improvement in the techniques of subduing matter to spirit is always attended by an increase in vulgarity. Only an artist of exceptional austerity can make a temperate use of the resources of a highly developed technology. Significantly enough, many sensitive artists of this age have adopted towards modern technique an attitude analogous to that of a hermit towards the pleasures of the world. Fearful of temptation, they retire into the desert—an artificial desert of their own making, a little oasis of technical aridity in the midst of the prevailing luxuriance. They are perhaps wise. Personally, however, I should have admired them more if they had faced the problem a little more courageously— gone out into the luxuriance and tried to master it. But that is by the way.

Advances in technology have led not only to vulgarity,

but also, indirectly, to the lowering of qualitative standards in all the popular arts. Process reproduction and the
rotary press have made possible the indefinite multiplica-
tion of writing and pictures. Universal education and
relatively high wages have created an enormous public
who know how to read and can afford to buy reading
matter and pictorial seeing matter. A great industry has
been called into existence in order to supply these com-
modities. Now, artistic talent is a very rare phenomenon;
whence it follows (as I have already remarked) that,
at every epoch and in all countries, most art has been
bad. But the proportion of trash in the total artistic
output is greater now than at any other period. That it
must be so is a matter of simple arithmetic. The population of Western Europe has a little more than doubled
during the last century. But the amount of reading- and
seeing-matter has increased, I should imagine, at least
twenty and possibly fifty or even a hundred times. If
there were n men of talent in a population of x millions,
there will presumably be $2n$ men of talent among $2x$
millions. The situation may be summed up thus. For every
page of print and pictures published a century ago, twenty
or perhaps even a hundred pages are published today.
But for every man of talent then living, there are now
only two men of talent. It may be of course that, thanks
to universal education, many potential talents which in
the past would have been stillborn are now enabled
to realize themselves. Let us assume, then, that there are
now three or even four men of talent to every one of
earlier times. It still remains true to say that the consumption of reading- and seeing-matter has far outstripped
the natural production of gifted writers and draftsmen.
It is the same with hearing-matter. Prosperity, the gramo-
phone and the radio have created an audience of hearers
who consume an amount of hearing-matter that has increased out of all proportion to the increase of population and the consequent natural increase of talented
musicians. It follows from all this that in all the arts
the output of trash is both absolutely and relatively
greater than it was in the past; and that it must remain
greater for just so long as the world continues to consume the present inordinate quantities of reading-matter,
seeing-matter, and hearing-matter.

So far I have spoken only of technical improvements

in the handling of materials. There have also been purely aesthetic advances in the technique of expression. Of these the most startling are to be found in the domain of music. Beethoven made it possible to give direct and poignant expression to a great number of thoughts and feelings which, owing to the absence of a suitable idiom, were inexpressible by even the most highly gifted of his predeceesors. Beethoven's aesthetic discoveries were exploited by other men in order to express thoughts and feelings of greatly inferior quality. The same thing happened in the case of all the great musical innovators of the nineteenth and early twentieth centuries. Thanks to Beethoven, to Berlioz, to Wagner (himself a sad vulgarian), to Rimsky-Korsakov, to Debussy, to Stravinsky, the modern jazz composer is in a position to express (with what an appalling technical efficiency!) every shade of all the baser emotions, from a baboonlike lust to a nauseating self-commiseration, from the mindless mass hysteria of howling mobs to a languishing masturbatory *"Träumerei."* The first popular waltz, as I pointed out some years ago, was *"Ach, du lieber Augustin."* Compare that innocently silly little tune with a successful waltz or blues of today. The distance traveled has been enormous. Towards what goal? One shudders to imagine it. And the joke, the atrocious and deplorable joke, is that this Gadarene progress has been made possible by the labors of some of the most noble and delicate spirits known to history.

What is the upshot of it all? So far as I can see, it is this: that the vulgarity which characterizes our industrial civilization is part of the inevitable result or concomitant of our prosperity, our universal instruction, our technological progress, our urbanization. Mr. Leavis and Mr. Thompson seem to think that the remedy for vulgarity and the general lowering of qualitative standards lies in better education; and certainly something can be done by teaching such children as are teachable to distinguish between the good and the bad, the bogus and the genuine. But I doubt whether education can restore us to complete emotional and artistic health. The psychological, social, and economic forces, now making towards vulgarization, are too strong to be resisted by a handful of school teachers (themselves, incidentally, more or less seriously infected by the disease they are supposed to cure). A change in the existing organization of society might do some good. For example, it might be possible, while preserving the advantages of machine production, to reintroduce, to some extent, the practice of handicrafts. Freed from the burden of competition, the organizers of industry could afford to create and artificially preserve little Red Indian Reservations of craftsmanship in the midst of a world of machines. Again, the state could train its citizens for a leisure in which the practice of handicrafts should play an important part. That love of "hobbies," so common in every class of society, could be systematized, could be given a new, more dignified status, a higher social significance. The psychological effects of such a policy would probably be excellent. But it does not follow that, because a man is contented, he will produce good art. I see no reason to suppose that the arts and crafts of a prosperous, technically efficient and relatively well-educated society would possess even the negative virtues of peasant art. For these negative virtues, as I have already shown, are the result of poverty and ignorance. A society of civilized handicraftsmen could never blindly accept an old tradition. There would always be attempts at originality—attempts foredoomed, in the great majority of cases, to failure; for only highly talented artists can hope to be original with success. The partial restoration of handicraft culture would probably make for personal happiness and social stability, but would do little, so far as I can see, to cure vulgarity. Vulgarity is the price we must pay for prosperity, education, and self-consciousness. Nor must we forget the influence of quantity upon quality. So long as population remains at its present density, ugliness is inevitable. For, reduplicated a million times, even the most beautiful object becomes hideous. Even more hideous will seem the endless repetitions of objects originally and intrinsically ugly. And intrinsically ugly they must be; for, in a large, prosperous, and educated population, it is impossible that the level of popular art should be high. It is impossible because, as I have shown, the consumption of the arts has increased far more rapidly than the natural production of men of talent. Great quantity inevitably creates bad quality and multiplies it till it becomes a nightmare.

So far, then, as the popular arts are concerned, the

prospect is none too good. Perhaps the wisest thing to do is to abandon them to their inevitable vulgarity and ineptitude and to concentrate all available resources on the training of a minority that shall be capable of appreciating the higher activities of the spirit. *Il faut cultiver notre oasis.*

12

On Art, Sanity, and Mysticism●

How significant is the enormous heightening, under mescalin, of the perception of color! For certain animals it is biologically very important to be able to distinguish certain hues. But beyond the limits of their utilitarian spectrum, most creatures are completely color blind. Bees, for example, spend most of their time "deflowering the fresh virgins of the spring"; but, as Von Frisch has shown, they can recognize only a very few colors. Man's highly developed color sense is a biological luxury— inestimably precious to him as an intellectual and spiritual being, but unnecessary to his survival as an animal. To judge by the adjectives which Homer puts into their mouths, the heroes of the Trojan War hardly excelled the bees in their capacity to distinguish colors. In this respect, at least, mankind's advance has been prodigious.

Mescalin raises all colors to a higher power and makes the percipient aware of innumerable fine shades of difference, to which, at ordinary times, he is completely blind. It would seem that, for Mind at Large, the so-called secondary characters of things are primary. Unlike Locke, it evidently feels that colors are more important,

● From *The Doors of Perception,* 1954. This passage is selected from Mr. Huxley's interpretation of his experiences while under the effects of the drug mescalin.

better worth attending to, than masses, positions, and dimensions. Like mescalin takers, many mystics perceive supernaturally brilliant colors, not only with the inward eye, but even in the objective world around them. Similar reports are made by psychics and sensitives. There are certain mediums to whom the mescalin taker's brief revelation is a matter, during long periods, of daily and hourly experience.

From this long but indispensable excursion into the realm of theory, we may now return to the miraculous facts—four bamboo chair legs in the middle of a room. Like Wordsworth's daffodils, they brought all manner of wealth—the gift, beyond price, of a new direct insight into the very Nature of Things, together with a more modest treasure of understanding in the field, especially, of the arts.

A rose is a rose is a rose. But these chair legs were chair legs were St. Michael and all angels. Four or five hours after the event, when the effects of a cerebral sugar shortage were wearing off, I was taken for a little tour of the city, which included a visit, towards sundown, to what is modestly claimed to be the World's Biggest Drug Store. At the back of the W.B.D.S., among the toys, the greeting cards, and the comics, stood a row, surprisingly enough, of art books. I picked up the first volume that came to hand. It was on Van Gogh, and the picture at which the book opened was "The Chair"— that astounding portrait of a *Ding an Sich*, which the mad painter saw, with a kind of adoring terror, and tried to render on his canvas. But it was a task to which the power even of genius proved wholly inadequate. The chair Van Gogh had seen was obviously the same in essence as the chair I had seen. But, though incomparably more real than the chairs of ordinary perception, the chair in his picture remained no more than an unusually expressive symbol of the fact. The fact had been manifested Suchness; this was only an emblem. Such emblems are sources of true knowledge about the Nature of Things, and this true knowledge may serve to prepare the mind which accepts it for immediate insights on its own account. But that is all. However expressive, symbols can never be the things they stand for.

It would be interesting, in this context, to make a study of the works of art available to the great knowers

of Suchness. What sort of pictures did Eckhart look at?
What sculptures and paintings played a part in the religious experience of St. John of the Cross, of Hakuin,
of Hui-neng, of William Law? The questions are beyond
my power to answer; but I strongly suspect that most of
the great knowers of Suchness paid very little attention
to art—some refusing to have anything to do with it at
all, others being content with what a critical eye would
regard as second-rate, or even, tenth-rate, works. (To a
person whose transfigured and transfiguring mind can
see the All in every *this*, the first-rateness or tenth-rate-
ness of even a religious painting will be a matter of the
most sovereign indifference.) Art, I suppose, is only for
beginners, or else for those resolute dead-enders, who
have made up their minds to be content with the *ersatz*
of Suchness, with symbols rather than with what they
signify, with the elegantly composed recipe in lieu of
actual dinner.

I returned the Van Gogh to its rack and picked up
the volume standing next to it. It was a book on Botticelli. I turned the pages. "The Birth of Venus"—never
one of my favorites. "Mars and Venus," that loveliness
so passionately denounced by poor Ruskin at the height
of his long-drawn sexual tragedy. The marvelously rich
and intricate "Calumny of Apelles." And then a somewhat less familiar and not very good picture, "Judith."
My attention was arrested and I gazed in fascination,
not at the pale neurotic heroine or her attendant, not at
the victim's hairy head or the vernal landscape in the
background, but at the purplish silk of Judith's pleated
bodice and long wind-blown skirts.

This was something I had seen before—seen that very
morning, between the flowers and the furniture, when
I looked down by chance, and went on passionately staring by choice, at my own crossed legs. Those folds
in the trousers—what a labyrinth of endlessly significant
complexity! And the texture of the gray flannel—how
rich, how deeply, mysteriously sumptuous! And here they
were again, in Botticelli's picture.

Civilized human beings wear clothes, therefore there
can be no portraiture, no mythological or historical storytelling without representations of folded textiles. But
though it may account for the origins, mere tailoring can
never explain the luxuriant development of drapery as a

major theme of all the plastic arts. Artists, it is obvious, have always loved drapery for its own sake—or, rather, for their own. When you paint or carve drapery, you are painting or carving forms which, for all practical purposes, are nonrepresentational—the kind of unconditioned forms on which artists even in the most naturalistic tradition like to let themselves go. In the average Madonna or Apostle the strictly human, fully representational element accounts for about ten per cent of the whole. All the rest consists of many colored variations on the inexhaustible theme of crumpled wool or linen. And these nonrepresentational nine tenths of a Madonna or an Apostle may be just as important qualitatively as they are in quantity. Very often they set the tone of the whole work of art, they state the key in which the theme is being rendered, they express the mood, the temperament, the attitude to life of the artist. Stoical serenity reveals itself in the smooth surfaces, the broad untortured folds of Piero's draperies. Torn between fact and wish, between cynicism and idealism, Bernini tempers the all but caricatural verisimilitude of his faces with enormous sartorial abstractions, which are the embodiment, in stone or bronze, of the everlasting commonplaces of rhetoric— the heroism, the holiness, the sublimity to which mankind perpetually aspires, for the most part in vain. And here are El Greco's disquietingly visceral skirts and mantles; here are the sharp, twisting, flamelike folds in which Cosimo Tura clothes his figures: in the first, traditional spirituality breaks down into a nameless physiological yearning; in the second, there writhes an agonized sense of the world's essential strangeness and hostility. Or consider Watteau; his men and women play lutes, get ready for balls and harlequinades, embark, on velvet lawns and under noble trees, for the Cythera of every lover's dream; their enormous melancholy and the flayed, excruciating sensibility of their creator find expression, not in the actions recorded, not in the gestures and the faces portrayed, but in the relief and texture of their taffeta skirts, their satin capes and doublets. Not an inch of smooth surface here, not a moment of peace or confidence, only a silken wilderness of countless tiny pleats and wrinkles, with an incessant modulation—inner uncertainty rendered with the perfect assurance of a master hand—of tone into tone, of one indeterminate color into another. In life, man proposes, God disposes. In the plastic arts the proposing is done by the subject matter; that which disposes is ultimately the artist's temperament, proximately (at least in portraiture, history, and genre) the carved or painted drapery. Between them, these two may decree that a *fête galante* shall move to tears, that a crucifixion shall be serene to the point of cheerfulness, that a stigmatization shall be almost intolerably sexy, that the likeness of a prodigy of female brainlessness (I am thinking now of Ingres' incomparable Mme Moitessier) shall express the austerest, the most uncompromising intellectuality.

But this is not the whole story. Draperies, as I had now discovered, are much more than devices for the introduction of nonrepresentational forms into naturalistic paintings and sculptures. What the rest of us see only under the influence of mescalin, the artist is congenitally equipped to see all the time. His perception is not limited to what is biologically or socially useful. A little of the knowledge belonging to Mind at Large oozes past the reducing valve of brain and ego, into his consciousness. It is knowledge of the intrinsic significance of every existent. For the artist as for the mescalin taker draperies are living hieroglyphs that stand in some peculiarly expressive way for the unfathomable mystery of pure being. More even than the chair, though less perhaps than those wholly supernatural flowers, the folds of my gray flannel trousers were charged with "is-ness." To what they owed this privileged status, I cannot say. Is it, perhaps, because the forms of folded drapery are so strange and dramatic that they catch the eye and in this way force the miraculous fact of sheer existence upon the attention? Who knows? What is important is less the reason for the experience than the experience itself. Poring over Judith's skirts, there in the World's Biggest Drug Store, I knew that Botticelli—and not Botticelli alone, but many others too—had looked at draperies with the same transfigured and transfiguring eyes as had been mine that morning. They had seen the *Istigkeit*, the Allness and Infinity of folded cloth and had done their best to render it in paint or stone. Necessarily, of course, without success. For the glory and the wonder of pure existence belong to another order, beyond the power of even the highest art to express. But in Judith's skirt I could clearly see what, if I had been a painter of genius, I might have made of my old gray flannels. Not much, heaven knows, in comparison with the reality; but enough to delight generation after generation of beholders, enough to make them understand at least a little of the true significance of what, in our pathetic imbecility, we call "mere things" and disregard in favor of television.

"This is how one ought to see," I kept saying as I looked down at my trousers, or glanced at the jeweled books in the shelves, at the legs of my infinitely more than Van Goghian chair. "This is how one ought to see, how things really are." And yet there were reservations. For if one always saw like this, one would never want to do anything else. Just looking, just being the divine Not-self of flower, of book, of chair, of flannel. That would be enough. But in that case what about other people? What about human relations? In the recording of that morning's conversations I find the question constantly repeated, "What about human relations?" How could one reconcile this timeless bliss of seeing as one ought to see with the temporal duties of doing what one ought to do and feeling as one ought to feel? "One ought to be able," I said, "to see these trousers as infinitely important and human beings as still more infinitely important." One ought—but in practice it seemed to be impossible. This participation in the manifest glory of things left no room, so to speak, for the ordinary, the necessary concerns of human existence, above all for concerns involving persons. For persons are selves and, in one respect at least, I was now a Not-self, simultaneously perceiving and being the Not-self of the things around me. To this newborn Not-self, the behavior, the appearance, the very thought of the self it had momentarily ceased to be, and of other selves, its onetime fellows, seemed not indeed distasteful (for distastefulness was not one of the categories in terms of which I was thinking), but enormously irrelevant. Compelled by the investigator to analyze and report on what I was doing (and how I longed to be left alone with Eternity in a flower, Infinity in four chair legs, and the Absolute in the folds of a pair of flannel trousers!) I realized that I was deliberately avoiding the eyes of those who were with me in the room, deliberately refraining from being too much aware of them. One was my wife, the other a man I respected and greatly liked; but both belonged to the world from which, for the moment, mescalin had delivered me —the world of selves, of time, of moral judgments and utilitarian considerations, the world (and it was this aspect of human life which I wished, above all else, to forget) of self-assertion, of cocksureness, of overvalued words and idolatrously worshiped notions.

At this stage of the proceedings I was handed a large colored reproduction of the well-known self-portrait by Cézanne—the head and shoulders of a man in a large straw hat, red-cheeked, red-lipped, with rich black whiskers and a dark unfriendly eye. It is a magnificent painting; but it was not as a painting that I now saw it. For the head promptly took on a third dimension and came to life as a small goblinlike man looking out through a window in the page before me. I started to laugh. And when they asked me why, "What pretensions!" I kept repeating. "Who on earth does he think he is?" The question was not addressed to Cézanne in particular, but to the human species at large. Who did they all think they were?

"It's like Arnold Bennett in the Dolomites," I said, suddenly remembering a scene, happily immortalized in a snapshot, of A. B., some four or five years before his death, toddling along a wintry road at Cortina d'Ampezzo. Around him lay the virgin snow; in the background was a more than gothic aspiration of red crags. And there was dear, kind, unhappy A. B., consciously overacting the role of his favorite character in fiction, himself, the Card in person. There he went, toddling slowly in the bright Alpine sunshine, his thumbs in the armholes of a yellow waistcoat which bulged, a little lower down, with the graceful curve of a Regency bow window at Brighton—his head thrown back as though to aim some stammered utterance, howitzerlike, at the blue dome of heaven. What he actually said, I have forgotten; but what his whole manner, air, and posture fairly shouted was, "I'm as good as those damned mountains." And in some ways, of course, he was infinitely better; but not, as he knew very well, in the way his favorite character in fiction liked to imagine.

Successfully (whatever that may mean) or unsuccessfully, we all overact the part of our favorite character in fiction. And the fact, the almost infinitely unlikely fact, of actually being Cézanne makes no difference. For the consummate painter, with his little pipeline to Mind at Large bypassing the brain valve and ego-filter, was also and just as genuinely this whiskered goblin with the unfriendly eye.

For relief I turned back to the folds in my trousers. "This is how one ought to see," I repeated yet again. And I might have added, "These are the sort of things one ought to look at." Things without pretensions, satisfied to be merely themselves, sufficient in their Suchness, not acting a part, not trying, insanely, to go it alone, in isolation from the Dharma-Body, in Luciferian defiance of the grace of God.

"The nearest approach to this," I said, "would be a Vermeer."

Yes, a Vermeer. For that mysterious artist was trebly gifted—with the vision that perceives the Dharma-Body as the hedge at the bottom of the garden, with the talent to render as much of that vision as the limitations of human capacity permit, and with the prudence to confine himself in his paintings to the more manageable aspects of reality; for though Vermeer represented human beings, he was always a painter of still life. Cézanne, who told his female sitters to do their best to look like apples, tried to paint portraits in the same spirit. But his pippin-like women are more nearly related to Plato's Ideas than to the Dharma-Body in the hedge. They are Eternity and Infinity seen, not in sand or flower, but in the abstractions of some very superior brand of geometry. Vermeer never asked his girls to look like apples. On the contrary, he insisted on their being girls to the very limit—but always with the proviso that they refrain from behaving girlishly. They might sit or quietly stand but never giggle, never display self-consciousness, never say their prayers or pine for absent sweethearts, never gossip, never gaze enviously at other women's babies, never flirt, never love or hate or work. In the act of doing any of these things they would doubtless become more intensely themselves, but would cease, for that very reason, to manifest their divine essential Not-self. In Blake's phrase, the doors of Vermeer's perception were only partially cleansed. A single panel had become almost perfectly transparent; the rest of the door was still muddy. The essential Not-self could be perceived very clearly in things and in living creatures on the hither side of good and evil. In human beings it was visible only when they were in repose, their minds untroubled, their bodies motionless. In these circumstances Vermeer could see Suchness in all its heavenly beauty—could see and, in some small measure, render it in a subtle and sumptuous still life. Vermeer is undoubtedly the greatest painter of human still lives. But there have been others, for example, Vermeer's French contemporaries, the Le Nain brothers. They set out, I suppose, to be genre painters; but what they actually produced was a series of human still lives, in which their cleansed perception of the infinite significance of all things is rendered not, as with Vermeer, by subtle enrichment of color and texture, but by a heightened clarity, an obsessive distinctness of form, within an austere, almost monochromatic tonality. In our day we have had Vuillard, the painter, at his best, of unforgettably splendid pictures of the Dharma-Body manifested in a bourgeois bedroom, of the Absolute blazing away in the midst of some stockbroker's family in a suburban garden, taking tea.

> Ce qui fait que l'ancien bandagiste renie
> Le comptoir dont le faste alléchait les passants,
> C'est son jardin d'Auteuil, où, veufs de tout encens,
> Les Zinnias ont l'air d'être en tôle vernie.

For Laurent Tailhade the spectacle was merely obscene. But if the retired rubber goods merchant had sat still enough, Vuillard would have seen in him only the Dharma-Body, would have painted, in the zinnias, the goldfish pool, the villa's Moorish tower and Chinese lanterns, a corner of Eden before the Fall.

But meanwhile my question remained unanswered. How was this cleansed perception to be reconciled with a proper concern with human relations, with the necessary chores and duties, to say nothing of charity and practical compassion? The age-old debate between the actives and the contemplatives was being renewed—renewed, so far as I was concerned, with an unprecedented poignancy. For until this morning I had known contemplation only in its humbler, its more ordinary forms—as discursive thinking; as a rapt absorption in poetry or painting or music; as a patient waiting upon those inspirations, without which even the prosiest writer cannot hope to accomplish anything; as occasional glimpses, in Nature, of Wordsworth's "something far more deeply interfused"; as systematic silence leading, sometimes, to hints of an "obscure knowledge." But now I knew contemplation at its height. At its height, but not yet in its fullness. For in its fullness the way of Mary includes the way of Martha and raises it, so to speak, to its own higher power. Mescalin opens up the way of Mary, but shuts the door on that of Martha. It gives access to contemplation —but to a contemplation that is incompatible with action and even with the will to action, the very thought of action. In the intervals between his revelations the mescalin taker is apt to feel that, though in one way everything is supremely as it should be, in another there is something wrong. His problem is essentially the same as that which confronts the quietist, the *arhat* and, on another level, the landscape painter and the painter of human still lives. Mescalin can never solve that problem; it can only pose it, apocalyptically, for those to whom it had never before presented itself. The full and final solution can be found only by those who are prepared to implement the right kind of *Weltanschauung* by means of the right kind of behavior and the right kind of constant and unstrained alertness. Over against the quietist stands the active-contemplative, the saint, the man who, in Eckhart's phrase, is ready to come down from the seventh heaven in order to bring a cup of water to his sick brother. Over against the *arhat*, retreating from appearances into an entirely transcendental Nirvana, stands the Bodhisattva, for whom Suchness and the world of contingencies are one, and for whose boundless compassion every one of those contingencies is an occasion not only for transfiguring insight, but also for the most practical charity. And in the universe of art, over against Vermeer and the other painters of human still lives, over against the masters of Chinese and Japanese landscape painting, over against Constable and Turner, against Sisley and Seurat and Cézanne, stands the all-inclusive art of Rembrandt. These are enormous names, inaccessible eminences. For myself, on this memorable May morning, I could only be grateful for an experience which had shown me, more clearly than I had ever seen it before, the true nature of the challenge and the completely liberating response.

Let me add, before we leave this subject, that there is no form of contemplation, even the most quietistic, which is without its ethical values. Half at least of all morality is negative and consists in keeping out of mischief. The Lord's Prayer is less than fifty words long, and six of those words are devoted to asking God not to lead us into temptation. The one-sided contemplative leaves undone many things that he ought to do; but to make up for it, he refrains from doing a host of things he ought not to do. The sum of evil, Pascal remarked, would be much diminished if men could only learn to sit quietly in their rooms. The contemplative whose perception has been cleansed does not have to stay in his room. He can go about his business, so completely satisfied to see and be a part of the divine Order of Things that he will never even be tempted to indulge in what Traherne called "the dirty Devices of the world." When we feel ourselves to be sole heirs of the universe, when "the sea flows in our veins . . . and the stars are our jewels," when all things are perceived as infinite and holy, what motive can we have for covetousness or self-assertion, for the pursuit of power or the drearier forms of pleasure? Contemplatives are not likely to become gamblers, or procurers, or drunkards; they do not as a rule preach intolerance, or make war; do not find it necessary to rob, swindle, or grind the faces of the poor. And to these enormous negative virtues we may add another which, though hard to define, is both positive and important. The *arhat* and the quietist may not practice contemplation in its fullness; but if they practice it at all, they may bring back enlightening reports of another, a transcendent country of the mind; and if they practice it in the height, they will become conduits through which some beneficent influence can flow out of that other country into a world of darkened selves, chronically dying for lack of it.

Meanwhile I had turned, at the investigator's request, from the portrait of Cézanne to what was going on, inside my head, when I shut my eyes. This time, the inscape was curiously unrewarding. The field of vision was filled with brightly colored, constantly changing structures that seemed to be made of plastic or enameled tin.

"Cheap," I commented. "Trivial. Like things in a five-and-ten." And all this shoddiness existed in a closed, cramped universe. "It's as though one were below decks in a ship," I said. "A five-and-ten-cent ship."

And as I looked, it became very clear that this five-and-ten-cent ship was in some way connected with human pretensions, with the portrait of Cézanne, with A. B. among the Dolomites overacting his favorite character in fiction. This suffocating interior of a dime-store ship was my own personal self; these gimcrack mobiles of tin and plastic were my personal contributions to the universe.

I felt the lesson to be salutary, but was sorry, none the less, that it had had to be administered at this moment and in this form. As a rule the mescalin taker discovers an inner world as manifestly a datum, as self-evidently "infinite and holy," as that transfigured outer world which I had seen with my eyes open. From the first, my own case had been different. Mescalin had endowed me temporarily with the power to see things with my eyes shut; but it could not, or at least on this occasion did not, reveal an inscape remotely comparable to my flowers or chair or flannels "out there." What it had allowed me to perceive inside was not the Dharma-Body, in images, but my own mind; not Suchness, but a set of symbols—in other words, a homemade substitute for Suchness.

Most visualizers are transformed by mescalin into visionaries. Some of them—and they are perhaps more numerous than is generally supposed—require no transformation; they are visionaries all the time. The mental species to which Blake belonged is fairly widely distributed even in the urban-industrial societies of the present day. The poet-artist's uniqueness does not consist in the fact that (to quote from his *Descriptive Catalogue*) he actually *saw* "those wonderful originals called in the Sacred Scriptures the Cherubim." It does not consist in the fact that "these wonderful originals seen in my visions, were some of them one hundred feet in height . . . all containing mythological and recondite meaning." It consists solely in his ability to render, in words or (somewhat less successfully) in line and color, some hint at least of a not excessively uncommon experience. The untalented visionary may perceive an inner reality no less tremendous, beautiful, and significant than the world beheld by Blake; but he lacks altogether the ability to express, in literary or plastic symbols, what he has seen.

From the records of religion and the surviving monuments of poetry and the plastic arts it is very plain that, at most times and in most places, men have attached more importance to the inscape than to objective existents, have felt that what they saw with their eyes shut possessed a spiritually higher significance than what they saw with their eyes open. The reason? Familiarity breeds contempt, and how to survive is a problem ranging in urgency from the chronically tedious to the excruciating. The outer world is what we wake up to every morning of our lives, is the place where, willy-nilly, we must try to make our living. In the inner world there is neither work nor monotony. We visit it only in dreams and musings, and its strangeness is such that we never find the same world on two successive occasions. What wonder, then, if human beings in their search for the divine have generally preferred to look within! Generally, but not always. In their art no less than in their religion, the Taoists and the Zen Buddhists looked beyond visions to the Void, and through the Void at "the ten thousand things" of objective reality. Because of their doctrine of the Word made flesh, Christians should have been able, from the first, to adopt a similar attitude towards the universe around them. But because of the doctrine of the Fall, they found it very hard to do so. As recently as three hundred years ago an expression of thoroughgoing world denial and even world condemnation was both orthodox and comprehensible. "We should feel wonder at nothing at all in Nature except only the Incarnation of Christ." In the seventeenth century, Lallemant's phrase seemed to make sense. Today it has the ring of madness.

In China the rise of landscape painting to the rank of a major art form took place about a thousand, in Japan about six hundred and in Europe about three hundred, years ago. The equation of Dharma-Body with hedge was made by those Zen Masters, who wedded Taoist naturalism with Buddhist transcendentalism. It was, therefore, only in the Far East that landscape painters consciously regarded their art as religious. In the West religious painting was a matter of portraying sacred personages, of illustrating hallowed texts. Landscape painters regarded themselves as secularists. Today we recognize in Seurat one of the supreme masters of what may be called mystical landscape painting. And yet this man who was able, more effectively than any other, to render the One in the many, became quite indignant when somebody praised him for the "poetry" of his work. "I merely apply the System," he protested. In other words he was merely a *pointilliste* and, in his own eyes, nothing else. A similar anecdote is told of John Constable. One day towards the end of his life, Blake met Constable at Hampstead and was shown one of the younger artist's sketches. In spite of his contempt for naturalistic art, the old visionary knew a good thing when he saw it—except, of course, when it was by Rubens. "This is not drawing," he cried, "this is inspiration!" "I had meant it to be drawing," was Constable's characteristic answer. Both men were right. It *was* drawing, precise and veracious, and at the same time it *was* inspiration—inspiration of an order at least as high as Blake's. The pine trees on the Heath had actually been seen as identical with the Dharma-Body. The sketch was a rendering, necessarily imperfect but still profoundly impressive, of what a cleansed perception had revealed to the open eyes of a great painter. From a contemplation, in the tradition of Wordsworth and Whitman, of the Dharma-Body as hedge, and from visions, such as Blake's, of the "wonderful originals" within the mind, contemporary poets have retreated into an investigation of the personal, as opposed to the more than personal, subconscious and to a rendering, in highly abstract terms, not of the given, objective fact, but of mere scientific and theological notions. And something similar has happened in the field of painting, where we have witnessed a general retreat from landscape, the predominant art form of the nineteenth century. This retreat from landscape has not been into that other, inner divine Datum, with which most of the traditional schools of the past were concerned, that Archetypal World, where men have always found the raw materials of myth and religion. No, it has been a retreat from the outward Datum into the personal subconscious, into a mental world more squalid and more tightly closed than even the world of conscious personality. These contraptions of tin and highly colored plastic—where had I seen them before? In every picture gallery that exhibits the latest in nonrepresentational art.

And now someone produced a phonograph and put a record on the turntable. I listened with pleasure, but experienced nothing comparable to my seen apocalypses of flowers or flannel. Would a naturally gifted musician *hear* the revelations which, for me, had been exclusively visual? It would be interesting to make the experiment. Meanwhile, though not transfigured, though retaining its normal quality and intensity, the music contributed not a little to my understanding of what had happened to me and of the wider problems which those happenings had raised.

Instrumental music, oddly enough, left me rather cold. Mozart's C minor Piano Concerto was interrupted after the first movement, and a recording of some madrigals by Gesualdo took its place.

"These voices," I said appreciatively, "these voices— they're a kind of bridge back to the human world."

And a bridge they remained even while singing the most startlingly chromatic of the mad prince's compositions. Through the uneven phrases of the madrigals, the music pursued its course, never sticking to the same key for two bars together. In Gesualdo, that fantastic character out of a Webster melodrama, psychological disintegration had exaggerated, had pushed to the extreme limit, a tendency inherent in modal as opposed to fully tonal music. The resulting works sounded as though they might have been written by the later Schönberg.

"And yet," I felt myself constrained to say, as I listened to these strange products of a Counter Reformation psychosis working upon a late medieval art form, "and yet it does not matter that he's all in bits. The whole is disorganized. But each individual fragment is in order, is a representative of a Higher Order. The Highest Order prevails even in the disintegration. The totality is present even in the broken pieces. More clearly present, perhaps, than in a completely coherent work. At least you aren't lulled into a sense of false security by some merely human, merely fabricated order. You have to rely on your immediate perception of the ultimate order. So in a certain sense disintegration may have its advantages. But of course it's dangerous, horribly dangerous. Suppose you couldn't get back, out of the chaos. . . ."

From Gesualdo's madrigals we jumped, across a gulf of three centuries, to Alban Berg and the *Lyric Suite*.

"This," I announced in advance, "is going to be hell."

But, as it turned out, I was wrong. Actually the

music sounded rather funny. Dredged up from the personal subconscious, agony succeeded twelve-tone agony; but what struck me was only the essential incongruity between a psychological disintegration even completer than Gesualdo's and the prodigious resources, in talent and technique, employed in its expression.

"Isn't he sorry for himself!" I commented with a derisive lack of sympathy. And then, "*Katzenmusik*—learned *Katzenmusik*." And finally, after a few more minutes of the anguish, "Who cares what his feelings are? Why can't he pay attention to something else?"

As a criticism of what is undoubtedly a very remarkable work, it was unfair and inadequate—but not, I think, irrelevant. I cite it for what it is worth and because that is how, in a state of pure contemplation, I reacted to the *Lyric Suite*.

When it was over, the investigator suggested a walk in the garden. I was willing; and though my body seemed to have dissociated itself almost completely from my mind—or, to be more accurate, though my awareness of the transfigured outer world was no longer accompanied by an awareness of my physical organism—I found myself able to get up, open the French window, and walk out with only a minimum of hesitation. It was odd, of course, to feel that "I" was not the same as these arms and legs "out there," as this wholly objective trunk and neck and even head. It was odd; but one soon got used to it. And anyhow the body seemed perfectly well able to look after itself. In reality, of course, it always does look after itself. All that the conscious ego can do is to formulate wishes, which are then carried out by forces which it controls very little and understands not at all. When it does anything more—when it tries too hard, for example, when it worries, when it becomes apprehensive about the future—it lowers the effectiveness of those forces and may even cause the devitalized body to fall ill. In my present state, awareness was not referred to as ego; it was, to to speak, on its own. This meant that the physiological intelligence controlling the body was also on its own. For the moment that interfering neurotic who, in waking hours, tries to run the show, was blessedly out of the way.

From the French window I walked out under a kind of pergola covered in part by a climbing rose tree, in part by laths, one inch wide with half an inch of space between them. The sun was shining and the shadows of the laths made a zebralike pattern on the ground and across the seat and back of a garden chair, which was standing at this end of the pergola. That chair—shall I ever forget it? Where the shadows fell on the canvas upholstery, stripes of a deep but glowing indigo alternated with stripes of an incandescence so intensely bright that it was hard to believe that they could be made of anything but blue fire. For what seemed an immensely long time I gazed without knowing, even without wishing to know, what it was that confronted me. At any other time I would have seen a chair barred with alternate light and shade. Today the percept had swallowed up the concept. I was so completely absorbed in looking, so thunderstruck by what I actually saw, that I could not be aware of anything else. Garden furniture, laths, sunlight, shadow—these were no more than names and notions, mere verbalizations, for utilitarian or scientific purposes, after the event. The event was this succession of azure furnace doors separated by gulfs of unfathomable gentian. It was inexpressibly wonderful, wonderful to the point, almost, of being terrifying. And suddenly I had an inkling of what it must feel like to be mad. Schizophrenia has its heavens as well as its hells and purgatories. I remember what an old friend, dead these many years, told me about his mad wife. One day in the early stages of the disease, when she still had her lucid intervals he had gone to talk to her about their children. She listened for a time, then cut him short. How could he bear to waste his time on a couple of absent children, when all that really mattered, here and now, was the unspeakable beauty of the patterns he made, in this brown tweed jacket, every time he moved his arms? Alas, this paradise of cleansed perception, of pure one-sided contemplation, was not to endure. The blissful intermissions became rarer, became briefer, until finally there were no more of them; there was only horror.

Most takers of mescalin experience only the heavenly part of schizophrenia. The drug brings hell and purgatory only to those who have had a recent case of jaundice, or who suffer from periodical depressions or a chronic anxiety. If, like the other drugs of remotely comparable power, mescalin were notoriously toxic, the taking of it would be enough, of itself, to cause anxiety. But the reasonably healthy person knows in advance that, so far as he is concerned, mescalin is completely innocuous, that its effects will pass off after eight or ten hours, leaving no hangover and consequently no craving for a renewal of the dose. Fortified by this knowledge, he embarks upon the experiment without fear—in other words, without any disposition to convert an unprecedently strange and other than human experience into something appalling, something actually diabolical.

Confronted by a chair which looked like the Last Judgment—or, to be more accurate, by a Last Judgment which, after a long time and with considerable difficulty, I recognized as a chair—I found myself all at once on the brink of panic. This, I suddenly felt, was going too far. Too far, even though the going was into intenser beauty, deeper significance. The fear, as I analyze it in retrospect, was of being overwhelmed, of disintegrating under a pressure of reality greater than a mind, accustomed to living most of the time in a cosy world of symbols, could possibly bear. The literature of religious experience abounds in references to the pains and terrors overwhelming those who have come, too suddenly, face to face with some manifestation of the *Mysterium tremendum.* In theological language, this fear is due to the incompatibility between man's egotism and the divine purity, between man's self-aggravated separateness and the infinity of God. Following Boehme and William Law, we may say that, by unregenerate souls, the divine Light at its full blaze can be apprehended only as a burning, purgatorial fire. An almost identical doctrine is to be found in *The Tibetan Book of the Dead,* where the departed soul is described as shrinking in agony from the Pure Light of the Void, and even from the lesser, tempered Lights, in order to rush headlong into the comforting darkness of selfhood as a reborn human being, or even as a beast, an unhappy ghost, a denizen of hell. Anything rather than the burning brightness of unmitigated Reality—anything!

The schizophrenic is a soul not merely unregenerate, but desperately sick into the bargain. His sickness consists in the inability to take refuge from inner and outer reality (as the sane person habitually does) in the home-made universe of common sense—the strictly human world of useful notions, shared symbols and socially acceptable conventions. The schizophrenic is like a man permanently under the influence of mescalin, and therefore unable to shut off the experience of a reality which he is not holy enough to live with, which he cannot explain away because it is the most stubborn of primary facts, and which, because it never permits him to look at the world with merely human eyes, scares him into interpreting its unremitting strangeness, its burning intensity of significance, as the manifestations of human or even cosmic malevolence, calling for the most desperate counter-measures, from murderous violence at one end of the scale to catatonia, or psychological suicide, at the other. And once embarked upon the downward, the infernal road, one would never be able to stop. That, now, was only too obvious.

13

Adonis and the Alphabet •

Twenty miles north of Beirut we crossed a river. Not much of a river, in terms of size and water; but what a volume of myth, what a length of history! The bridge on which we had halted spanned the River Adonis. We looked over the parapet and were a little disappointed to find the water pellucid, unstained, at this late season, by the red earth of the Lebanon, the blood, if you prefer, of the dying god. To the east, high up in a gorge among the mountains, at the very place where Adonis lost his life, had stood the temple to which uncounted thousands of his worshipers climbed every year on arduous pilgrimage. And at Byblos, a few miles beyond the river, was the sanctuary of Adonis's lover. For the Greeks she was Aphrodite; for Solomon, who built a high place for her at Jerusalem, Ashtaroth; she was Ishtar in Babylonia, Astarte in Phoenicia, Atargatis for the Syrians—and, for Shakespeare, the heroine of his earliest poem.

"Fondling," she saith, "since I have hemm'd thee here
Within the circuit of this ivory pale,
I'll be a park, and thou shalt be my deer;
Feed where thou wilt, on mountain or in dale:
    Graze on my lips; and if those hills be dry,
    Stray lower, where the pleasant fountains lie."

• From *Tomorrow and Tomorrow and Tomorrow*, 1956.

We have come a long way, in this rococo Venus and
her reluctant boy, from the Dea Syria and the Corn
Spirit, from the drama of death and resurrection acted
out, symbolically, to the accompaniment of ritual coup-
lings and sacred prostitution, of the wailings of half-
naked women and the self-castrations of frenzied youths.
"Graze on my lips, stray lower. . . ." The cosmic has
become the comic; an enormous mystery has been transformed into a charming piece of near impropriety. This
is the way a world ends, the old, dark world of chthonic
deities and fertility cults—not (to parody Mr. Eliot) with
a bang, but a simper. And a good thing, too, on the whole.
Bang may be impressive; but what a bore in the long run,
how crude and brutal! Those denunciatory rumblings of
Hebrew prophets, those endless persecutions, those noisy
revivals of what each revivalist regards as True Religion,
those ham preachers with their thrilling voices and their
all too noble gestures, those tragedians eloquently gloat-
ing over disaster, those Carlylean moralists, Christian or
Stoic, bellowing away about the wickedness of being happy
and the abominableness of nature—surely, surely we have
had enough of them. Shakespeare's way of dealing
with the fertility religions is humaner than the Inquisi-
tion's and at least as effective. Both as literature and as
morals, *Venus and Adonis* is better than the *Malleus
Maleficarum*. As for grazing on lips and straying lower
—even at their most depraved these amusements are a
thousand times less wicked than torturing people, and
even burning them alive, because they prefer an
older conception of God to the one that is currently
fashionable among clergymen. But even so, Shakespeare's
is not the final answer. We have had enough, and more
than enough, of prophets, revivalists, and tragedians. But
we have also had enough of the satirists and debunkers,
of the writers of farces and the tellers of bawdy stories,
to whom long-suffering humanity has turned for an
antidote to all those Jeremiahs and Savonarolas, and
portentous Dantes, those preachers of crusades and
heresy hunters, ancient and modern. *Heads* implies *tails;*
simper is merely the obverse of bang, Félicia of Laura,
Bouvard et Pecuchet of *Paradise Lost*. There is no escape
except into the divine equanimity, which reconciles all
the opposites and so transfigures the world.

We got into the car again and drove on between the

sea and the mountains. A few minutes later the coastal highway had become the main street of a small town. We were in Jebeil, with the monuments of the Crusades towering ruinously overhead and the remains of Byblos—of half a dozen Bybloses, Roman, Greek, Phoenician, Colonial-Egyptian, Chalcolithic, Neolithic—emerging, under the spades of the archaeologists, from the earth beneath our feet.

There is no description of ancient Byblos. Lucian, in *The Syrian Goddess,* tells us that he visited the temple, but not what it looked like, nor what were the rites of Adonis in which he took part. And did he really think that the annual arrival of the Holy Head was a miracle? It is hard in the light of his later, total skepticism, to believe it. And yet the fact remains that, in *The Syrian Goddess,* he called it a miracle. The Holy Head belonged, presumably, to Osiris and came all the way from Egypt, floating on the waves and driven by mysteriously purposeful winds, which brought it punctually, after a seven-day crossing, to the land of Osiris's counterpart, Adonis. "I saw it," Lucian affirms; and there is no reason to doubt his word. After all, Chaucer and his contemporaries had all seen the *pigges bones* in the Pardoner's crystal reliquary.

Byblos, of course, was much more than a place of pilgrimage. It was a port, the oldest in Phoenicia, and a clearing house for trade between Egypt, Syria, and the further East on the one hand and Europe and Asia Minor on the other. The proof of this lies embedded in two Greek words, *byblos* and *biblion.* Byblos was the common name for papyrus. We find it in Herodotus and, much earlier, in Homer, who has Odysseus make fast the doors of his house with "byblian tackle," in other words, ropes of papyrus fiber. To the Greeks of Ionia and, later, of Europe, string and paper were brought by Phoenician traders, whose home port gave its name to the finished article as well as to the Egyptian plant which supplied the raw material. A Greek would call for a sheet of byblos or a ball of byblian twine, just as, centuries later, an Englishman would ask for a yard of damask or a pound of damsons. And when the byblos came in rolls and had writing on it, the thing was a biblion, a bible or, as we should say (since we used to do our writing on tablets of beechwood), a book. And this Phoenician city, I reflected as we strolled through its narrow spaces and enormous times, had had another, more than merely etymological connection with literature. For it was here, about thirty-five centuries ago, that some nameless genius invented, or at least perfected, the ABC.

The discovery of this fact was due to a happy accident. In 1922 a landslide revealed an underground chamber and a huge sarcophagus. The archaeologists went to work and had soon unearthed a whole cemetery of royal tombs. One of these contained the sarcophagus of King Ahiram, who reigned in the thirteenth century before our era. On it had been carved an inscription in Phoenician characters. The alphabet, it was clear, had been in use hundreds of years earlier than had previously been supposed. King Ahiram's coffin is now in the Beirut Museum—that fascinating repository of perhaps the ugliest works of art ever created by man; for the Phoenicians (heaven knows why) seem to have been incapable of producing anything but monstrosities. No, I exaggerate; they were capable sometimes of producing cutenesses. Their figurines of hippopotami, for example, might have been modeled by Walt Disney. But if art was not their strong point, commerce undoubtedly was; and it must have been in the interests of commercial efficiency that one of them invented the new and enormously simpler system of writing which was destined to replace cuneiform and hieroglyphics throughout the Near East and Europe. As a man of letters, I felt I ought to lay a wreath on the tomb of the Unknown Letter-Maker of Byblos.

It was Sunday, and in the Crusader's elegant little church a Maronite service was in progress. The words of an incomprehensible liturgy reverberated under the vaults, and above the heads of the congregation a family of sparrows was going unconcernedly about its business. Nobody paid any attention to their noisy impudence. The little creatures were taken for granted. Along with the ancient stones, the altar, the intoning priest, they were an accepted feature of the Sunday landscape, an element in the sacred situation. In this part of the world, birds seem to be perfectly compatible with monotheism. These Maronite sparrows are matched by the Mohammedan pigeons in the Omayyad Mosque at Damascus. That splendid sanctuary is alive with wings and cooing, and when droppings fall on the head of some grave and bearded worshiper—we actually saw it happen—there is no indignation, only a tolerant smile. Birds, after all, are God's creatures; and if Allah chooses not to provide them with a colon and a capacity for prolonged retention, who are we that we should dare to complain? Let us rather give thanks that dogs were not allowed to fly.

The dove was sacred in ancient Syria, and Atargatis was, among many other things, a Fish Goddess and the patroness of every animal except the pig. Within the precincts of her temple at Hierapolis, in northern Syria, there was a lake with an altar in it, and a congregation of carp; also a kind of holy zoo, where eagles, oxen, lions, and bears wandered harmlessly and at liberty among the worshipers. Ancient traditions die hard, and perhaps the birds we had seen owed their immunity, in mosque and church, to the buried memories of a religion far older than either Islam or Christianity. Animals, say the theologians, have no souls. Having no souls, they have no rights, and may be treated by human beings as though they were mere things. In certain circumstances, indeed, they deserve a treatment even worse than that which we ordinarily accord to things. Blessed Cecilia, a thirteenth-century Roman nun, has told how St. Dominic came one evening to preach, from behind the grille, to the Sisters of her convent. His theme was devils; and hardly had he begun his sermon, when "the enemy of mankind came on the scene in the shape of a sparrow and began to fly through the air, hopping even on the Sisters' heads, so that they could have handled him had they been so minded, and all this to hinder the preaching. St. Dominic, observing this, called Sister Maximilla and said: 'Get up and catch him, and bring him here to me.' She got up and putting out her hand, had no difficulty in seizing hold of him, and handed him out through the window to St. Dominic. St. Dominic held him fast in one hand, and commenced plucking off his feathers with the other, saying the while: 'You wretch, you rogue!' When he had plucked him clean of all his feathers, amidst much laughter from the Brothers and Sisters, and awful shrieks of the sparrow, he pitched him out, saying: 'Fly now if you can, enemy of mankind! You can cry out and trouble us, but you cannot hurt us.' "

What an ugly little picture it is! An intelligent and highly educated man wallowing in the voluntary ignorance of the lowest kind of superstition; a saint indulging his paranoid fancies to the point where they justified him in behaving like a sadist; a group of devout monks and nuns laughing full-throatedly at the shrieks and writhings of a tortured bird. Our own age is certainly bad; but in many respects the Age of Faith was even worse. Take, for example, this matter of torturing animals. There were a few humanitarians in the Middle Ages. Chaucer's Prioress, who could not bear to see a dog being beaten, was one of them. St Hugh of Avalon was another. This older contemporary of St. Dominic had a pet swan and, instead of plucking birds alive, used to feed and tame them. And then, of course, there was St. Francis—though not St. Francis's followers. His rustic disciple, Brother Juniper, once heard a sick man express a desire for fried pig's trotters, and immediately rushed out of the house and hacked the feet off a living hog. When the saint rebuked him, it was not, as one might have expected, for an act of barbarous cruelty, but because he had damaged a valuable piece of private property. There were other early humanitarians—but not many. In Mme de Rambure's anthology, *L'Église et la Pitié envers les Animaux,* the exploits of medieval animal lovers fill no more than a hundred pages. English Common Law took no cognizance of acts of cruelty towards the brute creation; and to judge from Hogarth's gruesome picture of children tormenting, with every refinement of sadistic beastliness, their dogs, cats, and birds, popular morality was as blind, in this respect, as the law. It was not until 1822 that the first piece of legislation on behalf of animals was enacted by Parliament. By 1876, the Royal Commission on Vivisection could state in its report that "the infliction upon animals of any unnecessary pain is justly abhorrent to the moral sense of Your Majesty's subjects generally." This was a far cry from Hogarth and St. Dominic, a change of heart and thought that marked perhaps the beginning of a religious revolution. The old, all too human bumptiousness which had been consecrated by verse twenty-six of the first chapter of Genesis, the doctrine that man is a being apart from the rest of creation and may do with it what he pleases, was giving place, under the influence of scientific knowledge, to a view of the world at once more realistic and more charitable. That which the theologians and the philosophers had been at such pains to divide was coming together again in a system of thought and feeling that bore, at last, some resemblance to the system of facts in nature.

Spiritual progress is always in an ascending spiral. Animal instinct gives place to human will and then to grace, guidance, inspiration, which are simply instinct on a higher level. Or consider the progress of consciousness. First there is the infant's undifferentiated awareness, next comes discrimination and discursive reasoning, and finally (if the individual wishes to transcend himself) there is a rise which is also a return towards an obscure knowledge of the whole, a realization of the timeless and the nondual in time and multiplicity. Similarly, in religion, there is the primitive worship of the god who is immanent in nature, next the worship of divine transcendence, and then, on the intellectual level, the philosophy of scientific monism and, on the existential level, the mystical experience of the One, which corresponds, two stories higher up, to the felt pantheism of the origins. St. Dominic was the preacher and, at the same time, the victim of a theological system which, in spite of the doctrine of the Incarnation, stressed the transcendence of God, the hatefulness of nature, the alienation of man from the rest of the creation. This fact explains his behavior, but does not completely excuse it. Tradition is strong, but not irresistible. Some measure of moral, intellectual, and spiritual independence is always possible— though it may, of course, be exceedingly dangerous, as the Albigensians found in St. Dominic's day and as ideological heretics discover in ours, to assert one's right to such independence. In this particular case, however, neither life nor conscience was in danger. There was no dogma equating sparrows with devils. The saint *could* have behaved rationally and charitably; if he behaved as he did, it was, I suppose, because he enjoyed being superstitious (*superstition* equals *concupiscence,* says Pascal), and also, no doubt, because twelve years of medieval higher education—twelve years, that is to say, of memorizing dead men's words and playing logical games with them—had left him with a notion of reality even more distorted, in some respects, than that of the ignorant peasant or artisan.

And this brings us back to the Unknown Letter-Maker; for we live, each one of us, immersed in language, and our thoughts, feelings, and behavior are, to a much greater extent than we care to admit, determined by the words and syntax of our native tongue and even by the signs through which those words and that syntax are made visible in writing. In the West it is only recently that, thanks to the logicians, the semanticists, the students of linguistics and metalinguistics, we have become fully aware of the part played by language as a virtual philosophy, a source of ontological postulates, a conditioner of thought and even perception, a molder of sentiments, a creator of behavior patterns. To the Indians, these ideas have been familiar for centuries. In every system of Hindu philosophy the phenomenal world is called *nama-rupa*, "name-and-form." This, at first glance, strikes us as odd. But after all (to quote the words of Heinrich Zimmer), "the possibilities for thought, practical or otherwise, at any given period are rigidly limited by the range and wealth of the available linguistic coinage. . . . The totality of this currency is called, in Indian philosophy, *naman* (Latin *nomen*, our word 'name'). The very substance, on and by which the mind operates when thinking, consists of this name-treasury of notions. *Naman* is the internal realm of concepts, which corresponds to the external realm of perceived 'forms,' the Sanskrit term for the latter being *rupa*. . . . *Rupa* is the outer counterpart of *naman; naman* the interior of *rupa*. *Nama-rupa* therefore denotes, on the one hand, man, the experiencing and thinking individual, man as endowed with mind and senses; and, on the other, all the means and objects of thought and perception. *Nama-rupa* is the whole world, subjective and objective, as observed and known." • But no language is perfect, no vocabulary is adequate to the wealth of the given universe, no pattern of words and sentences, however rich, however subtle, can do justice to the interconnected Gestalts with which experience presents us. Consequently the phenomenal forms of our name-conditioned universe are "by nature delusory and fallacious." Wisdom comes only to those who have learned how to talk and read and write without taking language more seriously than it deserves. As the only begetter of civilization and even of our humanity, language must be taken very seriously. Seriously, too, as an instrument

• Heinrich Zimmer, *Philosophies of India*, p. 23. New York, Pantheon Books Inc., 1951.

(when used with due caution) for thinking about the relationships between phenomena. But it must never be taken seriously when it is used, as in the old credal religions and their modern political counterparts, as being in any way the equivalent of immediate experience or as being a source of true knowledge about the nature of things. In an unsystematic way, the great medieval mystics, such as Eckhart and Tauler and the author of *The Cloud of Unknowing,* were acutely aware of the danger of taking language as seriously as it was taken by most of their contemporaries. But their warnings were couched in general terms, and their ignorance of any language but Latin and their native dialect made it impossible for them to formulate any effective criticism. For example, they did not, and could not, see that Aristotle's logic was a systematization of Greek grammar, which makes a certain amount of sense for those who speak an Indo-European language, but not for those who speak Chinese or for those who have learned the artificial languages of mathematics and modern logic; and that, therefore, it cannot be regarded (as it was regarded for so many centuries) as Logic with a large L, the final and definitive formulation of the laws of thought. Similarly, they did not, and could not, know that the age-old preoccupation of Western philosophers with the notion of substance was the natural consequence of their speaking a language in which there were clearly distinguishable parts of speech, a verb "to be," and sentences containing subjects and predicates. " 'Substance,' " says Bertrand Russell in his *History of Western Philosophy,* "is a metaphysical mistake due to transference to the world-structure of the structure of sentences composed of a subject and a predicate." And what about "essence"? The question is relevant only in the domain of language. "A *word* may have an essence, a *thing* cannot." In Chinese there are no fixed parts of speech, sentences do not take the subject-predicate form, and there is no verb meaning "to be." Consequently, except under foreign influence, Chinese philosophers have never formulated the idea of "substance," and never projected the word into the universe.

Their concern has always been with the relationships between things, not with their "essences"; with the "how" of experience rather than the inferred "what." If the

Arian controversy had reached China, one can imagine the native theologians speculating about the simultaneous threeness and oneness of the Persons, but never dividing, or not dividing, the Substance.

Western science began with the ideas of essence and substance, which were implicit in the Indo-European languages and had been made explicit in Greek philosophy and Latin theology; but it has been compelled, by the inner logic of the scientific process, to get rid of these notions and adopt instead an up-to-date, critical version of the Chinese view of things.

Language exists in two forms, the spoken and the written. As knowledge accumulated, and formal education was made more widely available, written language became progressively more and more important. *Littera scripta manet, volat irrevocabile verbum;* writing abides, the spoken word flies off and cannot be recalled. Socrates, who is remembered solely because Xenophon and Plato wrote about him, was himself an enemy of writing. Wisdom and a knowledge of metaphysical and moral truth cannot, he maintained, be conveyed in books, but only by means of rhetoric and dialectic. The Chinese sages, it may be remarked, were of a diametrically opposite opinion. For them, rhetoric and dialectic were beneath contempt. Serious philosophical ideas could be conveyed only in writing—and only, of course, in the kind of writing current in China, where language is rendered visible by means of a complicated system of signs, some of which (the pictograms) are actually representations of the things denoted, others (the ideograms) are compound symbols standing for ideas, and yet others (the phonograms) represent certain of the sounds which occur most commonly in the spoken language. Before the invention of the alphabet, the civilized peoples of the Near East employed one or other of two very ancient systems of writing—the hieroglyphic writing of Egypt and the cuneiform of Sumeria and, later, of Babylonia, Assyria, and Persia. Both systems were fundamentally similar to the Chinese, inasmuch as both made use of hundreds of signs, some pictographic, some ideographic, and some phonographic. The inventors of the alphabet performed the extraordinary feat of reducing these hundreds of signs to less than thirty. These twenty-odd consonants and vowels were so judiciously chosen that, by means of them, every word in every language could be rendered, not indeed perfectly, but well enough for most practical purposes—and rendered, what was more, in a form which indicated, more or less, how the word was to be pronounced. Efficiency in business and government; universal education; encyclopedias and dictionaries; the possibility of expressing one's meaning unequivocally and with the maximum of precision—these are a few of the benefits for which we have to thank the Unknown Letter-Maker. The ABC has been an enormous blessing, but like most blessings, not entirely unmixed. Rendered alphabetically, a word remains strictly itself. Rendered by means of pictograms, ideograms, and phonograms, a word becomes something else, as well as itself. The Chinese interest in relations rather than substance is due in part, as we have seen, to the idiosyncrasies of a language in which there are no fixed parts of speech and no word for "to be"; in part to the nature of Chinese writing. "Chinese thought," says Professor Chang Tun-Sun, "is not based upon the law of identity, but takes as its starting point relative orientation, or rather the relation of opposites." (For example, "non-resistance means strength," "fluency stutters," "*yin* entails *yang*." This last pair of correlated opposites is fundamental in Chinese thought, which regards the positive principle as dependent, for its existence, upon the negative, and the negative upon the positive. Brought up on Latin grammar and the ABC, St. Dominic could see only the differences between things, not their togetherness. God was one thing and Nature, since the Fall, something other and alien, something which willingly lent itself to the Enemy of Mankind, so that a sparrow was really the Devil in disguise and must be tortured, just as the Albigensians must be tortured for going one stage further and affirming that the Devil had actually created the material world.) The Chinese system of thought is "probably related to the nature of Chinese characters. Being ideographic, Chinese characters put emphasis on the signs and symbols of objects. The Chinese are interested in the interrelation between the different signs, without being bothered by the substance underlying them. . . . The characteristic of Chinese thought lies in its exclusive attention to the correlational implications between different signs."

When words are alphabetically rendered, they remain,

as I have said, merely themselves. Spelled out, a name is still that particular name, and the corresponding form is still that particular form. The ABC confirms the phenomenal world of *nama-rupa*. In English, for example, the notion of "good" is rendered by the four letters, g-o-o-d. In Chinese, the same idea is represented by a combination of the sign for "woman" with the sign for "child." How touching! But now consider the Chinese word *fang*. *Fang* has many different meanings, but is represented by only one character, originally applied to *fang*, signifying "square"—a character which is a kind of picture or diagram of two boats tied together. When this sign stands for *fang* in any of its other meanings, it is used as a phonogram and has to be combined with another sign, so as to be distinguishable from "square." Thus, the sign for "woman" plus the phonogram for *fang* means "hinder." *Woman* plus *child* equals *good*. But this good has its price; for a man who has a wife and children has given hostages to fortune. The good of one context is the hindrance of another. What a wealth of ideas is implicit in the writing of these two common words! No wonder if the Chinese paid so much attention to "the correlational implications between different signs."

The universe is a many-dimensional pattern, infinite in extent, infinite in duration, infinite in significance, and infinitely aware, we may surmise, of its own infinities. Within the cosmic order, every component pattern, every object and event, is related to every other; there is a co-varying togetherness of all things. But, by creatures like ourselves, most of the interconnections within the general Gestalt are, and will always be unrecognized. For us, "the world is full of a number of things," which we tend to see as so many independent entities. And we are confirmed in this tendency by alphabetic writing. For alphabetic writing creates an illusion of clarity and separateness. The words we read are written in such a way that they seem to be exclusively themselves, and this makes us believe that we know what's what, that a rose is a rose is a rose. But in fact a rose is a rose-plus is a rose-minus is a rose to the nth. The *what* we think we know is never only *what*. Besides, as an underlying substance, *what* is unknowable and non-existent. *What* exists only when it is known by the liberated and transfigured consciousness, which experiences the paradox of the absoluteness of relationships, the infinity and universality of particulars. This experience is what Eckhart calls the experience of "isness"—which is entirely different from the notion of being or the dogma of substance. For the unliberated, untransfigured mind, all that is knowable is the *how* of relationships. The characters employed in the older systems of writing helped men to remember this all-important fact. That "woman" plus a certain phonogram (which was originally a pictogram, representing two boats tied together, and stood for "square") should actually mean "hinder," is a most salutary reminder that the universe is bottomlessly odd. Lucian, Astarte, the alphabet, sparrows in church, St. Dominic, the Albigenses—what a rich mixed bag of disparate items! But, ultimately, nothing is irrelevant to anything else. There is a togetherness of all things in an endless hierarchy of living and interacting patterns.

Conditioned by their culture, their language, their position in time, their temperament, character, and intelligence, men have paid attention now to one set of patterns, now to another. Today we have it in our power to perceive, infer, and understand a far wider area of reality than was open to our ancestors. Nature, language, history, human behavior—our knowledge of these things is incomparably wider than that which was available in the past. But width, unfortunately, is all too often the enemy of depth. Clear knowledge of the Whole outside us requires to be supplemented by an obscure knowledge of the Whole within. Moreover, the clear external knowledge must be carried inwards, as far as analysis and introspection can take it, while the obscure knowledge within must be projected outwards, so that our theoretical conviction of the world's unity may be transformed into an intuition, a constant realization. How easy it is to say what ought to be done! And how difficult, alas, to do it and, therefore, how unlikely that, except by very few, it will ever be done!

II: CRITICISM

There are few things more melancholy than the spectacle
of literary fossilization. A great writer comes into being,
lives, labors, and dies. Time passes; year by year the
sediment of muddy comment and criticism thickens round
the great man's bones. The sediment sets firm; what was
once a living organism becomes a thing of marble. On
the attainment of total fossilization the great man has
become a classic. It becomes increasingly difficult for the
members of each succeeding generation to remember that
the stony objects which fill the museum cases were once
alive. It is often a work of considerable labor to reconstruct
the living animal from the fossil shape. But the trouble
is generally worth taking. And in no case is it more
worth while than in Chaucer's.

With Chaucer the ordinary fossilizing process, to which
every classical author is subject, has been complicated
by the petrifaction of his language. Five hundred years
have almost sufficed to turn the most living of poets into
ᴀ substitute on the modern sides of schools for the mental
gymnastic of Latin and Greek. Prophetically, Chaucer
saw the fate that awaited him and appealed against
his doom:

• From *On the Margin*, 1923.

Ye know eke that, in form of speech is change
Within a thousand years, and wordes tho
That hadden price, now wonder nice and strange
Us thinketh them; and yet they spake them so,
And sped as well in love as men now do.

The body of his poetry may have grown old, but its
spirit is still young and immortal. To know that spirit—
and not to know it is to ignore something that is of
unique importance in the history of our literature—it is
necessary to make the effort of becoming familiar with
the body it informs and gives life to. The antique language and versification, so "wonder nice and strange" to
our ears, are obstacles in the path of most of those who
read for pleasure's sake (not that any reader worthy of the
name ever reads for anything else but pleasure); to the
pedants they are an end in themselves. Theirs is the
carcass, but not the soul. Between those who are daunted
by his superficial difficulties and those who take too much
delight in them Chaucer finds but few sympathetic
readers. I hope in these pages to be able to give a few
of the reasons that make Chaucer so well worth reading.

Chaucer's art is, by its very largeness and objectiveness,
extremely difficult to subject to critical analysis. Confronted by it, Dryden could only exclaim, "Here is God's
plenty!"—and the exclamation proves, when all is said, to
be the most adequate and satisfying of all criticisms. All
that the critic can hope to do is to expand and to illus-
trate Dryden's exemplary brevity.

"God's plenty!"—the phrase is a peculiarly happy one.
It calls up a vision of the prodigal earth, of harvest
fields, of innumerable beasts and birds, of teeming life.
And it is in the heart of this living and material world of
Nature that Chaucer lives. He is the poet of earth, supremely content to walk, desiring no wings. Many English poets have loved the earth for the sake of something—
a dream, a reality, call it which you will—that lies behind
it. But there have been few, and, except for Chaucer,
no poets of greatness, who have been in love with earth
for its own sake, with Nature in the sense of something
inevitably material, something that is the opposite of the
supernatural. Supreme over everything in this world he
sees the natural order, the "law of kind," as he calls it.
The teachings of most of the great prophets and poets
are simply protests against the law of kind. Chaucer does

not protest, he accepts. It is precisely this acceptance that makes him unique among English poets. He does not go to Nature as the symbol of some further spiritual reality; hills, flowers, sea, and clouds are not, for him, transparencies through which the workings of a great soul are visible. No, they are opaque; he likes them for what they are, things pleasant and beautiful, and not the less delicious because they are definitely of the earth earthy. Human beings, in the same way, he takes as he finds, noble and beastish, but, on the whole, wonderfully decent. He has none of that strong ethical bias which is usually to be found in the English mind. He is not horrified by the behavior of his fellow-beings, and he has no desire to reform them. Their characters, their motives interest him, and he stands looking on at them, a happy spectator. This serenity of detachment, this placid acceptance of things and people as they are, is emphasized if we compare the poetry of Chaucer with that of his contemporary, Langland, or whoever it was that wrote *Piers Plowman.*

The historians tell us that the later years of the fourteenth century were among the most disagreeable periods of our national history. English prosperity was at a very low ebb. The Black Death had exterminated nearly a third of the working population of the islands, a fact which, aggravated by the frenzied legislation of the Government, had led to the unprecedented labor troubles that culminated in the peasants' revolt. Clerical corruption and lawlessness were rife. All things considered, even our own age is preferable to that in which Chaucer lived. Langland does not spare denunciation; he is appalled by the wickedness about him, scandalized at the openly confessed vices that have almost ceased to pay to virtue the tribute of hypocrisy. Indignation is the inspiration of *Piers Plowman,* the righteous indignation of the prophet. But to read Chaucer one would imagine that there was nothing in fourteenth-century England to be indignant about. It is true that the Pardoner, the Friar, the Shipman, the Miller, and, in fact, most of the Canterbury pilgrims are rogues and scoundrels; but, then, they are such "merry harlots" too. It is true that the Monk prefers hunting to praying, that, in these latter days when fairies are no more, "there is none other incubus" but the friar, that "purse is the Archdeacon's hell," and the Summoner a villain of the first magnitude; but Chaucer can only regard these things as primarily humorous. The fact of people not practicing what they preach is an unfailing source of amusement to him. Where Langland cries aloud in anger, threatening the world with hell-fire, Chaucer looks on and smiles. To the great political crisis of his time he makes but one reference, and that a comic one:

> So hideous was the noyse, ah *benedicite!*
> Certes he Jakke Straw, and his meyné,
> Ne maden schoutes never half so schrille,
> Whan that they wolden eny Flemyng kille,
> As thilke day was mad upon the fox.

Peasants may revolt, priests break their vows, lawyers lie and cheat, and the world in general indulge its sensual appetites; why try and prevent them, why protest? After all, they are all simply being natural, they are all following the law of kind. A reasonable man, like himself, "flees fro the pres and dwelles with soothfastnesse." But reasonable men are few, and it is the nature of human beings to be the unreasonable sport of instinct and passion, just as it is the nature of the daisy to open its eye to the sun and of the goldfinch to be a spritely and "gaylard" creature. The law of kind has always and in everything domination; there is no rubbing nature against the hair. For

> God it wot, there may no man embrace
> As to destreyne a thing, the which nature
> Hath naturelly set in a creature.
> Take any brid, and put him in a cage,
> And do all thine entent and thy corrage
> To foster it tendrely with meat and drynke,
> And with alle the deyntees thou canst bethinke,
> And keep it all so kyndly as thou may;
> Although his cage of gold be never so gay,
> Yet hath this brid, by twenty thousand fold,
> Lever in a forest, that is wyld and cold,
> Gon ete wormes, and such wrecchidnes;
> For ever this brid will doon his busynes
> To scape out of his cage when that he may;
> His liberté the brid desireth aye . . .
> Lo, heer hath kynd his dominacioun,
> And appetyt flemeth (banishes) discrescioun.
> Also a she wolf hath a vilayne kynde,
> The lewideste wolf that she may fynde,

Or least of reputacioun, him will sche take,
In tyme whan hir lust to have a make.
Alle this ensaumples tell I by these men
That ben untrewe, and nothing by wommen.

(As the story from which these lines are quoted happens to be about an unfaithful wife, it seems that, in making the female sex immune from the action of the law of kind, Chaucer is indulging a little in irony.)

For men han ever a licorous appetit
On lower thing to parforme her delit
Than on her wyves, ben then never so faire,
He never so trewe, ne so debonaire.

Nature, deplorable as some of its manifestations may be, must always and inevitably assert itself. The law of kind has power even over immortal souls. This fact is the source of the poet's constantly expressed dislike of celibacy and asceticism. The doctrine that upholds the superiority of the state of virginity over that of wedlock is, to begin with (he holds), a danger to the race. It encourages a process which we may be permitted to call dysgenics—the carrying on of the species by the worst members. The Host's words to the Monk are memorable:

Allas! why wearest thou so wide a cope?
God give me sorwe! and I were a pope
Nought only thou, but every mighty man,
Though he were shore brode upon his pan (head)
Should han a wife; for all this world is lorn;
Religioun hath take up all the corn
Of tredyng, and we burel (humble) men ben shrimpes;
Of feble trees there cometh wrecchid impes.
This maketh that our heires ben so sclendere
And feble, that they may not wel engendere.

But it is not merely dangerous; it is antinatural. That is the theme of the "Wife of Bath's Prologue." Counsels of perfection are all very well when they are given to those

That wolde lyve parfytly;
But, lordyngs, by your leve, that am not I.

The bulk of us must live as the law of kind enjoins.

It is characteristic of Chaucer's conception of the world, that the highest praise he can bestow on anything is to assert of it. that it possesses in the highest degree the qualities of its own particular kind. Thus of Cressida he says:

> She was not with the least of her stature,
> But all her limbes so well answering
> Weren to womanhood, that creature
> Nas never lesse mannish in seeming.

The horse of brass in the "Squire's Tale" is

> So well proportioned to be strong,
> Right as it were a steed of Lombardye,
> Thereto so *horsely* and so quick of eye.

Everything that is perfect of its kind is admirable, even though the kind may not be an exalted one. It is, for instance, a joy to see the way in which the Canon sweats:

> A cloote-leaf (dock leaf) he had under his hood
> For sweat, and for to keep his head from heat.
> But it was joye for to see him sweat;
> His forehead dropped as a stillatorie
> Were full of plantain or of peritorie.

The Canon is supreme in the category of sweaters, the very type and idea of perspiring humanity; therefore he is admirable and joyous to behold, even as a horse that is supremely horsely or a woman less mannish than anything one could imagine. In the same way it is a delight to behold the Pardoner preaching to the people. In its own kind his charlatanism is perfect and deserves admiration:

> Mine handes and my tonge gon so yerne,
> That it is joye to see my busynesse.

This manner of saying of things that they are joyous, or, very often, heavenly, is typical of Chaucer. He looks out on the world with a delight that never grows old or weary. The sights and sounds of daily life, all the lavish beauty of the earth fill him with a pleasure which he can only express by calling it a "joy" or a "heaven." It "joye was to see" Cressida and her maidens playing together; and

> So aungellyke was her native beauté
> That like a thing immortal seemede she,
> As doth an heavenish parfit creature.

The peacock has angel's feathers; a girl's voice is heavenly to hear:

Antigone the shene
Gan on a Trojan song to singen clear,
That it an heaven was her voice to hear.

One could go on indefinitely multiplying quotations that testify to Chaucer's exquisite sensibility to sensuous beauty and his immediate, almost exclamatory response to it. Above all, he is moved by the beauty of "young, fresh folkes, he and she"; by the grace and swiftness of living things, birds and animals; by flowers and placid, luminous, parklike landscapes.

It is interesting to note how frequently Chaucer speaks of animals. Like many other sages, he perceives that an animal is, in a certain sense, more human in character than a man. For an animal bears the same relation to a man as a caricature to a portrait. In a way a caricature is truer than a portrait. It reveals all the weaknesses and absurdities that flesh is heir to. The portrait brings out the greatness and dignity of the spirit that inhabits the often ridiculous flesh. It is not merely that Chaucer has written regular fables, though the "Nun's Priest's Tale" puts him among the great fabulists of the world, and there is also much definitely fabular matter in the *Parliament of Fowls*. No, his references to the beasts are not confined to his animal stories alone; they are scattered broadcast throughout his works. He relies for much of his psychology and for much of his most vivid description on the comparison of man, in his character and appearance (which with Chaucer are always indissolubly blended), with the beasts. Take, for example, that enchanting simile in which Troilus, stubbornly antinatural in refusing to love as the law of kind enjoins him, is compared to the corn-fed horse, who has to be taught good behavior and sound philosophy under the whip:

As proude Bayard ginneth for to skip
Out of the way, so pricketh him his corn,
Till he a lash have of the longe whip,
Then thinketh he, "Though I prance all biforn,
First in the trace, full fat and newe shorn,
Yet am I but an horse, and horses' law
I must endure and with my feeres draw."

Or, again, women with too pronounced a taste for fine apparel are likened to the cat:

> And if the cattes skin be sleek and gay,
> She will not dwell in housé half a day,
> But forth she will, ere any day be dawet
> To show her skin and gon a caterwrawet.

In his descriptions of the personal appearance of his characters Chaucer makes constant use of animal characteristics. Human beings, both beautiful and hideous, are largely described in terms of animals. It is interesting to see how often in that exquisite description of Alisoun, the carpenter's wife, Chaucer produces his clearest and sharpest effects by a reference to some beast or bird:

> Fair was this younge wife, and therewithal
> As any weasel her body gent and small . . .
> But of her song it was as loud and yern
> As is the swallow chittering on a barn.
> Thereto she coulde skip and make a game
> As any kid or calf following his dame.
> Her mouth was sweet as bragot is or meath,
> Or hoard of apples, laid in hay or heath.
> Wincing she was, as is a jolly colt,
> Long as a mast and upright as a bolt.

Again and again in Chaucer's poems do we find such similitudes, and the result is always a picture of extraordinary precision and liveliness. Here, for example, are a few:

> Gaylard he was as goldfinch in the shaw,

or,

> Such glaring eyen had he as an hare;

or,

> As piled (bald) as an ape was his skull.

The self-indulgent friars are
>   Like Jovinian,

> Fat as a whale, and walken as a swan.

The Pardoner describes his own preaching in these words:

> Then pain I me to stretche forth my neck
> And east and west upon the people I beck,
> As doth a dove, sitting on a barn.

Very often, too, Chaucer derives his happiest metaphors

from birds and beasts. Of Troy in its misfortune and decline he says: Fortune

> Gan pull away the feathers bright of Troy
> From day to day.

Love-sick Troilus soliloquizes thus:

> He said: "O fool, now art thou in the snare
> That whilom japedest at lovés pain,
> Now art thou hent, now gnaw thin owné chain."

The metaphor of Troy's bright feathers reminds me of a very beautiful simile borrowed from the life of the plants:

> And as in winter leavés been bereft,
> Each after other, till the tree be bare,
> So that there nis but bark and branches left,
> Lieth Troilus, bereft of each welfare,
> Ybounden in the blacke bark of care.

And this, in turn, reminds me of that couplet in which Chaucer compares a girl to a flowering pear tree:

> She was well more blissful on to see
> Than is the newe parjonette tree.

Chaucer is as much at home among the stars as he is among the birds and beasts and flowers of earth. There are some literary men of today who are not merely not ashamed to confess their total ignorance of all facts of a "scientific" order, but even make a boast of it. Chaucer would have regarded such persons with pity and contempt. His own knowledge of astronomy was wide and exact. Those whose education has been as horribly imperfect as my own will always find some difficulty in following him as he moves with easy assurance through the heavens. Still, it is possible without knowing any mathematics to appreciate Chaucer's descriptions of the great pageant of the sun and stars as they march in triumph from mansion to mansion through the year. He does not always trouble to take out his astrolabe and measure the progress of "Phebus, with his rosy cart"; he can record the god's movements in more general terms that may be understood even by the literary man of nineteen hundred and twenty. Here, for example, is a description of "the colde frosty seisoun of Decembre," in which matters celestial and earthly are mingled to make a picture of extraordinary richness:

> Phebus wox old and hewed like latoun,
> That in his hoté declinacioun
> Shone as the burned gold, with streames bright;
> But now in Capricorn adown he light,
> Where as he shone full pale; I dare well sayn
> The bitter frostes with the sleet and rain
> Destroyed hath the green in every yerd.
> Janus sit by the fire with double beard,
> And drinketh of his bugle horn the wine;
> Beforn him stont the brawn of tusked swine,
> And *"noel"* cryeth every lusty man.

In astrology he does not seem to have believed. The magnificent passage in the "Man of Law's Tale," where it is said that

> In the starres, clearer than is glass,
> Is written, God wot, whoso can it read,
> The death of every man withouten drede,

is balanced by the categorical statement found in the scientific and educational treatise on the astrolabe, that judicial astrology is mere deceit.

His scepticism with regard to astrology is not surprising. Highly as he prizes authority, he prefers the evidence of experience, and where that evidence is lacking he is content to profess a quiet agnosticism. His respect for the law of kind is accompanied by a complementary mistrust of all that does not appear to belong to the natural order of things. There are moments when he doubts even the fundamental beliefs of the Church:

> A thousand sythes have I herd men telle
> That there is joye in heaven and peyne in helle;
> And I accorde well that it be so.
> But natheless, this wot I well also
> That there is none that dwelleth in this countree
> That either hath in helle or heaven y-be.

Of the fate of the spirit after death he speaks in much the same style:

> His spiryt changed was, and wente there
> As I came never, I cannot tellen where;
> Therefore I stint, I nam no divinistre;
> Of soules fynde I not in this registre,

Ne me list not th' opiniouns to telle
Of hem, though that they witten where they dwelle.

He has no patience with superstitions. Belief in dreams, in
auguries, fear of the "raveness qualm or schrychynge of
thise owles" are all unbefitting to a self-respecting man:

To trowen on it bothe false and foul is;
Alas, alas, so noble a creature
Ah is a man shall dreaden such ordure!

By an absurd pun he turns all Calchas's magic arts of
prophecy to ridicule:

So when this Calkus knew by calkulynge,
And eke by answer of this Apollo
That Grekes sholden such a people bringe,
Through which that Troye muste ben fordo,
He cast anon out of the town to go.

It would not be making a fanciful comparison to say
that Chaucer in many respects resembles Anatole France.
Both men possess a profound love of this world for its own
sake, coupled with a profound and gentle scepticism
about all that lies beyond this world. To both of them the
lavish beauty of Nature is a never-failing and all-sufficient
source of happiness. Neither of them are ascetics; in pain
and privation they see nothing but evil. To both of them
the notion that self-denial and self-mortification are necessarily righteous and productive of good is wholly alien.
Both of them are apostles of sweetness and light, of
humanity and reasonableness. Unbounded tolerance of human weakness and a pity, not the less sincere for being
a little ironical, characterize them both. Deep knowledge
of the evils and horrors of this unintelligible world makes
them all the more attached to its kindly beauty. But in
at least one important respect Chaucer shows himself to
be the greater, the completer spirit. He possesses, what
Anatole France does not, an imaginative as well as an
intellectual comprehension of things. Faced by the mul-
titudinous variety of human character, Anatole France
exhibits a curious impotence of imagination. He does
not understand characters in the sense that, say, Tolstoy
understands them; he cannot, by the power of imagination, get inside them, become what he contemplates.
None of the persons of his creation are complete characters; they cannot be looked at from every side; they

are portrayed, as it were, in the flat and not in three dimensions. But Chaucer has the power of getting into someone else's character. His understanding of the men and women of whom he writes is complete; his slightest character sketches are always solid and three-dimensional. The prologue to the *Canterbury Tales*, in which the effects are almost entirely produced by the description of external physical features, furnishes us with the most obvious example of his three-dimensional drawing. Or, again, take that description in the "Merchant's Tale" of old January and his young wife May after their wedding night. It is wholly a description of external details, yet the result is not a superficial picture. We are given a glimpse of the characters in their entirety:

Thus laboureth he till that the day gan dawe,
And then he taketh a sop in fine clarré,
And upright in his bed then sitteth he.
And after that he sang full loud and clear,
And kissed his wife and made wanton cheer.
He was all coltish, full of ragerye,
And full of jargon as a flecked pye.
The slacké skin about his necké shaketh,
While that he sang, so chanteth he and craketh.
But God wot what that May thought in her heart,
When she him saw up sitting in his shirt,
In his night cap and with his necke lean;
She praiseth not his playing worth a bean.

But these are all slight sketches. For full-length portraits of character we must turn to *Troilus and Cressida*, a work which, though it was written, before the fullest maturity of Chaucer's powers, is in many ways his most remarkable achievement, and one, moreover, which has never been rivalled for beauty and insight in the whole field of English narrative poetry. When one sees with what certainty and precision Chaucer describes every movement of Cressida's spirit from the first moment she hears of Troilus' love for her to the moment when she is unfaithful to him, one can only wonder why the novel of character should have been so slow to make its appearance. It was not until the eighteenth century that narrative artists, using prose as their medium instead of verse, began to rediscover the secrets that were familiar to Chaucer in the fourteenth.

Troilus and Cressida was written, as we have said,

before Chaucer had learnt to make the fullest use of his powers. In coloring it is fainter, less sharp and brilliant than the best of the *Canterbury Tales*. The character studies are there, carefully and accurately worked out; but we miss the bright vividness of presentation with which Chaucer was to endow his later art. The characters are all alive and completely seen and understood. But they move, as it were, behind a veil—the veil of that poetic convention which had, in the earliest poems, almost completely shrouded Chaucer's genius, and which, as he grew up, as he adventured and discovered, grew thinner and thinner, and finally vanished like gauzy mist in the sunlight. When *Troilus and Cressida* was written the mist had not completely dissipated, and the figures of his creation, complete in conception and execution as they are, are seen a little dimly because of the interposed veil.

The only moment in the poem when Chaucer's insight seems to fail him is at the very end; he has to account for Cressida's unfaithfulness, and he is at a loss to know how he shall do it. Shakespeare, when he rehandled the theme, had no such difficulty. His version of the story, planned on much coarser lines than Chaucer's, leads obviously and inevitably to the foreordained conclusion; his Cressida is a minx who simply lives up to her character. What could be more simple? But to Chaucer the problem is not so simple. His Cressida is not a minx. From the moment he first sets eyes on her Chaucer, like his own unhappy Troilus, falls head over ears in love. Beautiful, gentle, gay; possessing, it is true, somewhat "tendre wittes," but making up for her lack of skill in ratiocination by the "sudden avysements" of intuition; vain, but not disagreeably so, of her good looks and of her power over so great and noble a knight as Troilus; slow to feel love, but once she has yielded, rendering back to Troilus passion for passion; in a word, the "least mannish" of all possible creatures—she is to Chaucer the ideal of gracious and courtly womanhood. But, alas, the old story tells us that Cressida jilted her Troilus for that gross prize-fighter of a man, Diomed. The woman whom Chaucer has made his ideal proves to be no better than she should be; there is a flaw in the crystal. Chaucer is infinitely reluctant to admit the fact. But the old story is specific in its statement; indeed, its whole point consists in Cressida's in-

fidelity. Called upon to explain his heroine's fall, Chaucer
is completely at a loss. He makes a few halfhearted attempts to solve the problem, and then gives it up, falling
back on authority. The old clerks say it was so, therefore it must be so, and that's that. The fact is that
Chaucer pitched his version of the story in a different
key from that which is found in the "olde bokes," with
the result that the note on which he is compelled by his
respect for authority to close is completely out of harmony with the rest of the music. It is this that accounts
for the chief, and indeed the only defect of, the poem—
its hurried and boggled conclusion.

I cannot leave Cressida without some mention of the
doom which was prepared for her by one of Chaucer's
worthiest disciples, Robert Henryson, in some ways the
best of the Scottish poets of the fifteenth and sixteenth
centuries. Shocked by the fact that, in Chaucer's poem,
Cressida receives no punishment for her infidelity, Henryson composed a short sequel, *The Testament of Cresseid*,
to show that poetic justice was duly performed. Diomed,
we are told, grew weary as soon as he had "all his ap-
petyte and mair, fulfillit on this fair ladie" and cast her
off, to become a common drab.

> O fair Cresseid! the flour and *A per se*
> Of Troy and Greece, how wast thou fortunait!
> To change in filth all thy feminitie
> And be with fleshly lust sa maculait,
> And go amang the Grekis, air and`late
> So giglot-like.

In her misery she curses Venus and Cupid for having
caused her to love only to lead her to this degradation:

> The seed of love was sowen in my face
> And ay grew green through your supply and grace.
> But now, alas! that seed with frost is slain,
> And I fra lovers left, and all forlane

In revenge Cupid and his mother summon a council of
gods and condemn the *A per se* of Greece and Troy to
be a hideous leper. And so she goes forth with the other
lepers, armed with bowl and clapper, to beg her bread.
One day Troilus rides past the place where she is sitting
by the roadside near the gates of Troy:

Then upon him she cast up both her een,
  And with ane blenk it cam into his thocht,
That he some time before her face had seen,
  But she was in such plight he knew her nocht,
  Yet then her look into his mind it brocht
The sweet visage and amorous blenking
Of fair Cresseid, one sometime his own darling.

He throws her an alms and the poor creature dies. And
so the moral sense is satisfied. There is a good deal of
superfluous mythology and unnecessary verbiage in *The
Testament of Cresseid,* but the main lines of the poem are
firmly and powerfully drawn. Of all the disciples of
Chaucer, from Hoccleve and the Monk of Bury down to
Mr. Masefield, Henryson may deservedly claim to stand
the highest.

2

Ben Jonson[*]

It comes as something of a surprise to find that the niche reserved for Ben Jonson in the English Men of Letters Series [**] has only now been filled. One expected somehow that he would have been among the first of the great ones to be enshrined; but no, he has had a long time to wait; and Adam Smith, and Sydney Smith, and Hazlitt, and Fanny Burney have gone before him into the temple of fame. Now, however, his monument has at last been made, with Professor Gregory Smith's qualified version of "O rare Ben Jonson!" duly and definitively carved upon it.

What is it that makes us, almost as a matter of course, number Ben Jonson among the great? Why should we expect him to be an early candidate for immortality, or why, indeed, should he be admitted to the English Men of Letters Series at all? These are difficult questions to answer; for when we come to consider the matter we find ourselves unable to give any very glowing account of Ben or his greatness. It is hard to say that one likes his work; one cannot honestly call him a good poet or a supreme dramatist. And yet, unsympathetic as he is, uninteresting as he often can be, we still go on respecting and admiring

[*] From *On the Margin*, 1923.
[**] G. Gregory Smith, *Ben Jonson*. (English Men of Letters Series.) London, Macmillan & Co., Ltd., 1919.

him, because, in spite of everything, we are conscious, obscurely but certainly, that he was a great man.

He had little influence on his successors; the comedy of humors died without any but an abortive issue. Shadwell, the mountain-bellied "Og, from a treason tavern rolling home," is not a disciple that any man would have much pride in claiming. No raking up of literary history will make Ben Jonson great as a founder of a school or an inspirer of others. His greatness is a greatness of character. There is something almost alarming in the spectacle of this formidable figure advancing with tanklike irresistibility towards the goal he had set himself to attain. No sirens of romance can seduce him, no shock of opposition unseat him in his career. He proceeds along the course theoretically mapped out at the inception of his literary life, never deviating from this narrow way till the very end—till the time when, in his old age, he wrote that exquisite pastoral, *The Sad Shepherd,* which is so complete and absolute a denial of all his lifelong principles. But *The Sad Shepherd* is a weakness, albeit a triumphant weakness. Ben, as he liked to look upon himself, as he has again and again revealed himself to us, is the artist with principles, protesting against the anarchic absence of principle among the geniuses and charlatans, the poets and ranters of his age.

The true artificer will not run away from nature as he were afraid of her; or depart from life and the likeness of truth; but speak to the capacity of his hearers. And though his language differ from the vulgar somewhat, it shall not fly from all humanity, with the Tamerlanes and Tamer-Chams of the late age, which had nothing in them but the scenical strutting and furious vociferation to warrant them to the ignorant gapers. He knows it is his only art, so to carry it as none but artificers perceive it. In the meantime, perhaps, he is called barren, dull, lean, a poor writer, or by what contumelious word can come in their cheeks, by these men who without labour, judgment, knowledge, or almost sense, are received or preferred before him.

In these sentences from *Discoveries* Ben Jonson paints his own picture—portrait of the artist as a true artificer —setting forth, in its most general form, and with no distracting details of the humors or the moral purpose of art, his own theory of the artist's true function and nature.

Jonson's theory was no idle speculation, no mere thing of words and air, but a creed, a principle, a categorical imperative, conditioning and informing his whole work. And study of the poet must, therefore, begin with the formulation of his theory, and must go on, as Professor Gregory Smith's excellent essay does indeed proceed, to show in detail how the theory was applied and worked out in each individual composition.

A good deal of nonsense has been talked at one time or another about artistic theories. The artist is told that he should have no theories, that he should warble native wood-notes wild, that he should "sing," be wholly spontaneous, should starve his brain and cultivate his heart and spleen; that an artistic theory cramps the style, stops up the Helicons of inspiration, and so on, and so on. The foolish and sentimental conception of the artist, to which these anti-intellectual doctrines are a corollary, dates from the time of romanticism and survives among the foolish and sentimental of today. A consciously practiced theory of art has never spoiled a good artist, has never damned up inspiration, but rather, and in most cases profitably, canalized it. Even the Romantics had theories and were wild and emotional on principle.

Theories are above all necessary at moments when old traditions are breaking up, when all is chaos and in flux. At such moments an artist formulates his theory and clings to it through thick and thin; clings to it as the one firm raft of security in the midst of the surrounding unrest. Thus, when the neoclassicism, of which Ben was one of the remote ancestors, was crumbling into the nothingness of *The Loves of the Plants* and *The Triumphs of Temper*, Wordsworth found salvation by the promulgation of a new theory of poetry, which he put into practice systematically and to the verge of absurdity in *Lyrical Ballads*. Similarly in the shipwreck of the old tradition of painting we find the artists of the present day clinging desperately to intellectual formulas as their only hope in the chaos. The only occasions, in fact, when the artist can afford entirely to dispense with theory occur in periods when a well-established tradition reigns supreme and unquestioned. And then the absence of theory is more apparent than real; for the tradition in which he is working is a theory, originally formulated by someone else, which he accepts unconsciously and as though it were the law of Nature itself.

The beginning of the seventeenth century was not one of these periods of placidity and calm acceptance. It was a moment of growth and decay together, of fermentation. The fabulous efflorescence of the Renaissance had already grown rank. With that extravagance of energy which characterized them in all things, the Elizabethans had exaggerated the traditions of their literature into insincerity. All artistic traditions end, in due course, by being reduced to the absurd; but the Elizabethans crammed the growth and decline of a century into a few years. One after another they transfigured and then destroyed every species of art they touched. Euphuism, Petrarchism, Spenserism, the sonnet, the drama—some lasted a little longer than others, but they all exploded in the end, these beautiful iridescent bubbles blown too big by the enthusiasm of their makers.

But in the midst of this unstable luxuriance voices of protest were to be heard, reactions against the main romantic current were discernible. Each in his own way and in his own sphere, Donne and Ben Jonson protested against the exaggerations of the age. At a time when sonneteers in legions were quibbling about the blackness of their ladies' eyes or the golden wires of their hair, when Platonists protested in melodious chorus that they were not in love with "red and white" but with the ideal and divine beauty of which peachblossom complexions were but inadequate shadows, at a time when love-poetry had become, with rare exceptions, fantastically unreal, Donne called it back, a little grossly perhaps, to facts with the dry remark:

> Love's not so pure and abstract as they use
> To say, who have no mistress but their muse.

There have been poets who have written more lyrically than Donne, more fervently about certain amorous emotions, but not one who has formulated so rational a philosophy of love as a whole, who has seen all the facts so clearly and judged them so soundly. Donne laid down no literary theory. His followers took from him all that was relatively unimportant—the harshness, itself a protest against Spenserian facility, the conceits, the sensuality tempered by mysticism—but the important and original quality of Donne's work, the psychological realism, they could not, through sheer incapacity, transfer into their own poetry. Donne's immediate influence was on the whole bad. Any influence for good he may have had has been on poets of a much later date.

The other great literary Protestant of the time was the curious subject of our examination, Ben Jonson. Like Donne he was a realist. He had no use for claptrap, or rant, or romanticism. His aim was to give his audiences real facts flavored with sound morality. He failed to be a great realist, partly because he lacked the imaginative insight to perceive more than the most obvious and superficial reality, and partly because he was so much preoccupied with the sound morality that he was prepared to sacrifice truth to satire; so that in place of characters he gives us humors, not minds, but personified moral qualities.

Ben hated romanticism; for, whatever may have been his bodily habits, however infinite his capacity for drinking sack, he belonged intellectually to the party of sobriety. In all ages the drunks and the sobers have confronted one another, each party loud in derision and condemnation of the defects which it observes in the other. "The Tamerlanes and Tamer-Chams of the late age" accuse the sober Ben of being "barren, dull, lean, a poor writer." Ben retorts that they "have nothing in them but the scenical strutting and furious vociferation to warrant them to the ignorant gapers." At another period it is the Hernanis and the Rollas who reproach that paragon of dryness, the almost fiendishly sober Stendhal, with his grocer's style. Stendhal in his turn remarks: "*En paraissant, vers 1803, le* Génie *de Chateaubriand m'a semblé ridicule.*" And today? We have our sobers and our drunks, our Hardy and our Belloc, our Santayana and our Chesterton. The distinction is eternally valid. Our personal sympathies may lie with one or the other; but it is obvious that we could dispense with neither. Ben, then, was one of the sobers, protesting with might and main against the extravagant behavior of the drunks, an intellectual insisting that there was no way of arriving at truth except by intellectual processes, an apotheosis of the Plain Man determined to stand no nonsense about anything. Ben's poetical achievement, such as it is, is the achievement of one who relied on no mysterious inspiration, but on those solid qualities of sense, perseverance, and sound judgment which any decent citizen of a decent country may be expected to possess. That he himself possessed, hidden somewhere in the obscure crypts and recesses of his mind, other rarer spiritual qualities is proved by the existence of his additions to *The Spanish Tragedy*—if, indeed, they are his, which there is no cogent reason to doubt—and his last fragment of a master-piece, *The Sad Shepherd*. But these qualities, as Professor Gregory Smith points out, he seems deliberately to have suppressed; locked them away, at the bidding of his imperious theory, in the strange dark places from which, at the beginning and the very end of his career, they emerged. He might have been a great romantic, one of the sublime inebriates; he chose rather to be classical and sober. Working solely with the logical intellect and rejecting as dangerous the aid of those uncontrolled illogical elements of imagination, he produced work that is in its own way excellent. It is well-wrought, strong, heavy with learning and what the Chaucerians would call "high sentence." The emotional intensity and brevity excepted, it possesses all the qualities of the French classical drama. But the quality which characterizes the best Elizabethan and indeed the best English poetry of all periods, the power of moving in two worlds at once, it lacks. Jonson, like the French dramatists of the seventeenth century, moves on a level, directly towards some logical goal. The road over which his great contemporaries take us is not level; it is, as it were, tilted and uneven, so that as we proceed along it we are momently shot off at a tangent from the solid earth of logical meaning into superior regions where the intellectual laws of gravity have no control. The mistake of Jonson and the classicists in general consists in supposing that nothing is of value that is not susceptible of logical analysis; whereas the truth is that the greatest triumphs of art take place in a world that is not wholly of the intellect, but lies somewhere between it and the inenarrable, but, to those who have penetrated it, supremely real, world of the mystic. In his fear and dislike of nonsense, Jonson put away from himself not only the Tamer-Chams and the fustian of the late age, but also most of the beauty it had created.

With the romantic emotions of his predecessors and contemporaries Jonson abandoned much of the characteristically Elizabethan form of their poetry. That extraordinary melodiousness which distinguishes the Elizabethan lyric is not to be found in any of Ben's writing. The poems by which we remember him—"Cynthia," "Drink to Me Only," "It is Not Growing Like a Tree"—are classically well-made (though the cavalier lyrists were to do better in the same style); but it is not for any musical qualities that we remember them. One can understand Ben's critical contempt for those purely formal devices for producing musical richness in which the Elizabethans delighted.

> Eyes, why did you bring unto me these graces,
> Grac'd to yield wonder out of her true measure,
> Measure of all joyes' stay to phansie traces
>   Module of pleasure.

The device is childish in its formality, the words, in their obscurity, almost devoid of significance. But what matter, since the stanza is a triumphant of sonorous beauty? The Elizabethans devised many ingenuities of this sort; the minor poets exploited them until they became ridiculous; the major poets employed them with greater discretion, playing subtle variations (as in Shakespeare's sonnets) on the crude theme. When writers had something to say, their thoughts, poured into these copiously elaborate forms, were molded to the grandest poetical eloquence. A minor poet, like Lord Brooke, from whose works we have just quoted a specimen of pure formalism, could produce, in his moments of inspiration, such magnificent lines as:

> The mind of Man is this world's true dimension,
>   And knowledge is the measure·of the mind;

or these, of the nethermost hell:

> A place there is upon no centre placed,
> Deepe under depthes, as farre as in the skie
> Above the earth; darke, infinitely spaced:
> Pluto the king, the kingdome, miserie.

Even into comic poetry the Elizabethans imported the grand manner. The anonymous author of

> Tee-hee, tee-hee! Oh, sweet delight
> He tickles this age, who can
> Call Tullia's ape marmosite
> And Leda's goose a swan,

knew the secret of that rich, facile music which all those who wrote in the grand Elizabethan tradition could produce. Jonson, like Donne, reacted against the facility and floridity of this technique, but in a different way. Donne's protest took the form of a conceited subtlety of thought combined with a harshness of meter. Jonson's classical training inclined him towards clarity, solidity of sense, and economy of form. He stands, as a lyrist halfway between the Elizabethans and the cavalier song writers; he has broken away from the old tradition, but has not yet made himself entirely at home in the new. At the best he achieves a minor perfection of point and neatness. At the worst he falls into that dryness and dullness with which he knew he could be reproached.

We have seen from the passage concerning the true artificer that Jonson fully realized the risk he was running. He recurs more than once in *Discoveries* to the same theme, "Some men to avoid redundancy run into that [a "thin, flagging, poor, starved" style]; and while they strive to have no ill-blood or juice, they lose their good." The good that Jonson lost was a great one. And in the same way we see today how a fear of becoming sentimental, or "chocolate-boxy," drives many of the younger poets and artists to shrink from treating of the great emotions or the obvious lavish beauty of the earth. But to eschew a good because the corruption of it is very bad is surely a sign of weakness and a folly.

Having lost the realm of romantic beauty—lost it deliberately and of set purpose—Ben Jonson devoted the whole of his immense energy to protraying and reforming the ugly world of fact. But his reforming satiric intentions interfered, as we have already shown, with his realistic intentions, and instead of recreating in his art the actual world of men, he invented the wholly intellectual and therefore wholly unreal universe of Humors. It is an odd new world, amusing to look at from the safe distance that separates stage from stalls; but not a place one could ever wish to live in—one's neighbors, fools, knaves, hypocrites, and bears would make the most pleasing prospect intolerable. And over it all is diffused the atmosphere of Jonson's humor. It is a curious kind of humor, very different from anything that passes under that name today, from the humor of *Punch,* or *A Kiss for Cinderella.* One has only to read *Volpone*—or, better still, go to see it when it is acted this year by the Phoenix Society for the revival of old plays—to realize that Ben's conception of a joke differed materially from ours. Humor has never been the same since Rousseau invented humanitarianism. Syphilis and broken legs were still a great deal more comic in Smollett's day than in our own. There is a cruelty, a heartlessness about much of the older humor which is sometimes shocking, sometimes, in its less extreme forms, pleasantly astringent and stimulating after the orgies of quaint pathos and sentimental comedy in which we are nowadays forced to indulge. There is not a pathetic line in *Volpone;* all the characters are profoundly unpleasant, and the fun is almost as grim as fun can be. Its heartlessness is not the brilliant, cynical heartlessness of the later Restoration comedy, but something ponderous and vast. It reminds us of one of those enormous, painful jokes which fate sometimes plays on humanity. There is no alleviation, no purging by pity and terror. It requires a very hearty sense of humor to digest it. We have reason to admire our ancestors for their ability to enjoy this kind of comedy as it should be enjoyed. It would get very little appreciation from a London audience of today.

In the other comedies the fun is not so grim; but there is a certain hardness and brutality about them all—due, of course, ultimately to the fact that the characters are not human, but rather marionettes of wood and metal that collide and belabor one another, like the ferocious puppets of the Punch and Judy show, without feeling the painfulness of the proceeding. Shakespeare's comedy is not heartless, because the characters are human and sensitive. Our modern sentimentality is a corruption, a softening of genuine humanity. We need a few more Jonsons and Congreves, some more plays like *Volpone,* or that inimitable *Marriage à la Mode* of Dryden, in which the curtain goes up on a lady singing the outrageously cynical song that begins:

> Why should a foolish marriage vow,
>   That long ago was made,
> Constrain us to each other now
>   When pleasure is decayed?

Too much heartlessness is intolerable (how soon one turns, revolted, from the literature of the Restoration!), but a little of it now and then is bracing, a tonic for relaxed sensibilities. A little ruthless laughter clears the air as nothing else can do; it is good for us, every now and then, to see our ideals laughed at, our conception of nobility caricatured; it is good for solemnity's nose to be tweaked, it is good for human pomposity to be made to look mean and ridiculous. It should be the great social function—as Marinetti has pointed out—of the music halls, to provide this cruel and unsparing laughter, to make a buffoonery of all the solemnly accepted grandeurs and nobilities. A good dose of this mockery, administered twice a year at the equinoxes, should purge our minds of much waste matter, make nimble our spirits and brighten the eye to look more clearly and truthfully on the world about us.

Ben's reduction of human beings to a series of rather unpleasant Humors is sound and medicinal. Humors do not, of course, exist in actuality; they are true only as caricatures are true. There are times when we wonder whether a caricature is not, after all, truer than a photograph; there are others when it seems a stupid lie. But at all times a caricature is disquieting; and it is very good for most of us to be made uncomfortable.

3

Crébillon the Younger•

Prophecy is mainly interesting for the light it throws on the age in which it is uttered. The Apocalypse, for example, tells us how a Christian felt about the world at the end of the first century. Manifestly ludicrous as a forecast, Mercier's *L'An 2440* is worth reading, because it shows us what were the ideals of an earnest and rather stupid Frenchman in the year 1770. And the ideals of an earnest and very intelligent Englishman of the early twentieth century may be studied, in all their process of development, in the long series of Mr. Well's prophetic books. Our notions of the future have something of that significance which Freud attributes to our dreams. And not our notions of the future only: our notions of the past as well. For if prophecy is an expression of our contemporary fears and wishes, so too, to a very great extent, is history—or at least what passes for history among the mass of ordinary unprofessional folk. Utopias, earthly paradises and earthly hells are flowers of the imagination which contrive to blossom and luxuriate even in the midst of the stoniest dates and documents, even within the fixed and narrow boundaries of established fact. The works of St. Thomas survive; we have a record of the acts of Innocent III. But that does not prevent our pic-

• From *Essays New and Old,* 1927.

tures of the Middle Ages from being as various and as highly colored as our pictures of Utopia, the Servile State or the New Jerusalem. We see the past through the refractive medium of our prejudices, our tastes, our contemporary fears and hopes. The facts of history exist; but they hardly trouble us. We select and interpret our documents till they square with our theories.

The eighteenth century is a period which has been interpreted and reinterpreted in the most surprisingly various ways: by its own philosophers (for the eighteenth century was highly self-conscious) as the age of reason and enlightenment; by the Romantics and their strange heirs, the Reactionaries and the Early Victorians, as the age of vice and spiritual drought; by the later nineteenth-century sceptics, who curiously combined the strictest Protestant morality with the most dogmatically anti-Christian philosophy, as an age of reason indeed, but of more than dubious character; by the Beardsleyites of the nineties, as an epoch of deliciously depraved frivolity, of futile and therefore truly aesthetic elegance. The popular conception of the eighteenth century at the present day is a mixture of Beardsley's and Voltaire's. We find its morals and its manners in the highest degree "amusing"; and when we want a stick to beat the corpses of the Eminent Victorians we apply to Hume or Gibbon, to Voltaire or Helvétius, to Horace Walpole or Madame du Deffand. For the simpler-minded among us, the eighteenth century is summed up by Mr. Nigel Playfair's version of *The Beggar's Opera*. The more sophisticated find their *dix-huitième* in the original French documents (judiciously selected) or in the ironic pages of Mr. Lytton Strachey.

Charming historical Utopia! A moment's thought, however, is sufficient to show how arbitrarily we have abstracted it from reality. For who, after all, were the most important, the most durable and influential men that the century produced? The names of Bach, Handel, and Mozart present themselves immediately to the mind; of Swedenborg and Wesley and Blake; of Dr. Johnson, Bishop Berkeley, and Kant. Of none of these can it be said that he fits very easily into the scheme of *The Beggar's Opera*. True, our pianists and conductors have tried, Procrustes-like, to squeeze the musicians into the *dix-huitième* mold. They play Bach mechanically, Handel lightly, Mozart frivolously, without feeling and therefore without sense, and call the process a "classical" interpretation. But let that pass. The fact remains that the greatest men of the eighteenth century are not in the least what we should call *dix-huitième*.

It must not be imagined, however, that our particular "eighteenth century" is completely mythical. Something like it did genuinely exist, during a couple of generations, among a small class of people in most European countries, especially France. The fact that we have chosen to re-create a whole historical epoch in the image of this intellectually free and morally licentious *dix-huitième* throws some light on our own problems, our own twentieth-century bugbears, our own desires. For a certain section of contemporary society the terms "modern" and "eighteenth century" are almost synonymous. Like our ancestors, we too are in revolt against intellectual authority and moral "prejudices." Perhaps the chief difference between them and us is that they believed in pure reason as well as extra-conjugal love; we Bergsonians do not.

One of the most characteristic representatives of this particular *dix-huitième* which we have chosen to exalt at the expense of all the other possible eighteenth centuries is Crébillon the Younger. We find in his novels all the qualities which we regard as typical of the period: elegance, frivolity, a complete absence of moral "prejudices," especially on the subject of love, a certain dry, spirit of detachment and analysis. *Le Sopha* and *La Nuit et le Moment* are documents which, taken by themselves, completely justify our current conception of the age in which they were written. For that reason alone they deserve to be read. One should always be prepared to quote authorities in support of one's theories. Moreover, they are worth reading for their own sakes. For Crébillon was a psychologist and, in his own limited field, one of the most acute of his age.

The typically modern method of presenting character differs from that employed by the novelists of the eighteenth century. In our novels we offer the facts in a so-to-speak raw state, leaving the reader to draw his own conclusions from them. The older psychologists treated the facts to a preliminary process of intellectual digestion; they gave their readers something more than the mere behavioristic material on which psychological judgments are based; they gave them the conclusions they themselves had already drawn from the facts. Compare Constant's *Adolphe* with the *Ulysses* of James Joyce; the difference of method is manifest. Crébillon is a characteristic eighteenth-century psychologist. With the dry intellectual precision of his age, he describes and comments on his characters, analyzes their behavior, draws conclusions, formulates generalizations. What a contemporary novelist would imply in twenty pages of description and talk, he expresses outright in two or three sentences that are an intellectual summing up of all the evidence. The novelist who employs the older method gains in definition and clarity what he loses in realism, in life, in expansive implication and suggestion. There is much to be said for both methods of presentation; most of all, perhaps, for a combination of the two.

So much for Crébillon's method of presenting character. It is time to consider the sort of people and the particular aspect of their characters which he liked to present. His heroes and heroines are the men and women of our own favorite *dix-huitième*—the eighteenth century whose representative man is rather Casanova than Bach, rather the Cardinal de Bernis than Wesley. They are aristocrats who fill their indefinite leisure with an amateur's interest in literature, art, and even science (see, for the scientific interests, Cléandre's story, in *La Nuit et le Moment,* of his physicophysiological argument with Julie); with talk and social intercourse, with gambling and country sports; and above all, with that most perfect of time killers, *l'amour.* Crébillon's main, his almost exclusive, preoccupation is with the last of these aristocratic amusements. And it in on his psychology of love—of a certain kind of love—that his claim to literary immortality must be based.

Crébillon's special province is that obscure borderland between soul and body, where physiology and psychology meet and mingle and are reciprocally complicated. It is a province of which, during the last century and in this country, at any rate, we have heard but the scantiest accounts. It was only with birth that physiology ever made its entrance into the Victorian novel, not with conception. In these matters, Crébillon's age was more scientific. The existence of physiology was frankly admitted at every stage of the reproductive process. It was mentioned in connection with every kind of love, from *l'amour passion* to *l'amour goût*. It was freely discussed, and its phenomena described, classified, and explained. The relations between the senses and the imagination, between love and pleasure, between desire and the affections are methodically defined in that literature of which Crébillon's stories are representative. And it is very right that they should be so defined. For no analysis of love can claim to be complete which ignores the physiological basis and accompaniment of the passion. Love, says Donne in his nearest approach to a versified epigram,

> Love's not so pure and abstract as they use
> To say, who have no mistress but their Muse.

The distinction between sacred and profane, spiritual and fleshly love is an arbitrary, gratuitous and metaphysical distinction. The most spiritual love is rooted in the flesh; the most sacred is only profane love sublimated and refined. To ignore these obvious facts is foolish and slightly dishonest. And indeed, they never have been ignored except by the psychologists of the nineteenth century. The writers of every other age have always admitted them. It was in aristocratic France, however, and during the eighteenth century, that they were most closely and accurately studied. Crébillon *fils* is one of the acutest, one of the most scientific of the students.

Scientific—I apply the epithet deliberately, not vaguely and at random. For Crébillon's attitude towards the phenomena of sex seems to me precisely that of the true scientific investigator. It is with a mind entirely open and unbiased that he approaches the subject. He contrives to forget that love is a matter of the most intimate human concern, that it has been from time immemorial the subject of philosophical speculation and moral precept. Making a clean sweep of all the prejudices, he sets to work, coolly and with detachment, as though the subject of his investigations were something as remote, as utterly divorced from good and evil, as spiral nebulae, liver flukes, or the aurora borealis.

Men have always tended to attribute to the objects of their intense emotions, and even to the emotions themselves, some kind of cosmical significance. Mystics and lovers, for example, have never been content to find the justification for their feelings in the feelings themselves: they have asked us to believe that these feelings possess a universal truth value as well as, for themselves, a personal behavior value. And they have invented cosmogonies and metaphysical systems to justify and explain their emotional attitudes. The fact that all these metaphysical systems are, scientifically speaking, almost certainly untrue in no way affects the value for the individual and for whole societies of the emotions and attitudes which gave them birth. Thus, mysticism will always be a beautiful and precious thing, even though it should be conclusively proved that all the philosophical systems based upon it are nonsensical. And one can be convinced of the superiority of spiritual to carnal, of "conjugial" to "scortatory" love without believing a word of Plato or Swedenborg.

In a quiet and entirely unpretentious way Crébillon was an expounder of the scientific truth about love— that its basis is physiological; that the intense and beautiful emotions which it arouses cannot be philosophically justified or explained, but should be gratefully accepted for what they are: feelings significant in themselves and of the highest practical importance for those who experience them. He is no vulgar and stupid cynic who denies the existence, because he cannot accept the current metaphysical explanation, of any feelings higher than the merely physical. "*Les plaisirs gagnent toujours à être ennoblis,*" says Crébillon, through the mouth of the Duke in *Le Hasard au Coin du Feu.* It is the man of science who speaks, the unprejudiced observer, the accepter of facts. Pleasure is a fact; so is nobility. He admits the existence of both. Pleasure gains by being ennobled: that is the practical, experimental justification of all the high, aspiring, seemingly infinite emotions evoked by love. True, it may be objected that Crébillon gives too little space in his analysis of love to that which ennobles pleasure and too much to pleasure pure and simple. He would have been more truly scientific if he had reversed the balance; for that which ennobles is of more practical significance, both to individuals and to societies, than that which is ennobled. We may excuse him, perhaps, by supposing that, in the society in which he lived (the Pompadour was his patroness), his opportunities for observing the ennobling passions were scarce in comparison with his opportunities for observing the raw physiological material on which such passions work.

But it is foolish as well as ungrateful to criticize an author for what he has failed to achieve. The reader's business is with what the writer has done, not with what he has left undone. And Crébillon, after all, did do something which, whatever its limitations was worth doing. What writer, for example, has spoken more acutely on the somewhat scabrous, but none the less important subject of feminine "temperament"? I cannot do better than quote a specimen of his analysis, with the generalization he draws from it. He is speaking here of a woman whose imagination is more ardent than her senses, and who, living in a society where this imagination is perpetually being fired, is for ever desperately trying to experience the pleasures of which she dreams.

> *Elle a l'imagination fort vive et fort déréglée, et quoique l'inutilité des épreuves qu'elle a faites en certain genre eût dû la corriger d'en faire, elle ne veut pas se persuader qu'elle soit née plus malheureuse qu'elle croit que d'autres ne le sont, et elle se flatte toujours qu'il est réservé au dernier qu'elle prend de la rendre aussi sensible qu'elle désire de l'être. Je ne doute même pas que cette idée ne soit la source de ses déréglements et de la peine qu'elle prend de jouer ce qu'elle ne sent pas. . . . Je dirai plus, c'est qu'aujourd'hui il est prouvé que ce sont les femmes à qui les plaisirs de l'amour sont les moins nécessaires qui les recherchent avec la plus de fureur, et que les trois quarts de celles qui se sont perdues avaient reçu de la nature tout ce qu'il leur fallait pour ne l'être pas.*

Admirable description of a type not at all uncommon in all societies where love-making is regarded as the proper study of womankind! The type, I repeat, is not uncommon; but Crébillon's succinct and accurate description of it is something almost unique.

Here is another passage in which he analyzes the motives of a different type of cold woman—a much more dangerous type, it may be remarked: the type to which all successful adventuresses belong.

> *Soit caprice, soit vanité, la chose du monde qui lui plaît le plus est d'inspirer de désirs; elle jouit du moins des tranports de son amant. D'ailleurs, la froideur de*

*ses sens n'empêche pas sa tête de s'animer, et si la
nature lui a refusé ce que l'on appelle le plaisir, elle
lui a en échange donné une sorte de volupté qui n'existe,
à la vérité, que dans ses idés; mais qui lui fait peut-être
éprouver quelque chose de plus délicat que ce qui ne
part que des sens. Pour vous* [adds Clitandre, address-
ing his companion], *pour vous, plus heureuse qu'elle,
vous avez, si je ne me trompe, rassemblé les deux.*

It would be possible to compile out of the works of
Crébillon a whole collection of such character sketches
and aphorisms. *What every Young Don Juan ought to
Know* might serve as title to this florilegium. It should be
placed in the hands of all those, women as well as men,
who propose to lead, professionally, the arduous and
difficult life of leisure. Here are a few of the aphorisms
which will deserve to find a place in this anthology of
psychological wisdom.

*Une jolie femme dépend bien moins d'elle-même que
des circonstances; et par malheur il s'en trouve tant, de
si peu prévues, de si pressantes, qu'il n'y a point à
s'étonner si, après plusieurs aventures, elle n'a connu ni
l'amour, ni son cœur. Il s'ensuit que ce qu'on croit la
dernière fantaisie d'une femme est bien souvent sa
première passion.*

*Les sens ont aussi leur délicatesse; à un certain point
on les émeut; qu'on le passe, on les révolte.*

*L'on n'occupe pas longtemps l'imagination d'une
femme sans aller jusqu'à son coeur, ou du moins sans
que par les effets cela ne revienne au même.*

Of Crébillon's life there is but little to say. It was quite
uneventful. The record of it, singularly scanty, contains
almost no unusual or surprising element. It was precisely
the life which you would expect the author of *Le Sopha*
to have led: a cheerful, social, literary life in the Paris of
Louis XV. Crébillon was born on St. Valentine's Day,
1770, thus achieving legitimacy by fifteen days; for his
parents were only married on the thirty-first of January.
His father was Prosper Jolyot de Crébillon, the tragic poet
who provoked the envy and the competitive rivalry of
Voltaire. I am not ashamed to say that I have never
read a line of the elder Crébillon's works. Life is not so
long that one can afford to spend even the briefest time
in the perusal of eighteenth-century French tragedians.

The literary career of the younger Crébillon began in the theater. In association with the actors Romagnesi, Biancolelli, and Riccoboni he composed a number of satirical pieces and parodies for the Italian comedians. It was at this period that he confided to Sébastien Mercier, *"qu'il n'avait encore achevé la lecture des tragédies de son père, mais que cela viendrait. Il regardait la tragédie française comme la farce la plus complète qu'ait pu inventer l'esprit humain."*

His first successful novel, *Tanzai et Néardarné, Historie Japonaise,* was published in 1734. It was so successful, indeed, and so Japanese, that Crébillon, accused of satirizing the Cardinal de Rohan and other important persons, was arrested and thrown into prison, from which, however, the good graces of a royal reader soon released him.

Tanzai was followed in 1736 by *Les Égarements du Cœur et de l'Esprit,* and in 1740 by *Le Sopha.* It was the epoch of Crébillon's social triumphs. He was for some time perpetual chairman of the famous dinners of the Caveau, and there were many other societies of which he was, officially or unofficially, the leading light.

In 1748 he married—somewhat tardily, for he had had a child by her two years before—an English wife, Lady Mary Howard. It is said that the poor lady squinted, was very ugly, awkward in society, shy, and deeply religious. Crébillon seems, none the less, to have been a model husband, while the marriage lasted; which was not very long, however, for Lady Mary died about 1756. Their only child died in infancy a short time after being legitimated.

It was in 1759 that the favor of Madame de Pompadour procured for Crébillon the post of Royal Censor of Literature. He performed his duties conscientiously and to the satisfaction of all parties concerned. On the death of his father, in 1762, he received a pension. In 1774 he became Police Censor as well as Royal Censor. In 1777 he died. For all practical purposes, however, he had been dead fifteen years or more. *"Il y a longtemps,"* said his obituarist, *"très longtemps même, qu'il avait eu le chagrin de se voir survivre à lui-même."* Melancholy fate! It caused his contemporaries to do him, towards the end, something less than justice. The most enthusiastic of his epitaphs is cool enough:

Dans ce tombeau gît Crébillon.
Qui? le fameux tragique—Non!
Celui qui le mieux peignit l'âme
Du petit-maître et de la femme.

The praise is faint. It is meant, perhaps, to damn. But it does not succeed in damning. To have been the best painter of anybody's soul, even the fop's, even the eighteenth-century lady's, is a fine achievement. "*Je fus étonnée,*" says one of Crébillon's characters, describing the charms of her lover's conversation, "*je fus étonnée de la sorte de consistance que les objets les plus frivoles semblaient prendre entre ses mains.*" The whole merit of that French eighteenth century, of which Crébillon was the representative man, consisted precisely in giving "a sort of consistency to the most frivolous objects." To lead a life of leisure gracefully is an art, and though we can all do nothing, few of us contrive to do it well. It is scarcely possible to imagine a life more hopelessly futile than that which was led by the men and women of the Old French aristocracy. Intrinsically, such a life seems ghastly in its emptiness and sterility. And yet, somehow, by sheer force of style, these frivolous creatures of the *dix-huitième* contrived to fill the emptiness, to coax the most charming and elegant flowers from the sterility of their existence. To the most futile of lives they gave "a sort of consistency"; they endowed nothingness with solidity and form. Crébillon shared this power with his contemporaries. The conquests of the *petit-maître,* the prompt surrenders of Célie and Cidalise and Julie—these are his theme. It seems unpromising in its smallness and its triviality. But by dint of treating it seriously—with the double seriousness of the scientific observer and the literary artist—he has made out of it something which we in our turn are compelled to take seriously. Like Célie, we are astonished.

"The Queen," writes Swift in one of his letters to Stella, "the Queen is well, but I fear she will be no long liver; for I am told she has sometimes the gout in her bowels (I hate the word bowels)." Yes, how he hated it! And not the word only—the things too, the harmless necessary tripes—he loathed and destested them with an intensity of hatred such as few men have ever been capable of. It was unbearable to him that men should go through life with guts and sweetbreads, with livers and lights, spleens and kidneys. That human beings should have to get rid of the waste products of metabolism and digestion was for Swift a source of excruciating suffering. And if the Yahoos were all his personal enemies, that was chiefly because they smelt of sweat and excrement, because they had genital organs and dugs, groins and hairy armpits; their moral shortcomings were of secondary importance. Swift's poems about women are more ferocious even than his prose about the Yahoos; his resentment against women for being warm-blooded mammifers was incredibly bitter. Read (with a bottle of smelling salts handy, if you happen to be delicately stomached) *The Lady's Dressing Room, Cassinus and Peter, A Beautiful Young Nymph Going to Bed*. Here is a moderately characteristic sample:

• From *Do What You Will*, 1929.

And first a dirty smock appeared,
Beneath the armpits well besmeared . . .
But oh! it turned poor Stephen's bowels,
When he beheld and smelt the towels,
Begummed, besmattered, and beslimed,
With dirt and sweat and earwax grimed.

Passing from description to philosophical reflection, we find such lines as these:

His foul imagination links
Each dame he sees with all her stinks;
And if unsavoury odors fly,
Conceives a lady standing by.

Nor can I refrain from mentioning that line, which Swift thought so much of that he made it the culmination of two several poems:

Oh, Celia, Celia, Celia . . . !

The monosyllabic verb, which the modesties of 1929, will not allow me to reprint, rhymes with "wits" and "fits."

Swift must have "hated the word bowels" to the verge of insanity: nothing short of the most violent love or the intensest loathing could possibly account for so obsessive a preoccupation with the visceral and excrementitious subject. Most of us dislike bad smells and offal; but so mildly that, unless they are actually forced upon our senses, we seldom think of them. Swift hated bowels with such a passionate abhorrence that he felt a perverse compulsion to bathe continually in the squelchy imagination of them. Human beings are always fascinated by what horrifies and disgusts them. The reasons are obscure and doubtless complicated. One of the sources of this apparent perversity is surely to be found in the almost universal craving for excitement. Life, for most people is a monotonous affair; they want to be thrilled, stimulated, excited, almost at all costs. The horrifying and disgusting are sources of strong emotion; therefore the horrifying and disgusting are pursued as goods. Most of us, I suppose, enjoy disgust and horror, at any rate in small doses. But we fairly quickly reach a point where the enjoyment turns into pain; when this happens we naturally do our best to avoid the source of the painful emotions. But there are at least two classes of people who are ready voluntarily to continue the pursuit of horrors and disgustfulnesses long after the majority of their fellows have begun to shrink from a pleasure which has become an intolerable pain. In the first class we find the congenitally insensitive —those who can be excited only by a relatively enormous stimulus. The extreme case is that of certain idiots for whom a surgical operation without anesthetics is a real pleasure. Under the knife and the cautery they begin at last to feel. Between this extreme of insensitiveness and the statistical normal there is no hiatus, but a continuous series of graded types, for all of whom the normal stimulus is to a greater or less degree inadequate. To the congenitally insensitive we must add those whose normal sensitiveness has, for one reason or another, decreased during the course of life. A familiar type is that of the ageing debauchee, habituated to a continuous excitement, but so much exhausted by his mode of life, so blunted and hardened, that he can only be excited by a more than normally powerful stimulus. Such insensitives can stomach doses of horror and disgust which would be mortal to the ordinary man.

But the insensitives are not the only lovers of horror and disgust. There is another class of men and women, often more than ordinarily sensitive, who deliberately seek out what pains and nauseates them for the sake of the extraordinary pleasure they derive from the overcoming of their repulsion. Take the case, for example, of the mystical Mme Guyon, who felt that her repugnance for unclean and unsavory objects was a weakness disgraceful in one who lived only for and with God. One day she determined to overcome this weakness, and, seeing on the ground a particularly revolting gob of phlegm and spittle, she picked it up and, in spite of intolerable retchings of disgust, put it in her mouth. Her nauseated horror was succeeded by a sentiment of joy, of profound exultation. A similar incident may be found in the biography of St. Francis of Assisi. Almost the first act of his religious life was to kiss the pustulent hand of one of those lepers, the sight and smell of whom had, up till that time, sickened him with disgust. Like Mme Guyon, he was rewarded for his pains with a feeling of rapturous happiness. Even the most unsaintly people have felt the glow of satisfaction which follows the accomplishment of some act in the teeth of an instinctive resistance. The pleasure of asserting the conscious will against one of those dark instinctive forces which consciousness rightly regards as its enemies, is for many people, and in certain circumstances, more than sufficient to outweigh the pain caused by the thwarting of the instinct. Our minds, like our bodies, are colonies of separate lives, existing in a state of chronically hostile symbiosis; the soul is in reality a great conglomeration of souls, the product of whose endless warfare at any given moment is our behavior at that moment. The pleasures attending the victory of conscious will have a special quality of their own, a quality which, for many temperaments, makes them preferable to any other kind of pleasure. Nietzsche advised men to be cruel to themselves, not because asceticism was pleasing to some hypothetical god, but because it was a good spiritual exercise, because it wound up the will and enhanced the sense of power and of conscious, voluntary life. To this delightful enhancement of the sense of power the believer, whose conscious will is fighting for what is imagined to be an absolute good, can add the no less delightful sense of being virtuous, the pleasing consciousness that he is pleasing God. Mme Guyon and St. Francis probably did not exaggerate when they described in such rapturous terms the joy evoked in them by their voluntary wallowings in filth.

Swift—to return from a long digression—Swift belonged, it seems to me, to a subspecies of the second category of horror-lovers. He was not one of those insensitives who can only respond to the most violent stimuli. On the contrary, he seems to have been more than normally sensitive. His "hatred of bowels" was the rationalization of an intense disgust. Why, then, did he pore so lingeringly on what revolted him? What was his reward? Was it the Nietzschean enhancement of the sense of power? Or was it the Christian's happy consciousness of pleasing God by the conquest of a weakness? No, it was certainly not for the love of God that the Dean of St. Patrick's humiliated himself in the excrement and offal. Was it, then, for love of himself, for the pleasure of asserting his will? A little, perhaps. But his real reward was the pain he suffered. He felt a compulsion to remind himself of his hatred of bowels, just as a man with a wound or an aching tooth feels a compulsion to touch the source of

his pain—to make sure that it is still there and still agonizing. With Swift, it was not a case of the pleasure of self-
assertion outweighing the pain of voluntarily-evoked disgust. For him the pain *was* the pleasure, or, at any rate,
it was the desirable end towards which his activities
were directed. He wished to suffer.

Swift's greatness lies in the intensity, the almost insane violence of that "hatred of bowels" which is the
essence of his misanthropy and which underlies the whole
of his work. As a doctrine, a philosophy of life, this
misanthropy is profoundly silly. Like Shelley's apocalyptic
philanthropy, it is a protest against reality, childish (for
it is only the child who refuses to accept the order of
things), like all such protests, from the fairy story to
the socialist's Utopia. Regarded as a political pamphlet
or the expression of a world view, *Gulliver* is as preposterous as *Prometheus Unbound*. Regarded as works of
art, as independent universes of discourse existing on
their own authority, like geometries harmoniously developed from a set of arbitrarily chosen axioms, they are
almost equally admirable. What interests me here, however, is the relation of these two works to the reality
outside themselves, not the inward, formal relation of
their component parts with one another. Considered, then,
merely as comments on reality, *Gulliver* and *Prometheus*
are seen, for all their astonishing difference, to have a
common origin—the refusal on the part of their authors
to accept the physical reality of the world. Shelley's refusal to accept the given reality took the form of a lyrical
and prophetic escape into the Golden Age that is to be
when kings and priests have been destroyed and the
worship of abstractions and metaphysical absolutes is substituted for that of the existing gods. Swift, on the contrary,
made no attempt to escape, but remained earth-bound,
rubbing his nose in all those aspects of physical reality
which most distressed him. His Houyhnhnm Utopia was
not one of those artificial paradises which men have
fabricated (out of such diverse materials as religious
myths, novels, and whisky) as a refuge from a world
with which they were unable to cope. He was not like
that Old Person of Bazing in Edward Lear's rhyme, who

purchased a steed
Which he rode at full speed
To escape from the people of Bazing

Swift's horse was not a means of transport into another and better world. A winged angel would have served that purpose better. If he "purchased a steed," it was in order that he might shame the disgusting Yahoos by parading its superiority. For Swift, the charm of the country of the Houhynhnms consisted, not in the beauty and virtue of the horses, but in the foulness of the degraded men.

When we look into the matter we find that the great, the unforgivable sin of the Yahoos consisted in the fact that they possessed bowels. Like so many of the Fathers of the Church, Swift could not forgive men and women for being vertebrate mammals as well as immortal souls. He could not forgive them, in a word, for actually existing. It is unnecessary for me to insist at length on the absurdity, the childish silliness, of this refusal to accept the universe as it is given. Abstractions are made from reality and labeled soul, spirit, and so forth; reality is then hated for not resembling these arbitrary abstractions from its total mass. It would be as sensible to hate flowers for not resembling the liquid perfume which can be distilled from them. A yet greater, but no less common, childishness is to hate reality because it does not resemble the fairy stories which men have invented to console themselves for the discomforts and difficulties of daily life, or to hate it because life does not seem to hold the significance which a favorite author happens to have attributed to it. Ivan Karamazov returning God his entrance ticket to life is a characteristic example of this last form of childishness. Ivan is distressed because the real universe bears so little resemblance to the providential machine of Christian theology, distressed because he can find no meaning or purpose in life. But the purpose of life, outside the mere continuance of living (already a most noble and beautiful end), is the purpose we put into it: its meaning is whatever we may choose to call the meaning. Life is not a crossword puzzle, with an answer settled in advance and a prize for the ingenious person who noses it out. The riddle of the universe has as many answers as the universe has living inhabitants. Each answer is a working hypothesis, in terms of which the answerer experiments with reality. The best answers are those which permit the answerer to live most fully, the worst are those which condemn him to partial or complete death. The most fantastic answers will serve their turn as working hypotheses. Thus, certain primitive peoples are convinced that they are blood brothers to crocodiles or parrots, and live in accordance with their belief—most efficiently, according to all accounts. We smile at their philosophy. But is it more ridiculous, after all, than that whch teaches that men are brothers, not to parrots, but to imaginary angels? Or that an abstraction called the soul is the essential reality of human nature, and the body is hardly more than an accident, an evil accident at that?

Of the possible reasons for Swift's insensate hatred of bowels I will say more later. It was a hatred to which, of course, he had a perfect right. Every man has an inalienable right to the psychological major premise of his philosophy of life, just as every man has an alienable right to his own liver. But his liver may be a bad liver: it may make him sluggish, ill-tempered, despairingly melancholy. It may, in a word, be a hindrance to living instead of a help. It is the same with a philosophy of life. Every man has a right to look at the world as he chooses; but his world view may be a bad one—a hindrance, like the defective liver, instead of a help to living. Judged by these standards, the Swiftian world view is obviously bad. To hate bowels, to hate the body and all its ways, as Swift hated them, is to hate at least half of man's entire vital activity. It is impossible to live completely without accepting life as a whole in all its manifestations. Swift's prodigious powers were marshalled on the side of death, not life. How instructive, in this context, is the comparison with Rabelais! Both men were scatological writers. Mass for mass, there is probably more dung and offal piled up in Rabelais' work than in Swift's. But how pleasant is the dung through which Gargantua wades, how almost delectable the offal! The muck is transfigured by love; for Rabelais loved the bowels which Swift so malignantly hated. His was the true *amor fati*: he accepted reality in its entirety, accepted with gratitude and delight this amazingly improbable world, where flowers spring from manure, and reverent Fathers of the Church, as in Harington's *Metamorphosis of Ajax*, meditate on the divine mysteries while seated on the privy; where the singers of the most mystically spiritual love, such as Dante, Petrarch, and Cavalcanti, have wives and rows of children; and where the violences of animal passion can give birth to sentiments of the most exquisite tenderness and refinement. In this most beautiful, ridiculous, and tragic world Swift has no part: he is shut out from it by hatred, by his childish resentment against reality for not being entirely different from what, in fact, it is. That the lovely Celia should obey the calls of nature like any cow or camel, is for Swift a real disaster. The wise and scientific Rabelaisian, on the other hand, would be distressed if she did not obey them, would prescribe a visit to Carlsbad or Montecatini. Swift would have liked Celia to be as bodiless as an abstraction: he was furious with her for being solid and healthy. One is amazed that a grown man should feel and think in a manner so essentially childish. That the hatred of bowels should have been the major premise of his philosophy when Swift was fifteen is comprehensible, but that it should have remained the major premise when he was forty requires some explanation.

At this distance of time and with only the most inadequate evidence on which to go, we cannot hope to explain with certainty: the best we can do is to hazard a guess, to suggest a possible hypothesis. That which I would suggest—and doubtless it has been suggested before—is that Swift's hatred of bowels was obscurely, but none the less closely, connected with that "temperamental coldness" which Sir Leslie Stephen attributes to the mysterious lover of Stella and Vanessa. That any man with a normal dosage of sexuality could have behaved quite so oddly as Swift behaved towards the women he loved seems certainly unlikely. We are almost forced by the surviving evidence to believe that some physical or psychological impediment debarred him from making love in the ordinary, the all too human manner. Now, when a man is not actually, or at any rate potentially, all too human, he does not for that reason become superhuman: on the contrary, he tends to become subhuman. Subhumanly silly, as Kant was silly in the intervals of writing the superhuman *Critique of Pure Reason;* or subhumanly malignant, as the too virtuous Calvin was malignant. Cut off by some accident of body or character from the beautiful and humorous, the rather absurd but sacred, but sublime and marvelous world of carnal passion and tenderness (and lacking the aid of the flesh, the spirit must remain forever ignorant of the highest, the profoundest, the intensest forms of love), Swift was prevented from growing to full human maturity. Remaining subhumanly childish, he continued all his life to resent reality for not resembling the abstractions and fairy-tale compensations of the philosophers and theologians. At the same time his separation from the human world, his sense of solitude, developed in him something of the subhuman malignity, the hate, the envious "righteous indignation" of the Puritan. The reverse of this ferocious hater was, as so often happens, a sentimentalist —a sentimentalist, moreover, of the worst kind; for, in the writer of the baby language which fills so much space in Swift's *Journal to Stella*, we see that most abject and repulsive type of sentimentalist (a type, it may be added, exceedingly common at the present time), the adult man who deliberately mimics the attitudes of childhood. The character of the age in which Swift lived was hard and virile: machinery, Taylorization, the highly organized division of labor, specialization, and humanitarianism had not yet begun to produce their dehumanizing effects. In the England of the early seventeen-hundreds, Swift was ashamed of his infantility. His baby language was a secret between himself and the two "sweet rogues" to whom he wrote his letters. In public he revealed only the Puritan, the Father-of-the-Church side of him—the respectably misanthropical obverse of the infantile medal. If he had lived two hundred years later in our routine-ridden, mechanized world of flabbily subhuman sentimentalists, he would not have been ashamed of his infantility: on the contrary, he would have been proud. His angers and his hatreds are what he would have hidden from the modern public. If Swift were alive today, he would be the adored, the baroneted, the Order-of-Merited author, not of *Gulliver*, not of *The Tale of a Tub*, not of the *Advice to Servants*, not of *The Lady's Dressing Room*, but of *A Kiss for Cinderella* and *Peter Pan*.

Baudelaire•

Inasmuch as he pursues an absolute, the absolute of evil, *"Le débauché est un grand philosophe."* (The *mot* is attributed to the moderately eminent French metaphysician Jules Lachelier). The debauchee is a great philosopher. As it stands, the assertion is a little too sweeping; it needs qualification. No doubt, the debauchee *was* a great philosopher, once. But ever since the day of Hume he has ceased to be a great philosopher and become a rather silly one. For though it may be sublime to pursue the demonstrably unattainable, it is also ridiculous. A man may spend a laborious and ascetic lifetime writing books on the selenography of the back-side of the moon; we may admire his single-mindedness (if single-mindedness happens to be a quality that strikes us as being admirable), but we must also laugh at his folly. To pursue the absolute is as demonstrably a waste of time as to speculate on the topography of the invisible portions of the moon. Inasmuch as he attempts to rationalize an absolute wickedness, the debauchee may be something of a heroic figure. But he is also something of a figure of fun. And as a philosopher he is, in spite of Professor Lachelier, silly.

Even the sublimest of the satanists are a little ridiculous. For they are mad, all mad; and, however tragical

• From *Do What You Will,* 1929.

and appalling their insanity may be, madmen are always ridiculous. Ridiculous in their enormous unawareness, in their blindness, in the fixity of their moods, their iron consistency, their unvarying reactions to all that appeals to their mania. Ridiculous, in a word, because they are inhuman. And similarly, even the sublimest satanists (and with them, of course, their looking-glass counterparts, the sublimest saints) are ridiculous as well as grand, because they share with the madman (and deliberately share) his partial blindness, his stiffness, his strained and focused and unwavering fixity of monomaniacal purpose, his inhumanity.

The contrary and at the same time the complement of inhuman rigidity and consistency is a certain inhuman liberty. Concentrated on his one idea, the madman is out of contact with everything else. He loses all touch with reality, and so is free from those limitations which the necessity of making vital adjustments to the outside world imposes on the same. In spite of their rigid consistency of thought and action, or rather because of it, the saint and the satanist are free, like the madman, to disregard everything but their fixed idea. Often this idea is of a kind which prevents them from having anything like the normal physical relationship with their fellows and with the world at large. When this happens, their inhuman liberty is complete, manifest in all its ghastly grotesqueness. What happens when the intellect and imagination are allowed to break away completely from the wholesome control of the body and the instincts is illustrated with incomparable power by Dostoevsky. Take, for example, *The Possessed*. In the whole of that extraordinary and horrible novel (and the same is true of all Dostoevsky's books) there is not one single character who has a decent physical relationship with anyone or anything whatsoever. Dostoevsky's people do not even eat normally, much less make love, or work, or enjoy nature. That would be much too easy and obvious for such parvenus of intelligence and consciousness as the Russians. Commonplace love, mere creative labor, vulgar enjoyment of real sensuous beauty—these are activities neither "spiritual" nor "sinful" enough for newly-conscious Christians, and altogether too "irrational" to satisfy ex-moujiks suddenly enriched with all the gradually accumulated cultural wealth of Europe. Dostoevsky's characters are typical Russian parvenus to consciousness. Unrestrained by the body, their intellect and imagination have become at once licentious and monomaniacal. And when at last they feel impelled to put their wild, unrestrained imaginings into practice—for it is impossible to go on staring at one's own navel without in in the long-run becoming a trifle bored—what happens? They go and commit suicide, or murder, or rape, according to the turn their monomanias happen to have taken. How tragic it all is! But also how stupid and grotesque! If Stavrogin could have gone to bed with women he liked, instead of sleeping, on satanically ascetic principles, with women he detested; if Kirillov had had a wife and a job of decent work; if Pyotr Stepanovitch had ever looked with pleasure at a landscape or played with a kitten—none of these tragedies, these fundamentally ludicrous and idiotic tragedies, would have taken place. The horrors that darken *The Possessed* and the other novels of Dostoevsky are tragedies of mental licentiousness. All Dostoevsky's characters (and Dostoevsky himself, one suspects, was rather like them) have licentious minds, utterly unrestrained by their bodies. They are all emotional onanists, wildly indulging themselves in the void of imagination. Occasionally they grow tired of their masturbations and try to make contact with the world. But they have lost all sense of reality, all knowledge of human values. All their attempts to realize their onanistic dreaming in practice result in catastrophe. It is inevitable. But however agonizing they may be (and Dostoevsky spares us nothing), these tragedies, I repeat, are fundamentally ludicrous and idiotic. They are the absurdly unnecessary tragedies of self-made madmen. We suffer in sympathy, but against our will; afterwards we must laugh. For these tragedies are nothing but stupid farces that have been carried too far.

Robert Burns, after Chaucer the least pretentious and portentous, the most completely and harmoniously human of all English poets, understood this well. His "Address to the Deil" has for epigraph two tremendous lines from *Paradise Lost*:

O Prince! O Chief of many thronèd pow'rs
That led th' embattled Seraphim to war!

The words go rumbling through the spaces of the Miltonic universe, reverberate in fearful thunder from the roof of hell, in solemn and celestial music from sphere after crystal sphere; but when at last they strike the earth, what very strange and even indecorous echoes are returned!

> O Thou! whatever title suit thee,
> Auld Hornie, Satan, Nick, or Clootie,
> Wha in yon cavern grim and sootie,
>   Closed under hatches,
> Spairges about the brunstane cootie,
>   To scaud poor wretches!

It is the voice of humanity, of sane and humorous and unpretentious humanity, that speaks. Larger than life and half as natural, Milton declaims the potent charms that call up Satan from the abyss; saint and fiend, they stand together, a pair of twins. They are sublime, but for that very reason ridiculous. For the Chief of many thronèd powers is also a comic character, grotesque, like some too villainous villain in an old melodrama—like some too virtuous hero, for that matter.

And the lesser satanists are like their masters. Don Juan, Cain, Heathcliff, Stavrogin—they are all of them figures of fun, in spite of their sublimity, or rather because of it. And the satanists of real life are almost as ridiculous as the satanists of literature. Almost; but not quite, because, unless he is stark, staring mad, the living satanist is never so stiffly consistent, never so utterly free from the normal human restraints, as the satanist in books. It is only when satanists fail to live up to the satanic character that we can take them seriously—for it is then that they begin to be human. When they sublimely succeed, we are compelled to laugh. "Laughter," said Baudelaire, "is satanic." Some laughter, perhaps. But by no means all. There is a whole gamut of humorous and unferocious laughter that is entirely and characteristically human. And I suspect that it was precisely this human laughter that Baudelaire, the satanist, described as satanic. His values were reversed. The mirth which men like Chaucer or Burns would have found friendly in its quality of humanness, Baudelaire necessarily found hostile and fiendish. For if the devil is man's worst enemy, man is also the devil's. The most powerful solvent of satanic as of any other superhuman pretensions is the good-humored laughter of human beings. Call the devil Nick or Auld Hornie, and he loses immediately all his impressiveness and half his formidableness. Hence Baudelaire's hatred of laughter; from his satanic point of view it was indeed diabolical. Satan must be dignified at all costs. In his superb and portentous carapace there must be no chink through which the shafts of men's mirth can enter. The laughter-proof armor in which Baudelaire passed his life was a "sober dandyism" of dress, a frigidly aristocratic manner, a more than English coldness. His clothes, according to Théophile Gautier, had

> *un cachet voulu de simplicité anglaise et comme l'intention de se séparer du genre artiste. . . . Contrairement aux mœurs un peu débraillés des artistes, Baudelaire se piquait de garder les plus étroites convenances, et sa politesse était excessive jusqu'à paraître maniérée. Il mesurait ses phrases, n'employait que les termes les plus choisis. . . . La charge, très en honneur à Pimodan, était dédaignée par lui comme artiste et grossière; mais il ne s'interdisait pas le paradoxe et l'outrance. D'un air très simple, très naturel et parfaitement détache . . . il avançait quelque axiome satanique monstrueux. Ses gestes étaient lents, rares et sobres, rapprochés du corps, car il avait en horreur la gesticulation méridionale. Il n'aimait pas non plus la volubilité de parole, et la froideur britannique lui semblait de bon goût. On peut dire de lui que c'était un dandy égaré dans la bohème mais y gardant son rang et ses manières et ce culte de soi-même qui caractérise l'homme imbu des principes de Brummell.*

What elaborate precautions against the possible laughter of humanity! Satan is a gentleman, and only on condition of remaining a gentleman can he be Satan. The moment he loses his Brummellesque dignity and becomes Auld Hornie or Auld Nick, he is just a poor devil, nothing more. If Baudelaire could sometimes have dropped his dandy's correctness, could sometimes have permitted himself to be called Clootie, he would have been certainly a happier and completer man and perhaps a better because a more comprehensive poet.

But he preferred to cling to his satanic dignity; he buckled his laughter-proof armor yet more tightly about him. It was as a kind of Black Prince that he confronted the world—a dark figure, tragical and terrific, but at the same time ludicrous in being too imposing, insufficiently supple.

"Sin," says St. Paul, "is not imputed when there is

no law. . . . Moreover, the law entered, that the offence might abound." Only a believer in absolute goodness can consciously pursue the absolute of evil; you cannot be a Satanist without being at the same time, potentially or actually, a Godist. Baudelaire was a Christian inside out, the photographic image in negative of a Father of the Church. His philosophy was orthodox—nay, more than orthodox, almost Jansenistic. His views on original sin (in modern times the touchstone of orthodoxy) were entirely sound. They were much sounder, for example, than those of Jesus. Jesus could say, speaking of little children, that "of such is the kingdom of heaven"; a sound Augustinian, Baudelaire called them *"des Satans en herbe."* He had the good Christian's contempt for the modern belief in progress. *"La croyance au progrès,"* he said, *"est une doctrine de Belges."* And when Baudelaire had said of a thing that it was Belgian he had called it the worst name in his vocabulary.

To this Christian, who accepted the doctrine of the Fall with all its consequences, Humanitarianism was simply criminal nonsense. Man was by nature malignant and stupid. The "universal silliness of every class, individual, sex, and age" filled him, as it filled Flaubert, with a chronic indignation. Those who, like the painter Wiertz (another Belgian!), believed in "the immortal principles of '89," he regarded almost as personal enemies. *"Le Christ des humanitaires,"* he writes in his notes on Wiertz. *"Peinture philosophique. Sottises analogues à celles de Victor à la fin des Contemplations. Abolition de la peine de mort, puissance infinie de l'homme!"* For the democrat's ingenuous faith in the power of education to make all men equally intelligent and virtuous he had nothing but contempt. One of his projects was to write an essay on the *"infamie de l'imprimerie, grand obstacle au développement du Beau."* Wholly Christian again was Baudelaire's attitude towards the question of individual responsibility. For the eighteenth-century humanitarians, who started from the axiom that man in a "state of nature" is virtuous and reasonable, there could not, logically, be such a thing as sin in the Christian, or crime in the legal, sense of the word; the individual was not to blame for his bad actions. The entire responsibility rested with the Environment, with Society, with Bad Laws, Priestcraft, Superstition, and so forth. For Baudelaire only the individual counted. Those who do wrong must bear the whole responsibility for their wrongdoing. And what actions, according to Baudelaire, are wrong? The answer is simple: they are the actions which the Church regards as sinful. St. Paul never hated the flesh and all its works more venomously than did Baudelaire; Prudentius never wrote of love with a fiercer vehemence of disgust. For the poet, as for the Christian moralists, the worst, because the most attractive, the commonest, the apparently most harmless sins were those of a sexual nature. Avoid them, then! was the command of the moralists. But Baudelaire was a looking-glass Christian; for him the categorical imperative was just the opposite of this. Indulgence is hateful to God; therefore (such is the logic of the satanists) indulge. *"La volupté unique et suprême de l'amour gît dans la certitude de faire le mal. Et l'homme et la femme savent de naissance que dans le mal se trouve toute volupté."* Baudelaire liked revolution for the same reason as he liked love. *"Moi, quand je consens à être républicain"* (he did a little desultory shooting from the barricades in 1848), *"je fais le mal, le sachant. . . . Je dis: Vive la Révolution! comme je dirais: Vive la Destruction! Vive la Mort! Nous avons tous l'esprit républicain dans les veines comme la vérole dans les os. Nous sommes démocratisés et syphilisés!"* He hated and despised the revolutionaries who imagined that they were acting for the benefit of the human race. *"Moi, je me fous du genre humain."* "A taste for vengeance and the natural pleasure of demolition" were what drove *him* to the barricades.

But politics and, in general, "action" (in the popular sense of the word) were distasteful to him. It was only theoretically that he "understood a man's deserting one cause for the sake of knowing what it would feel like to serve another." An invincible dislike of all causes but that of poetry prevented him from attempting the experiment in practice. And in the same way, when he said that "not only would he be happy to be the victim, but that he would not object to being the executioner—so as to feel the Revolution in both ways," it was only a matter of words. His own active participation in the Revolution was too brief to permit of his being either victim or executioner.

Much of Baudelaire's satanism even outside the sphere

of politics was confined to words. Inevitably: for Baudelaire liked his freedom, and in a well-policed society the
satanists who put their principles too freely into practice
get thrown into jail. From Baudelaire's conversation
you would have imagined that he was a mixture of
Gilles de Rais, Heliogabalus, and the Marquis de Sade.
At any rate, that was what he wanted you to imagine.
But reputations have a strange life of their own, over
which their subject has little or no control. Baudelaire
would have liked the world to regard him as the incarnation of all the gentlemanly wickednesses. Instead of which
—but let me quote his own words: *"Un jour une femme
me dit: C'est singulier; vous êtes fort convenable; je croyais
que vous étiez toujours ivre et que vous sentiez mauvais."*

To have the reputation of being unpleasantly smelly—
could anything have been more humiliating to the man
who saw himself as the Chief of many thronèd powers!
Those who knew him personally made, of course, no
such mistakes. Their friend was no vulgar Bohemian,
but a Dandy; if he was wicked, it was in the grand
manner, like a gentleman, not an artist. But they also
knew that a great deal of his aristocratic satanism was
purely Platonic and conversational. Baudelaire was a
practicing satanist only in those circumstances in which
active satanism is not interfered with by the police. All
satanisms of violence and fraud were thus ruled out.
He talked about treacheries and executions, but did not
act them. The most interesting of the legally tolerated
sins are those of the flesh. Baudelaire was therefore,
above all, a satanist of love. But not in the manner of
the ferocious Marquis, nor even of Don Juan. He did
not victimize his partners; he victimized only himself.
His cruelties were directed inwards. Harmlessly, one is
tempted to say; the harmless cruelties of an academic
satanist. And harmless, in one sense, they were. Baudelaire's path was not strewn with seduced young girls,
adulterous wives, and flagellated actresses. Regrettably,
perhaps. For this apparently harmless variety of satanism
is in certain ways the most harmful of all. The flagellator
and the seducer do a certain strictly limited amount of
damage among their feminine acquaintances. The self-vic-
timizing satanist is infinitely more destructive. For what
are a few virginities and a few square inches of tanned
cocotte-skin compared with the entire universe? The entire

universe—nothing less. The satanist who is his own victim defaces and defiles for himself the entire universe. And when, like Baudelaire, he happens to be a great poet, he defaces and defiles it for his readers. Your Sades and Juans are never ruinous on this enormous scale. For they enjoy their satanisms—not very wholeheartedly, perhaps, and always crazily; but still enjoy. They go their way caroling with Pippa: "Nick's in his Hades, all's right with the world." The self-victimizer has no enjoyments to rationalize into a jolly Browningesque philosophy. The world is hateful to him; he himself has made it so.

Baudelaire treated himself with a studied malignancy. He took pains to make the world as thoroughly disgusting for himself as he could. As an example of his satanic technique, let me quote this fragment of autobiography from one of his sonnets:

> *Une nuit que j'étais près d'une affreuse juive,*
> *Comme au long d'un cadavre un cadavre étendu,*
> *Je me pris à songer près de ce corps vendu*
> *A la triste beauté dont mon désir se prive.*

Appalling lines! Reading them, one seems to sink through layer after darkening, thickening layer of slimy horror. A shuddering pity takes hold of one. And then amazement, amazement at the thought that this revolting torture was self-inflicted.

Torture, torture—the word comes back to one hauntingly, again and again, as one reads the *Fleurs du Mal*. Baudelaire himself brooded over the notion. "Love is like a torture or a surgical operation. This idea can be developed in the bitterest way. Even when the two lovers are very much in love and full of reciprocal desires, one of the two will always be calmer or less possessed than the other. He, or she, is the operator, the executioner; the other is the patient, the victim." The tortures which Baudelaire inflicted on himself were not mere operations; they were more horrible than that. Between him and the "frightful Jewesses" there was not even the possibility of reciprocal desire—there was nothing but disgust. His tortures were mostly those of defilement. To be chained to a corpse, to be confined in the midst of rats and excrement—these were the punishments to which he satanically condemned himself. And even his respites from the frightful Jewesses were only milder tortures. That "sad beauty of whom his desire deprived itself" was a drunken Negress, whose vulgarity shocked every fiber of his soul, whose stupidity amazed and appalled him, who drained him of his money and showed her gratitude by cuckolding him whenever she had an opportunity.

> *Quand elle eut de mes os sucé toute la moelle,*
> *Et que languissamment je me tournai vers elle*
> *Pour lui rendre un baiser d'amour, je ne vis plus*
> *Qu'une outre aux flancs gluants, toute peine de pus.*

In spite of which, or because of which, Baudelaire remained indissolubly attached to his mulatto. After their most serious quarrel he lay in his bed for days, uncontrollably and incessantly weeping. In spite or because of the fact that she represented sex in its lowest form, he loved her.

But frightful Jewesses and hardly less frightful Negresses were not the only object of Baudelaire's love. For,

> *Quand chez les débauchés l'aube blanche et vermeille*
> *Entree en société de l'Idéal rongeur,*
> *Par l'opération d'un mystère vengeur*
> *Dans la brute assoupie un ange se réveille.*

In other words, that morning-after sentiment, that *omne-animal-triste* feeling which, according to the Ancients, tinges with melancholy the loves of every creature but the mare and the woman, is easily and naturally rationalized in terms of Christian-Platonic idealism. The angel in Baudelaire was never fast asleep. For, as I have already pointed out, a man cannot be a Satanist who is not the same time a Godist. Above the frightful Jewesses and Negresses among whom Baudelaire had condemned himself to pass his life, hovered a white-winged, white-nightgowned ideal of feminine purity. The lineaments of this angelic child of fancy were by the poet occasionally superimposed on those of a real, flesh-and-blood woman, who thereupon ceased to be a woman and became, in the words used by Baudelaire himself when writing to one of his deified lady friends (an artist's model in this case), *"un objet de culte"* which it was *"impossible de souiller."* Unhappily the "impossibility of defilement" was not so absolute as he could have wished. Idealization is a process which takes place only in the idealist's fancy: it has no perceptible effect upon the thing idealized. The "object of worship" remains incurably what it was—in this case a woman. This regrettable fact was personally rediscovered by Baudelaire in the most ridiculously humiliating circumstances. Mme Sabatier was a merry young widow who gave literary and artistic dinner parties. The Goncourts call her *"une vivandière de faunes";* and she herself, it would seem, was also a trifle faunesque in her tastes and habits. It was in this unlikely temple of plump luxuriant flesh and more than ordinarily warm blood that Baudelaire chose to lodge his divine ideal. The fauns' barmaid became for him an object of worship. For five years he adored, piously. Then, the publication of the *Fleurs du Mal* and the subsequent lawsuit having made him suddenly famous, Mme Sabatier decided, without solicitation on his part, to yield. Invited to treat his deity as a human, even an all too human being, Baudelaire found himself incapable of rising to the occasion. The lady was offended—justifiably. She reproached him. Baudelaire returned her reproaches. *"Il y a quelques jours,"* he wrote, *"tu étais une divinité, ce qui est si commode, ce qui est si beau, ce qui est si inviolable. Te voilà femme maintenant."* It was unforgivable. *"J'ai horreur de la passion,"* he went on to explain, *"parce que je la connais avec toutes ses ignominies."* As a matter of fact, Baudelaire knew very little about passion. He knew the defiling torture of submitting to the embraces of frightful Jewesses; and, in the arms of his Negress, he knew the madness, the fixed incurable monomania, of exclusive sensuality. At the other end of the scale he knew the worship of inviolable divinities—a worship, of which one of the conditions was precisely the joyless or frantic debauchery among the Jewesses and Negresses. For *"la femme dont on ne jouit point est celle qu'on aime. . . . Ce qui rend la maîtresse plus chère, c'est la débauche avec d'autres femmes. Ce qu'elle perd en jouissances sensuelles elle gagne en adoration."* These strange perversities were what Baudelaire called passion. Of the more normal amorous relationships he was wholly ignorant. We may doubt whether he ever embraced a woman he respected, or knew what it was to combine desire with esteem, and tenderness with passion. Indeed, he would have denied the very possibility of such combinations. His theory of love was the theory of those extreme, almost Manichean Christians who condemned indiscriminately every form of physical passion, and regarded even marriage as a sin. Between mind and body, spirit and matter, he had fixed an impassable gulf. Body was wholly bad; therefore, according to the logic of satanism, it had to be indulged as much and above all as sordidly as possible. Spirit was wholly good; therefore, when *"dans la brute assoupie un ange se réveille,"* there must be nothing in the nature of a (by definition) defiling physical contact.

Where love was concerned, Baudelaire, in the phrase of Ivan Karamazov, "returned God his entrance ticket." He refused to accept love; he wanted something better. With the result, of course, that he got something much worse and that love refused to accept *him*. The best is ever the enemy of the good, and nowhere more murderously the enemy than where love is concerned. Baudelaire's idea of the best love was a purely mental relationship, a conscious interbecoming of two hitherto separate beings. Ordinary, unideal love was for him an *"épouvantable jeu,"* because at least "one of the players must lose the government of himself." Moreover, *"dans l'amour, comme dans presque toutes les affaires humaines, l'entente cordiale est le résultat d'un malentendu. Ce malentendu, c'est le plaisir. L'homme crie: O mon ange! La femme roucoule: Maman! Maman! Et ces deux imbéciles sont persuadés qu'ils pensent de concert. Le gouffre infranchissable qui fait l'incommunicabilité reste infranchi."* But, after all, why shouldn't it remain uncrossed? And why shouldn't one sometimes lose the government of oneself? We may think ourselves happy that we do not possess a perfect and uninterrupted awareness of self and of others. How fatiguing existence would be if consciousness and will were never given a holiday, if there were no "frightful games," in the course of which one might occasionally lose one's head! How fatiguing! And also how trivial and petty! For, in love at any rate, a man loses his head for the sake of something bigger and more important than his own ego, of something not himself that makes for life. And then the horror of being wholly transparent to somebody else, wholly clear-sighted oneself! Thanks, however, to the body, there can be no complete awareness, because there can be no mingling of substance, no interbecoming. The body guarantees our privacy, that inmost privacy, which we must not attempt to violate under pain of betraying our manhood.

> Aye free, aff han' your story tell,
>   When wi' a bosom cronie;
> But still keep something to yoursel'
>   Ye scarcely tell to onie.

To none, indeed—even in love. The realization of Baudelaire's ideal would be a psychological catastrophe. But being a sound, if satanic, Christian, with a prejudice in favor of mind and spirit, and a contemptuous hatred of the body, Baudelaire could not understand this; on the contrary, he imagined that he was yearning for his own and humanity's highest good. When he saw that there was no prospect of his getting what he yearned for, he renounced love altogether in favor of self-tormenting debauchery on the one hand, and long-range adoration on the other.

With that sovereign good sense which, in spite of the strangenesses and absurdities of their beliefs, generally distinguished the actions of the men of the Middle Ages, the great Platonizing poets of the thirteenth and fourteenth centuries harmonized philosophy and the exigencies of daily living, the ideal and the real, in a manner incomparably more satisfactory. Thus, there was a Mrs. Dante as well as a Beatrice, there were no less than four little Dantes; Dante's friend and fellow-poet, Guido Cavalcanti, also had a wife and a family; and though Petrarch never married, two bastard children, borne by the same mother and at an interval of six years, testify to the fact that Laura's inordinately Platonic friend was only prevented by the accident of his having taken orders from being as good and faithful a husband as he was, by all accounts, a tenderly solicitous father. Admirably inconsistent, these poets sang the praises of sacred love, while making the very best of the profane variety in the arms of an esteemed and affectionate spouse. Their Platonic relationships existed on the margin of marriage or its equivalent, just as in the larger world, the monasteries existed on the margin of secular life. Monk and Platonic mistress testified to the existence of the spiritual ideal; those whose temperament impelled them to take extreme courses were at liberty to devote themselves to the ideal either in the cloister or in the poet's study. Whatever happened, the ideal was not to be allowed to invade the sanctities of normal domestic life. This, as we realize when we read the *Canterbury Tales* and the *Decameron*, remained throughout the Middle Ages most wholesomely pagan, in spite of Christianity. The Reformation upset the medieval balance. Stupidly consistent the Bible-reading Protestants abolished the monasteries and let loose the idealism, hitherto safely bottled up on the outskirts of normal life, on the devoted heads of ordinary men and women. For the monk was substituted the Puritan. It was a change deplorably for the worse. Confined to his private asylum on the margin of society, the monk had been harmless. The Puritan was free to range the world, blighting and persecuting as he went, free to make life poisonous, not only for himself, but for all who came near him. The Puritan was and is a social danger, a public and private nuisance of the most odious kind. Baudelaire was a Puritan inside out. Instead of asceticism and respectability he practised debauchery. The means he used were the opposite of those employed by the Puritans; but his motives and theirs, the ends that he and they achieved, were the same. He hated life as much as they did, and was as successful in destroying it.

Incapable of understanding the inconsistencies even of the medieval Christians, Baudelaire was still less capable of understanding the much more radical inconsistencies of the pagan Greeks. For the Greeks, all the Gods (or in other words all the aspects of human nature) were equally divine. The art of life consisted, for them, in giving every God his due. These dues were various. Thus, Apollo's due was very different from the debt a man owed to Dionysus. Indeed, one due might be incompatible with another; but every one was owed and, in its proper time and season, must be acknowledged. No God must be cheated and none overpaid. Baudelaire was utterly un-Hellenic. Only once or twice in all his work does he touch a pagan theme, and then it is as a puritanical Jansenist, as an early Father of the Church, that he treats it. Read, for example, the poem called "Lesbos." Here are a few characteristic extracts:

Laisse du vieux Platon se froncer l'œil austère;
Tu tires ton pardon de l'excès des baisers . . . .

Tu tires ton pardon de l'éternal martyre
Infligé sans relâche aux cœurs ambitieux . . . .

Qui des Dieux osera, Lesbos, être ton juge,
  Et condamner ton front pâli dans les travaux,
Si ses balances d'or n'ont pesé le déluge,
  Des larmes qu'à la mer ont versé tes ruisseaux?
Qui des Dieux osera, Lesbos, être ton juge?

To the contemporaries and the successors of Sappho these
lines would have been absolutely incomprehensible. All
this talk about pardon and martyrdom, judgment and
tears—the Greeks would have shaken their heads over it
in utter bewilderment. For them, love-making was not
something that required pardoning or judging. And what
did it matter, after all, if *"les Phyrnés l'une l'autre
s'attirent"*? To the Greeks it was a matter of almost perfect
indifference whether one made love with somebody of
one's own or somebody of the other sex. There is little
in Plato's writing and still less in the reputation he
enjoyed among his fellow Greeks to make us suppose that
he frowned very austerely on homosexual embraces. The
Gods, if one can credit their official biographers, were
as little likely to pass judgment on Lesbos as Plato. And
if one of them had taken it into his head to do so, is it
likely that he would have found many tears in the Lesbian
streams? None certainly of remorse or conscious guilt.
The only tears which Hellenic lovers ever seem to have
dropped were those, in youth, of unsatisfied desire and
those, when age had made them feeble and ugly, of
regret for pleasures irrevocably past. Occasionally, too,
they may have wept the *lacrimae rerum*. For, like all
realists, the Greeks were, at bottom, profoundly pessimistic.
In spite of its beauty, its inexhaustible strangeness and
rich diversity, the world, they perceived, is finally deplorable. Fate has no pity; old age and death lie in
wait at the end of every vista. It is therefore our duty
to make the best of the world and its loveliness while
we can—at any rate during the years of youth and
strength. Hedonism is the natural companion of pessi-
mism. Where there is laughter, there also you may expect to find the "tears of things." But as for tears of
repentance and remorse—who but a fool would want to
make the world more deplorable than it already is? who
but a life-hating criminal would want to increase the sum
of misery at the expense of man's small portion of precarious joy?

The earth is rich in silicon; but our bodies contain

hardly a trace of it. It is poor in phosphorus; yet in phosphorus we are rich. Sea water contains little lime and almost infinitely little copper; nevertheless, there is copper in the blood of certain crustaceans and in the shell of every mollusc abundance of lime. It is much the same in the psychological as in the physical world. We live in a spiritual environment in which, at any given moment, certain ideas and sentiments abound, certain others are rare. But in any individual mind the proportions may be reversed. For the environment does not flow into us mechanically; the living mind takes up from it only what suits it, or what it is capable of taking. What suits the majority of minds (which are but weak, underorganized beings) is of course the environment. But strong, original minds may and often do dislike their surroundings. What suits them may exist in only the smallest quantities in the spiritual medium they inhabit. But like the copper-blooded crustaceans, like the lime-shelled molluscs, they have a wonderful art to find and take up what they need. Baudelaire exemplifies this type. In the age of Buckle and Podsnap, of optimism and respectability, he was the most savage and gloomy of Augustinian Christians, the most conscientious of debauchees. Why? His private history provides the explanation. The key facts are these: he had a childish passion for his mother, and his mother, while he was still a boy, married a second husband. This marriage was a shock from which he never recovered. Whole tracts of his consciousness were suddenly ravaged by it. He had adored and idealized—the more extravagantly for the fact that his adoration and idealization had been mingled with a precocious and slightly perverse sensuality. The divinity was suddenly thrown down and violated. He hated the violator and everything that could remind him of the act of violation; he adored the memory of the yet inviolate divinity. The cynicism and perversity of adolescence got mixed in his hatred and made him take an agonizing and degrading pleasure in rehearsing in thought and, later, in act the scenes of violation. In the intervals, when he was exhausted, he worshipped a disembodied goddess. And this was what he went on doing all his life. Needing, like all men, a philosophical explanation for his actions, he found it in the semi-Manichean Christianity of the early monks and the Jansenists. A very slight twist was enough to turn the creed and ethics of Pascal into a self-torturing, world-destroying satanism. On the other face of the satanic medal were those tendencies towards "spiritual" love, so grotesquely exemplified in the case of Mme Sabatier.

Baudelaire was not merely a satanist. He was the poet of ennui, of that appalling boredom which can assume *"les proportions de l'immortalité."* The personal causes of this boredom are easily traceable. From quite early youth Baudelaire never enjoyed good health. Syphilis was in his blood: he drank too much; he took, in one form or another, large quantities of opium; he was an experimenter with hashish; he was chronically exhausted by a joyless and at last utterly pleasureless debauchery. In the physical circumstances it was difficult for a man to feel very gay and buoyant. His purse was as sick as his body. He was never out of debt; his creditors unceasingly harassed him; he lived in a perpetual state of anxiety. A neurosis of which one of the symptoms was a terrible depression was the result. This depression, he records, became almost unbearable during the autumn months—those terrible, dreary months—

Quand le ciel bas et lourd pèse comme un couvercle
Sur l'esprit gémissant en proie aux longs ennuis,
Et que de l'horizon embrassant tout le cercle
Il nous verse un jour noir plus triste que les nuits.

These are, I know, but summary and superficial generalizations; and though it would be easy, with the aid of the biographical documents which the labors of the Crépets, father and son, have placed at our disposal, to explain, in detail and plausibly enough, all the characteristic features of Baudelaire's poetry in terms of his personal history, I shall not attempt the task. For what above all interests me here is not Baudelaire as a man, but Baudelaire as an influence, a persisting force. For a force he is.

"*Avec Baudelaire,*" writes M. Paul Valéry, "*la poésie française sort enfin des frontières de la nation. Elle se fait lire dans le monde; elle s'impose comme la poésie même de la modernité; elle engendre l'imitation, elle féconde de nombreux esprits. . . . Je puis donc dire que, s'il est parmi nos poètes, des poètes plus grands et plus puissamment doués que Baudelaire, il n'en est de plus* important."

Baudelaire is now the most important of French, and indeed of European, poets. His poetry, which is the poetry of self-stultifying, world-destroying satanism and unutterable ennui, has come to be regarded "*comme la poésie même de la modernité.*" The fact is, surely, odd. Let us try to understand its significance.

The most important of modern poets was a satanist. Does this mean that his contemporary admirers are, like him, despairing absolute-hunters with a

> *goût de l'infini*
> *Qui partout dans le mal lui-même se proclame?*

No. For to be a Satanist, as I have said before, one must also be a Godist; and the present age is singularly Godless. Debauchery was a tragical affair in Baudelaire's day; it is now a merely medical one. We feel scientifically about our sins, not satanically. Why, then, do we admire this topsy-turvy Jansenist, for whom the only pleasure in love was the consciousness of doing wrong? We ought to despise him for being so hopelessly old-fashioned. And hopelessly old-fashioned we do find him; but only in the Christian and tragical interpretation of his actions. The actions themselves are perfectly up-to-date. "*Tes débauches sans soif et tes amours sans âme*" are indistinguishable from the extreme forms of the modern "Good Time." The joylessness of modern pleasures and modern love (which are, of course, the image of the "modern" pleasures and loves of imperial Rome as it approached its catastrophe) is even completer than the joylessness of Baudelaire's debauchery. For Baudelaire, the Christian satanist, had at least the stimulating consciousness that, in malignantly ruining the universe for himself, he was doing evil. The moderns fail to get even this "kick" out of their self- and world-destroying entertainments. They perversely do what they don't want to do, what fails to amuse them, and do not even have the pleasure of imagining that they are thereby committing a sin.

The flesh is diabolic, the spirit divine. Therefore, commands the satanist, indulge the flesh to satiety and beyond. The modernist philosophy and the modernist ethic are different. Neither the spirit nor the flesh, nor for that matter anything at all, is divine. The only important thing is that a man should be socially efficient. Passion is the enemy of efficiency. So don't let your instincts run away with you; on the other hand, don't repress them too much. Repression interferes with efficiency. Efficiency demands that you should neither give yourself completely away nor keep yourself completely back. Those who live by this godless philosophy and obey these purely medical commandments soon reduce their own lives and, consequently, the entire universe to a gray nothingness. In order not to be too unbearably conscious of this fact they surround themselves with an ever-increasing number of substitutes for genuine feeling. To create in themselves the illusion of being alive, they make a noise, they rush about, they hasten from distraction to distraction. Much to the profit of the shareholders in the great amusement industries. In a word, they have a Good Time.

Now, the better the time (in the modern sense of the term), the greater the boredom. Rivers found that the unhappy Melanesians literally and physically died of ennui when they were brought too suddenly in contact with modern amusements. We have grown gradually accustomed to the disease, and we therefore find it less lethal than do the South Sea islanders. We do not die outright of it; it is only gradually that we approach the fatal conclusion of the malady. It will come, that fatal conclusion, when men have entirely lost the art of amusing themselves; they will then simply perish of ennui. Modern creation-saving machinery has already begun to deprive them of this art. The progress of invention may confidently be expected to quicken the process. A few more triumphs in the style of the radio and the talkies, and the boredom which is now a mere discomfort will become an intolerable agony.

We turn to poetry for the perfect expression of our own feelings. In the *Fleurs du Mal* the modern finds all his own sufferings described—with what incomparable energy, in forms how memorably beautiful!

Je suis comme le roi d'un pays pluvieux,
Riche mais impuissant, jeune et pourtant très vieux!

It is *"la poésie même de la modernité."*

The Best Picture•

Borgo San Sepolcro is not very easy to get at. There is a small low-comedy railway across the hills from Arezzo. Or you can approach it up the Tiber valley from Perugia. Or, if you happen to be at Urbino, there is a motorbus which takes you to San Sepolcro, up and down through the Apennines, in something over seven hours. No joke, that journey, as I know by experience. But it is worth doing, though preferably in some other vehicle than the bus, for the sake of the Bocca Trabaria, that most beautiful of Apennine passes, between the Tiber valley and the upper valley of the Metauro. It was in the early spring that we crossed it. Our omnibus groaned and rattled slowly up a bleak northern slope, among bald rocks, withered grass, and still unbudded trees. It crossed the col and suddenly, as though by a miracle, the ground was yellow with innumerable primroses, each flower a little emblem of the sun that had called it into being.

And when at last one has arrived at San Sepolcro, what is there to be seen? A little town surrounded by walls, set in a broad flat valley between hills; some fine Renaissance palaces with pretty balconies of wrought iron; a not very interesting church, and finally, the best picture in the world.

• From *Essays New and Old,* 1927.

The best picture in the world is painted in fresco on the wall of a room in the town hall. Some unwittingly beneficent vandal had it covered, some time after it was painted, with a thick layer of plaster, under which it lay hidden for a century or two, to be revealed at last in a state of preservation remarkably perfect for a fresco of its date. Thanks to the vandals, the visitor who now enters the Palazzo dei Conservatori at Borgo San Sepolcro finds the stupendous "Resurrection" almost as Piero della Francesca left it. Its clear, yet subtly sober colors shine out from the wall with scarcely impaired freshness. Damp has blotted out nothing of the design, nor dirt obscured it. We need no imagination to help us figure forth its beauty; it stands there before us in entire and actual splendor, the greatest picture in the world.

The greatest picture in the world. . . . You smile. The expression is ludicrous, of course. Nothing is more futile than the occupation of those connoisseurs who spend their time compiling first and second elevens of the world's best painters, eights and fours of musicians, fifteens of poets, all-star troupes of architects, and so on. Nothing is so futile because there are a great many kinds of merit and an infinite variety of human beings. Is Fra Angelico a better artist than Rubens? Such questions, you insist, are meaningless. It is all a matter of personal taste. And up to a point this is true. But there does exist, none the less, an absolute standard of artistic merit. And it is a standard which is in the last resort a moral one. Whether a work of art is good or bad depends entirely on the quality of the character which expresses itself in the work. Not that all virtuous men are good artists, nor all artists conventionally virtuous. Longfellow was a bad poet, while Beethoven's dealings with his publishers were frankly dishonorable. But one can be dishonorable towards one's publishers and yet preserve the kind of virtue that is necessary to a good artist. That virtue is the virtue of integrity, of honesty towards oneself. Bad art is of two sorts: that which is merely dull, stupid, and incompetent, the negatively bad; and the positively bad, which is a lie and a sham. Very often the lie is so well told that almost everyone is taken in by it—for a time. In the end, however, lies are always found out. Fashion changes, the public learns to look with a different focus and, where a little while ago it saw an admirable work which actually moved its emotions, it now sees a sham. In the history of the arts we find innumerable shams of this kind, once taken as genuine, now seen to be false. The very names of most of them are now forgotten. Still, a dim rumor that Ossian once was read, that Bulwer was thought a great novelist and "Festus" Bailey a mighty poet still faintly reverberates. Their counterparts are busily earning praise and money at the present day. I often wonder if I am one of them. It is impossible to know. For one can be an artistic swindler without meaning to cheat and in the teeth of the most ardent desire to be honest.

Sometimes the charlatan is also a first-rate man of genius and then you have such strange artists as Wagner and Bernini, who can turn what is false and theatrical into something almost sublime.

That it is difficult to tell the genuine from the sham is proved by the fact that enormous numbers of people have made mistakes and continue to make them. Genuineness, as I have said, always triumphs in the long run. But at any given moment the majority of people, if they do not actually prefer the sham to the real, at least like it as much, paying an indiscriminate homage to both.

And now, after this little digression we can return to San Sepolcro and the greatest picture in the world. Great it is, absolutely great, because the man who painted it was genuinely noble as well as talented. And to me personally the most moving of pictures, because its author possessed almost more than any other painter those qualities of character which I most admire and because his purely aesthetic preoccupations are of a kind which I am by nature best fitted to understand. A natural, spontaneous and unpretentious grandeur—this is the leading quality of all Piero's work. He is majestic without being at all strained, theatrical, or hysterical—as Handel is majestic, not as Wagner. He achieves grandeur naturally with every gesture he makes, never consciously strains after it. Like Alberti, with whose architecture, as I hope to show, his painting has certain affinities, Piero seems to have been inspired by what I may call the religion of Plutarch's *Lives*—which is not Christianity, but a worship of what is admirable in man. Even his technically religious pictures are paeans in praise of human dignity. And he is everywhere intellectual.

With the drama of life and religion he is very little

concerned. His battle pictures at Arezzo are not dramatic compositions in spite of the many dramatic incidents they contain. All the turmoil, all the emotions of the scenes have been digested by the mind into a grave intellectual whole. It is as though Bach had written the 1812 Overture. Nor are the two superb pictures in the National Gallery—the "Nativity" and the "Baptism"—distinguished for any particular sympathy with the religious or emotional significance of the events portrayed. In the extraordinary "Flagellation at Urbino," the nominal subject of the picture recedes into the background on the left-hand side of the panel, where it serves to balance the three mysterious figures standing aloof in the right foreground. We seem to have nothing here but an experiment in composition, but an experiment so strange and so startingly successful that we do not regret the absence of dramatic significance and are entirely satisfied. The "Resurrection" at San Sepolcro is more dramatic. Piero has made the simple triangular composition symbolic of the subject. The base of the triangle is formed by the sepulcher; and the soldiers sleeping round it are made to indicate by their position the upward jet of the two sides, which meet at the apex in the face of the risen Christ, who is standing, a banner in his right hand, his left foot already raised and planted on the brim of the sepulcher, preparing to set out into the world. No geometrical arrangement could have been more simple or more apt. But the being who rises before our eyes from the tomb is more like a Plutarchian hero than the Christ of conventional religion. The body is perfectly developed, like that of a Greek athlete; so formidably strong that the wound in its muscular flank seems somehow an irrelevance. The face is stern and pensive, the eyes cold. The whole figure is expressive of physical and intellectual power. It is the resurrection of the classical ideal, incredibly much grander and more beautiful than the classical reality, from the tomb where it had lain so many hundred years.

Aesthetically, Piero's work has this resemblance to Alberti's: that it too is essentially an affair of masses. What Alberti is to Brunelleschi, Piero della Francesca is to his contemporary, Botticelli. Botticelli was fundamentally a draftsman, a maker of supple and resilient lines, thinking in terms of arabesques inscribed on the flat. Piero, on the contrary, has a passion for solidity as such. There is something in all his works that reminds one constantly of Egyptian sculpture. Piero has that Egyptian love of the smooth rounded surface that is the external symbol and expression of a mass. The faces of his personages look as though they were carved out of some very hard rock into which it had been impossible to engrave the details of a human physiognomy—the hollows, the lines and wrinkles of real life. They are ideal, like the faces of Egyptian gods and princes, surface meeting and marrying with curved unbroken surface in an almost geometrical fashion. Look, for example, at the faces of the women in Piero's fresco at Arezzo: "The Queen of Sheba recognizing the Holy Tree." They are all of one peculiar cast: the foreheads are high, rounded, and smooth; the necks are like cylinders of polished ivory; from the midst of the concave sockets the eyelids swell out in one uninterrupted curve into convexity; the cheeks are unbrokenly smooth, and the subtle curvature of their surfaces is indicated by a very delicate chiaroscuro which suggests more powerfully the solidity and mass of the flesh than the most spectacular Carvaggioesque light and shade could do.

Piero's passion for solidity betrays itself no less strikingly in his handling of the dresses and drapery of his figures. It is noticeable, for example, that wherever the subject permits, he makes his personages appear in curious headdresses that remind one by their solid geometrical qualities of those oddly shaped ceremonial hats or tiaras worn by the statues of Egyptian kings. Among the frescoes at Arezzo are several which illustrate this peculiarity. In that representing Heraclius restoring the True Cross to Jerusalem, all the ecclesiastical dignitaries are wearing enormously high headdresses, conical, trumpet-shaped, even rectangular. They are painted very smoothly with, it is obvious, a profound relish for their solidity. One or two similar headdresses, with many varieties of wonderfully rounded helmets, are lovingly represented in the battle pieces in the same place. The Duke of Urbino, in the well-known portrait at the Uffizi, is wearing a red cloth cap whose shape is somewhat like that of the "Brodrick" of the modern English soldier, but without the peak—a cylinder fitting round the head, topped by a projecting disk as the crown. Its smoothness and the roundness of its surfaces are emphasized in the picture.

Nor does Piero neglect the veils of his female figures. Though transparent and of lawn, they hang round the heads of his women in stiff folds, as though they were made of steel. Among clothes he has a special fondness for pleated bodices and tunics. The bulge and recession of the pleated stuff fascinates him, and he likes to trace the way in which the fluted folds follow the curve of the body beneath. To drapery he gives, as we might expect, a particular weight and richness. Perhaps his most exquisite handling of drapery is to be seen in the altarpiece of the *"Madonna della Misericordia,"* which now hangs near the "Resurrection" in the town hall at San Sepolcro. The central figure in this picture, which is one of the earliest of Piero's extant works, represents the Virgin, standing, and stretching out her arms, so as to cover two groups of suppliants on either side with the folds of her heavy blue mantle. The mantle and the Virgin's dress hang in simple perpendicular folds, like the flutings on the robe of the archaic bronze charioteer at the Louvre. Piero has painted these alternately convex and concave surfaces with a peculiar gusto.

It is not my intention to write a treatise on Piero della Francesca; that has been done sufficiently often and sufficiently badly to make it unnecessary for me to bury that consummate artist any deeper under layers of muddy comment. All I have meant to do in this place is to give the reasons why I like his works and my justifications for calling the "Resurrection" the greatest picture in the world. I am attracted to his character by his intellectual power; by his capacity for unaffectedly making the grand and noble gesture; by his pride in whatever is splendid in humanity. And in the artist I find peculiarly sympathetic the lover of solidity, the painter of smooth curving surfaces, the composer who builds with masses. For myself I prefer him to Botticelli, so much so indeed, that if it were necessary to sacrifice all Botticelli's works in order to save the "Resurrection," the "Nativity," the *"Madonna della Misericordia"* and the Arezzo frescoes, I should unhesitatingly commit the "Primavera" and all the rest of them to the flames. It is unfortunate for Peiro's reputation that his works should be comparatively few and in most cases rather difficult of access. With the exception of the "Nativity" and "Baptism" at the National Gallery, all the really important works of Piero are at

Arezzo, San Sepolcro, and Urbino. The portraits of the Duke and Duchess of Urbino with their respective triumphs, in the Uffizi, are charming and exceedingly "amusing"; but they do not represent Piero at his best. The altarpiece at Perugia and the Madonna with saints and donor at Milan are neither of them first-rate. The St. Jerome at Venice is goodish; so too is the damaged fresco of the "Malatesta," at Rimini. The Louvre possesses nothing, and Germany can only boast of a study of architecture, inferior to that at Urbino. Anybody, therefore, who wants to know Piero must go from London to Arezzo, San Sepolcro, and Urbino. Now Arezzo is a boring sort of town, and so ungrateful to its distinguished sons that there is no monument within its walls to the divine Aretino. I deplore Arezzo; but to Arezzo, nevertheless, you must go to see Piero's most considerable works. From Arezzo you must make your way to San Sepolcro, where the inn is only just tolerable, and to which the means of communication are so bad that, unless you come in your own car, you are fairly compelled to stay there. And from San Sepolcro you must travel by bus for seven hours across the Apennines to Urbino. Here, it is true, you have not only two admirable Pieros (the "Flagellation" and an architectural scene), but the most exquisite palace in Italy and very nearly a good hotel. Even on the most wearily reluctant tourist Urbino imposes itself; there is no escaping it; it must be seen. But in the case of Arezzo and San Sepolcro there is no such moral compulsion. Few tourists, in consequence, take the trouble to visit them.

If the principal works of Piero were to be seen in Florence, and those of Botticelli at San Sepolcro, I do not doubt that the public estimation of these two masters would be reversed. Artistic English spinsters would stand in rapturous contemplation before the story of the "True Cross," instead of before the "Primavera." Raptures depend largely upon the stars in Baedeker, and the stars are more freely distributed to works of art in accessible towns than to those in the inaccessible. If the Arena chapel were in the mountains of Calabria, instead of at Padua, we should all have heard a good deal less of Giotto.

But enough. The shade of Conxolus rises up to remind me that I am running into the error of those who measure merit by a scale of oddness and rarity.

Most of our mistakes are fundamentally grammatical. We create our own difficulties by employing an inadequate language to describe facts. Thus, to take one example, we are constantly giving the same name to more than one thing, and more than one name to the same thing. The results, when we come to argue, are deplorable. For we are using a language which does not adequately describe the things about which we are arguing.

The word "painter" is one of those names whose indiscriminate application has led to the worst results. All those who, for whatever reason and with whatever intentions, put brushes to canvas and make pictures, are called without distinction, painters. Deceived by the uniqueness of the name, aestheticians have tried to make us believe that there is a single painter-psychology, a single function of painting, a single standard of criticism. Fashion changes and the views of art critics with it. At the present time it is fashionable to believe in form to the exclusion of subject. Young people almost swoon away with excess of aesthetic emotion before a Matisse. Two generations ago they would have been wiping their eyes before the latest Landseer. (Ah, those more than human, those positively Christ-like dogs—how they moved, what lessons they

● From *Essays New and Old,* 1927.

taught! There had been no religious painting like Land-seer's since Carlo Dolci died.)

These historical considerations should make us chary of believing too exclusively in any single theory of art. One kind of painting, one set of ideas are fashionable at any given moment. They are made the basis of a theory which condemns all other kinds of painting and all preceding critical theories. The process constantly repeats itself.

At the present moment, it is true, we have achieved an unprecedently tolerant eclecticism. We are able, if we are up-to-date, to enjoy everything, from Negro sculpture to Locca della Robbia and from Magnasco to Byzantine mosaics. But it is an eclecticism achieved at the expense of almost the whole content of the various works of art considered. What we have learned to see in all these works is their formal qualities, which we abstract and arbitrarily call essential. The subject of the work, with all that the painter desired to express in it beyond his feelings about formal relations, contemporary criticism re-jects as unimportant. The young painter scrupulously avoids introducing into his pictures anything that might be mistaken for a story, or the expression of a view of life, while the young *Kunstforscher* turns, as though at an act of exhibitionism, from any manifestation by a contempo-rary of any such forbidden interest in drama or philosophy. True, the old masters are indulgently permitted to illus-trate stories and express their thoughts about the world. Poor devils, they knew no better! Your modern observer makes allowance for their ignorance and passes over in silence all that is not a matter of formal relations. The admirers of Giotto (as numerous today as were the ad-mirers of Guido Reni a hundred years ago) contrive to look at the master's frescoes without considering what they represent, or what the painter desired to express. Every germ of drama or meaning is disinfected out of them; only the composition is admired. The process is analogous to reading Latin verses without understanding them—simply for the sake of the rhythmical rumbling of the hexameters.

It would be absurd, of course, to deny the importance of formal relations. No picture can hold together without composition and no good painter is without some specific passion for form as such—just as no good writer is without a passion for words and the arrangement of words. It is obvious that no man can adequately express himself, unless he takes an interest in the terms which he proposes to use as his medium of expression. Not all painters are interested in the same sort of forms. Some, for example, have a passion for masses and the surfaces of solids. Others delight in lines. Some compose in three dimensions. Others like to make silhouettes on the flat. Some like to make the surface of the paint smooth and, as it were, translucent, so that the objects represented in the picture can be seen distinct and separate, as through a sheet of glass. Others (as for example Rembrandt) love to make a rich thick surface which shall absorb and draw together into one whole all the objects represented, and that in spite of the depth of the composition and the distance of the objects from the plane of the picture. All these purely aesthetic considerations are, as I have said, important. All artists are interested in them; but almost none are interested in them to the exclusion of everything else. It is very seldom indeed that we find a painter who can be inspired merely by his interest in form and texture to paint a picture. Good painters of "abstract" subjects or even of still lives are rare. Apples and solid geometry do not stimulate a man to express his feelings about form and make a composition. All thoughts and emotions are interdependent. In the words of the dear old song,

The roses round the door
Make me love mother more.

One feeling is excited by another. Our faculties work best in a congenial emotional atmosphere. For example, Mantegna's faculty for making noble arrangements of forms was stimulated by his feelings about heroic and godlike humanity. Expressing those feelings, which he found exciting, he also expressed—and in the most perfect manner of which he was capable—his feelings about masses, surfaces, solids, and voids. "The roses round the door"—his hero worship—"made him love mother more"— made him, by stimulating his faculty for composition, paint better. If Isabella d'Este had made him paint apples, table napkins, and bottles, he would have produced, being uninterested in these objects, a poor composition. And yet, from a purely formal point of view, apples, bottles, and napkins are quite as interesting as human bodies and faces. But Mantegna—and with him the majority of painters—did not happen to be very passionately interested in these inanimate objects. When one is bored one becomes boring.

The apples round the door
Make me a frightful bore.

Inevitably; unless I happen to be so exclusively interested in form that I can paint anything that has a shape; or unless I happen to possess some measure of that queer pantheism, that animistic superstition which made Van Gogh regard the humblest of common objects as being divinely or devilishly alive. *"Crains dans le mur aveugle un regard qui t'épie."* If a painter can do that, he will be able, like Van Gogh, to make pictures of cabbage fields and the bedrooms of cheap hotels that shall be as wildly dramatic as a Rape of the Sabines.

The contemporary fashion is to admire beyond all others the painter who can concentrate on the formal side of his art and produce pictures which are entirely devoid of literature. Old Renoir's apophthegm, *"Un peintre, voyez-vous, qui a le sentiment du téton et des fesses, est un homme sauvé,"* is considered by the purists suspiciously latitudinarian. A painter who has the sentiment of the pap and the buttocks is a painter who portrays real models with gusto. Your pure aesthete should only have a feeling for hemispheres, curved lines and surfaces. But this "sentiment of the buttocks" is common to all good painters. It is the lowest common measure of the whole profession. It is possible, like Mantegna, to have a passionate feeling for all that is solid, and at the same time to be a stoic philosopher and a hero-worshipper; possible, with Michelangelo, to have a complete realization of breasts and also an interest in the soul or, like Rubens, to have a sentiment for human greatness as well as for human rumps. The greater includes the less; great dramatic or reflective painters know everything that the aestheticians who paint geometrical pictures, apples, or buttocks know, and a great deal more besides. What they have to say about formal relations, though important, is only a part of what they have to express. The contemporary insistence on form to the exclusion of everything else is an absurdity. So was the older insistence on exact imitation and sentiment to the exclusion of form. There need be no exclusions. In spite of the single name, there are many different kinds of painters and all of them, with the exception of those who cannot paint, and those whose minds are trivial, vulgar, and tedious, have a right to exist.

All classifications and theories are made after the event; the facts must first occur before they can be tabulated and methodized. Reversing the historical process, we attack the facts forearmed with theoretical prejudice. Instead of considering each fact on its own merits, we ask how it fits into the theoretical scheme. At any given moment a number of meritorious facts fail to fit into the fashionable theory and have to be ignored. Thus El Greco's art failed to conform with the ideal of good painting held by Philip the Second and his contemporaries. The Sienese primitives seemed to the seventeenth and eighteenth centuries incompetent barbarians. Under the influence of Ruskin, the later nineteenth century contrived to dislike almost all architecture that was not Gothic. And the early twentieth century, under the influence of the French, deplores and ignores, in painting, all that is literary, reflective or dramatic.

In every age theory has caused men to like much that was bad and reject much that was good. The only prejudice that the ideal art critic should have is against the incompetent, the mentally dishonest, and the futile. The number of ways in which good pictures can be painted is quite incalculable, depending only on the variability of the human mind. Every good painter invents a new way of painting. Is this man a competent painter? Has he something to say, is he genuine? These are the questions a critic must ask himself. Not, Does he conform with my theory of imitation, or distortion, or moral purity, or significant form?

There is one painter against whom, it seems to me, theoretical prejudice has always most unfairly told. I mean the elder Breughel. Looking at his best paintings I find that I can honestly answer in the affirmative all the questions which a critic may legitimately put himself. He is highly competent aesthetically; he has plenty to say; his mind is curious, interesting, and powerful; and he has no false pretensions, is entirely honest. And yet he has never enjoyed the high reputation to which his merits entitle him. This is due, I think, to the fact that his work has never quite squared with any of the various critical theories which since his days have had a vogue in the aesthetic world.

A subtle colorist, a sure and powerful draftsman, and possessing powers of composition that enable him to marshal the innumerable figures with which his pictures are filled into pleasingly decorative groups (built up, as we see, when we try to analyze his methods of formal arrangement, out of individually flat, silhouettelike shapes standing in a succession of receding planes), Breughel can boast of purely aesthetic merits that ought to endear him even to the strictest sect of the Pharisees. Coated with this pure aesthetic jam, the bitter pill of his literature might easily, one would suppose, be swallowed. If Giotto's dalliance with sacred history be forgiven him, why may not Breughel be excused for being an anthropologist and a social philosopher? To which I tentatively answer: Giotto is forgiven, because we have so utterly ceased to believe in Catholic Christianity that we can easily ignore the subject matter of his pictures and concentrate only on their formal qualities; Breughel, on the other hand, is unforgivable because he made comments on humanity that are still interesting to us. From his subject matter we cannot escape; it touches us too closely to be ignored. That is why Breughel is despised by all up-to-date *Kunstforschers*.

And even in the past, when there was no theoretical objection to the mingling of literature and painting, Breughel failed, for another reason, to get his due. He was considered low, gross, a mere comedian, and as such unworthy of serious consideration. Thus, the *Encyclopaedia Britannica*, which in these matters may be safely relied on to give the current opinion of a couple of generations ago, informs us, in the eleven lines which it parsimoniously devotes to Peter Breughel that "the subjects of his pictures are chiefly humorous figures, like those of D. Teniers; and if he wants the delicate touch and silvery clearness of that master, he has abundant spirit and comic power."

Whoever wrote these words—and they might have been written by any one desirous, fifty years ago, of playing for safety and saying the right thing—can never have taken the trouble to look at any of the pictures painted by Breughel when he was a grown and accomplished artist.

In his youth, it is true, he did a great deal of hack

work for a dealer who specialized in caricatures and devils in the manner of Hieronymus Bosch. But his later pictures, painted when he had really mastered the secrets of his art, are not comic at all. They are studies of peasant life, they are allegories, they are religious pictures of the most strangely reflective cast, they are exquisitely poetical landscapes. Breughel died at the height of his powers. But there is enough of his mature work in existence—at Antwerp, at Brussels, at Naples, and above all at Vienna—to expose the fatuity of the classical verdict and exhibit him for what he was: the first landscape painter of his century, the acutest student of manners, and the wonderfully skillful pictorial expounder or suggester of a view of life. It is at Vienna, indeed, that Breughel's art can best be studied in all its aspects. For Vienna possesses practically all his best pictures of whatever kind. The scattered pictures at Antwerp, Brussels, Paris, Naples, and elsewhere give one but the faintest notion of Breughel's powers. In the Vienna galleries are collected more than a dozen of his pictures, all belonging to his last and best period. "The Tower of Babel," the great "Calvary," the "Numbering of the People at Bethlehem," the two winter landscapes and the "Autumn Landscape," the "Conversion of Saint Paul," the "Battle Between the Israelites and the Philistines," the "Marriage Feast" and the "Peasants' Dance"—all these admirable works are here. It is on these that he must be judged.

There are four landscapes at Vienna: the "Dark Day" ("January") and "Huntsmen in the Snow" ("February"), a November landscape (the "Return of the Cattle"), and the "Numbering of the People at Bethlehem" which in spite of its name is little more than a landscape with figures. This last, like the "February Landscape" and the "Massacre of the Innocents" at Brussels, is a study of snow. Snow scenes lent themselves particularly well to Breughel's style of painting. For a snowy background has the effect of making all dark or colored objects seen against it appear in the form of very distinct, sharp-edged silhouettes. Breughel does in all his compositions what the snow does in nature. All the objects in his pictures (which are composed in a manner that reminds one very much of the Japanese) are paper-thin silhouettes arranged, plane after plane, like the theatrical scenery in the depth of the stage. Consequently in the painting of snow scenes, where nature starts by imitating his habitual method, he achieves an almost disquieting degree of fundamental realism. Those hunters stepping down over the brow of the hill toward the snowy valley with its frozen ponds are Jack Frost himself and his crew. The crowds who move about the white streets of Bethlehem have their being in an absolute winter, and those ferocious troopers looting and innocent-hunting in the midst of a Christmas card landscape are a part of the very army of winter, and the innocents they kill are the young green shoots of the earth.

Breughel's method is less fundamentally compatible with the snowless landscapes of January and November. The different planes stand apart a little too flatly and distinctly. It needs a softer, bloomier kind of painting to recapture the intimate quality of such scenes as those he portrays in these two pictures. A born painter of autumn, for example, would have fused the beasts, the men, the trees, and the distant mountains into a hazier unity, melting all together, the near and the far, in the rich surface of his paint. Breughel painted too transparently and too flatly to be the perfect interpreter of such landscapes. Still, even in terms of his not entirely suitable convention he has done marvels. The "Autumn Day" is a thing of the most exquisite beauty. Here, as in the more somberly dramatic January landscape, he makes a subtle use of golds and yellows and browns, creating a sober yet luminous harmony of colors. The November landscape is entirely placid and serene; but in the "Dark Day" he has staged one of those natural dramas of the sky and earth—a conflict between light and darkness. Light breaks from under clouds along the horizon, shines up from the river in the valley that lies in the middle distance, glitters on the peaks of the mountains. The foreground, which represents the crest of a wooded hill, is dark; and the leafless trees growing on the slopes are black against the sky. These two pictures are the most beautiful sixteenth-century landscapes of which I have any knowledge. They are intensely poetical, yet sober and not excessively picturesque or romantic. Those fearful crags and beetling precipices of which the older painters were so fond do not appear in these examples of Breughel's maturest work.

Breughel's anthropology is as delightful as his nature poetry. He knew his Flemings, knew them intimately, both in their prosperity and during the miserable years of strife, of rebellion, of persecution, of war and consequent poverty which followed the advent of the Reformation in Flanders.

A Fleming himself, and so profoundly and ineradicably a Fleming that he was able to go to Italy, and, like his great countryman in the previous century, Roger van der Weyden, return without the faintest tincture of Italianism —he was perfectly qualified to be the natural historian of the Flemish folk. He exhibits them mostly in those moments of orgiastic gaiety with which they temper the laborious monotony of their daily lives: eating enormously, drinking, uncouthly dancing, indulging in that peculiarly Flemish scatological waggery. The "Wedding Feast" and the "Peasants' Dance," both at Vienna, are superb examples of this anthropological type of painting. Nor must we forget those two curious pictures, the "Battle Between Carnival and Lent" and the "Children's Games." They too show us certain aspects of the joyous side of Flemish life. But the view is not of an individual scene, casually seized at its height and reproduced. These two pictures are systematic and encyclopaedic. In one he illustrates all children's games; in the other all the amusements of carnival, with all the forces arrayed on the side of asceticism. In the same way he represents, in his extraordinary "Tower of Babel," all the processes of building. These pictures are handbooks of their respective subjects.

Breughel's fondness for generalizing and systematizing is further illustrated in his allegorical pieces. The "Triumph of Death," at the Prado, is appalling in its elaboration and completeness. The fantastic "*Dulle Griet*" at Antwerp is an almost equally elaborate triumph of evil. His illustrations to proverbs and parables belong to the same class. They show him to have been a man profoundly convinced of the reality of evil and of the horrors which this mortal life, not to mention eternity, hold in store for suffering humanity. The world is a horrible place; but in spite of this, or precisely because of this, men and women eat, drink, and dance, Carnival tilts against Lent and triumphs, if only for a moment; children play in the streets, people get married in the midst of gross rejoicings.

But of all Breughel's pictures the one most richly suggestive of reflection is not specifically allegorical or systematic. "Christ Carrying the Cross" is one of his largest canvases, thronged with small figures rhythmically grouped against a wide and romantic background. The composition is simple, pleasing in itself, and seems to spring out of the subject instead of being imposed on it. So much for pure aesthetics.

Of the Crucifixion and the Carrying of the Cross there are hundreds of representations by the most admirable and diverse masters. But of all that I have ever seen this Calvary of Breughel's is the most suggestive and, dramatically, the most appalling. For all other masters have painted these dreadful scenes from within, so to speak, outwards. For them Christ is the center, the divine hero of the tragedy; this is the fact from which they start; it affects and transforms all the other facts, justifying, in a sense, the horror of the drama and ranging all that surrounds the central figure in an ordered hierarchy of good and evil. Breughel, on the other hand, starts from the outside and works inwards. He represents the scene as it would have appeared to any casual spectator on the road to Golgotha on a certain spring morning in the year A.D. 33. Other artists have pretended to be angels, painting the scene with a knowledge of its significance. But Breughel resolutely remains a human onlooker. What he shows is a crowd of people walking briskly in holiday joyfulness up the slopes of a hill. On the top of the hill, which is seen in the middle distance on the right, are two crosses with thieves fastened to them, and between them a little hole in the ground in which another cross is soon to be planted. Round the crosses, on the bare hilltop stands a ring of people, who have come out with their picnic baskets to look on at the free entertainment offered by the ministers of justice. Those who have already taken their stand round the crosses are the prudent ones; in these days we should see them with campstools and thermos flasks, six hours ahead of time, in the vanguard of the queue for a Melba night at Covent Garden. The less provident or more adventurous people are in the crowd coming up the hill with the third and greatest of the criminals whose cross is to take the place of honor between the other two. In their anxiety not to miss any of the fun on the way up, they forget that they will have to take back seats at the actual place of execution. But it may be, of course, that they have reserved their places, up there. At Tyburn one could get an excellent seat in a private box for half a crown; with the ticket in one's pocket, one could follow the cart all the way from the prison, arrive with the criminal and yet have a perfect view of the performance. In these later days, when cranky humanitarianism has so far triumphed that hangings take place in private and Mrs. Thompson's screams are not even allowed to be recorded on the radio, we have to be content with reading about executions, not with seeing them. The impresarios who sold seats at Tyburn have been replaced by titled newspaper proprietors who sell juicy descriptions of Tyburn to a prodigiously much larger public. If people were still hanged at Marble Arch, Lord Riddell would be much less rich.

That eager, tremulous, lascivious interest in blood and beastliness which in these more civilized days we can only satisfy at one remove from reality in the pages of our newspapers, was franklier indulged in Breughel's day; the naïve ingenuous brute in man was less sophisticated, was given longer rope, and joyously barks and wags its tail round the appointed victim. Seen thus, impassively, from the outside, the tragedy does not purge or uplift; it appalls and makes desperate; or it may even inspire a kind of gruesome mirth. The same situation may often be either tragic or comic, according as it is seen through the eyes of those who suffer or those who look on. (Shift the point of vision a little and Macbeth could be paraphrased as a roaring farce.) Breughel makes a concession to the high tragic convention by placing in the foreground of his picture a little group made up of the holy women weeping and wringing their hands. They stand quite apart from the other figures in the picture and are fundamentally out of harmony with them, being painted in the style of Roger van der Weyden. A little oasis of passionate spirituality, an island of consciousness and comprehension in the midst of the pervading stupidity and brutishness. Why Breughel put them into his picture is difficult to guess; perhaps for the benefit of the conventionally religious, perhaps out of respect for tradition; or perhaps he found his own creation too depressing and added this noble irrelevance to reassure himself.

Variations on Goya •

There are anthologies of almost everything—from the best to the worst, from the historically significant to the eccentric, from the childish to the sublime. But there is one anthology, potentially the most interesting of them all, which, to the best of my knowledge, has never yet been compiled; I mean, the Anthology of Later Works.

To qualify for inclusion in such an anthology, the artist would have to pass several tests. First of all, he must have avoided a premature extinction and lived on into artistic and chronological maturity. Thus the last poems of Shelley, the last compositions of Schubert and even of Mozart would find no place in our collection. Consummate artists as they were, these men were still psychologically youthful when they died. For their full development they needed more time than their earthly destiny allowed them. Of a different order are those strange beings whose chronological age is out of all proportion to their maturity, not only as artists, but as human spirits. Thus, some of the letters written by Keats in his early twenties and many of the paintings which Seurat executed before his death at thirty-two might certainly qualify as Later Works. But, as a general rule, a certain minimum of time is needed for the ripening of such fruits. For the most part, our hypo-

• From *Themes and Variations*, 1950.

thetical anthologist will make his selections from the art of elderly and middle-aged men and women.

But by no means all middle-aged and elderly artists are capable of producing significant Later Works. For the last half century of a long life, Wordsworth preserved an almost unbroken record of dullness. And in this respect he does not stand alone. There are many, many others whose Later Works are their worst. All these must be excluded from our anthology, and I would pass a similar judgment on that other large class of Later Works which, though up to the standard of the earlier, are 'not significantly different from them. Haydn lived to a ripe old age and his right hand never forgot its cunning; but it also failed to learn a new cunning. Peter-Pan-like, he continued, as an old man, to write the same sort of thing he had written twenty, thirty, and forty years before. Where there is nothing to distinguish the creations of a man's maturity from those of his youth it is superfluous to include any of them in a selection of characteristically Later Works.

This leaves us, then, with the Later Works of those artists who have lived without ever ceasing to learn of life. The field is relatively narrow; but within it, what astonishing and sometimes what disquieting treasures! One thinks of the ineffable serenity of the slow movement of Beethoven's A minor Quartet, the peace passing all understanding of the orchestral prelude to the "Benedictus" of his *Missa Solemnis*. But this is not the old man's only mood; when he turns from the contemplation of eternal reality to a consideration of the human world, we are treated to the positively terrifying merriment of the last movement of his B-flat major Quartet—merriment quite inhuman, peals of violent and yet somehow abstract laughter echoing down from somewhere beyond the limits of the world. Of the same nature, but if possible even more disquieting, is the mirth which reverberates through the last act of Verdi's *Falstaff*, culminating in that extraordinary final chorus in which the aged genius makes his maturest comment on the world—not with bitterness or sarcasm or satire, but in a huge, contrapuntal paroxysm of detached and already posthumous laughter.

Turning to the other arts, we find something of the same nonhuman, posthumous quality in the Later Works of Yeats and, coupled with a prodigious majesty, in those of Piero della Francesca. And then, of course there is *The Tempest*—a work charged with something of the unearthly serenity of Beethoven's "Benedictus" but concluding in the most disappointing anticlimax, with Prospero giving up his magic for the sake (heaven help us!) of becoming once again a duke. And the same sort of all too human anticlimax saddens us at the end of the second part of *Faust*, with its implication that draining fens is Man's Final End, and that the achievement of this end automatically qualifies the drainer for the beatific vision.

And what about the last El Grecos—for example, that unimaginable "Immaculate Conception" at Toledo with its fantastic harmony of brilliant, ice-cold colors, its ecstatic gesticulations in a heaven with a third dimension no greater than that of a mine shaft, its deliquescence of flesh and flowers and drapery into a set of ectoplasmic abstractions? What about them, indeed? All we know is that, beautiful and supremely enigmatic, they will certainly take their place in our hypothetical anthology.

And finally, among these and all other extraordinary Later Works, we should have to number the paintings, drawings and etchings of Goya's final twenty-five or thirty years.

The difference between the young Goya and the old may be best studied and appreciated by starting in the basement of the Prado, where his cartoons for the tapestries are hung; climbing thence to the main floor, where there is a room full of his portraits of royal imbeciles, grandees, enchanting duchesses, *majas*, clothed and unclothed; walking thence to the smaller room containing the two great paintings of the "Second of May"—Napoleon's mamelukes cutting down the crowd and, at night, when the revolt has been quelled, the firing squads at work upon their victims by the light of lanterns; and finally mounting to the top floor where hang the etchings and drawings, together with those unutterably mysterious and disturbing "black paintings," with which the deaf and aging Goya elected to adorn the dining room of his house, the Quinta del Sordo. It is a progress from lighthearted eighteenth-century art, hardly at all unconventional in subject matter or in handling, through fashionable brilliancy and increasing virtuosity, to something quite timeless both in technique and spirit—the most powerful of commentaries on human crime and madness, made in terms of an artistic convention uniquely fitted to express precisely that extraordinary mingling of hatred and compassion, despair and sardonic humor, realism and fantasy.

"I show you sorrow," said the Buddha, "and the ending of sorrow"—the sorrow of the phenomenal world in which man, "like an angry ape, plays such fantastic tricks before high heaven as make the angels weep," and the ending of sorrow in the beatific vision, the unitive contemplation of transcendental reality. Apart from the fact that he is a great and, one might say, uniquely original artist, Goya is significant as being, in his Later Works, the almost perfect type of the man who knows only sorrow and not the ending of sorrow.

In spite of his virulent anticlericalism, Goya contrived to remain on sufficiently good terms with the Church to receive periodical commissions to paint religious pictures. Some of these, like the frescoes in the cupola of La Florida, are frankly and avowedly secular. But others are serious essays in religious painting. It is worth looking rather closely at what is probably the best of these religious pieces—the fine "Agony in the Garden." With outstretched arms, Christ raises toward the comforting angel a face whose expression is identical with that of the poor creatures whom we see, in a number of unforgettably painful etchings and paintings, kneeling or standing in an excruciating anticipation before the gun barrels of a French firing squad. There is no trace here of that loving confidence which, even in the darkest hours, fills the hearts of men and women who live continually in the presence of God; not so much as a hint of what François de Sales calls "holy indifference" to suffering and good fortune, of the fundamental equanimity, the peace passing all understanding, which belongs to those whose attention is firmly fixed upon a transcendental reality.

For Goya the transcendental reality did not exist. There is no evidence in his biography or his works that he ever had even the most distant personal experience of it. The only reality he knew was that of the world around him; and the longer he lived the more frightful did that world seem—the more frightful, that is to say, in the eyes of his rational self; for his animal high spirits went on bubbling up irrepressibly, whenever his body was free from pain or sickness, to the very end. As a young man in good health, with money and reputation, a fine position

and as many women as he wanted, he had found the
world a very agreeable place—absurd, of course, and with
enough of folly and roguery to furnish subject matter for
innumerable satirical drawings, but eminently worth living in. Then all of a sudden came deafness, and, after
the joyful dawn of the Revolution, Napoleon and French
imperialism and the atrocities of war; and, when Napoleon's hordes were gone, the unspeakable Ferdinand VII
and clerical reaction and the spectacle of Spaniards fighting among themselves; and all the time, like the drone of
a bagpipe accompanying the louder noises of what is
officially called history, the enormous stupidity of average
men and women, the chronic squalor of their superstitions, the bestiality of their occasional violences and orgies.

Realistically or in fantastic allegories, with a technical
mastery that only increased as he grew older, Goya recorded it all—not only the agonies endured by his people
at the hands of the invaders, but also the follies and
crimes committed by these same people in their dealings
with one another. The great canvases of the Madrid massacres and executions, the incomparable etchings of "War's
Disasters," fill us with an indignant compassion. But then
we turn to the *"Disparates"* and the *"Pinturas Negras."*
In these, with a sublimely impartial savagery, Goya sets
down exactly what he thinks of the martyrs of the Dos
de Mayo when they are not being martyred. Here, for
example, are two men—two Spaniards—sinking slowly toward death in an engulfing quicksand, but busily engaged
in knocking one another over the head with bludgeons.
And here is a rabble coming home from a pilgrimage—
scores of low faces, distorted as though by reflection in the
back of a spoon, all openmouthed and yelling. And all
the blank black eyes stare vacantly and idiotically in
different directions.

These creatures who haunt Goya's Later Works are
inexpressibly horrible, with the horror of mindlessness and
animality and spiritual darkness. And above the lower
depths where they obscenely pullulate is a world of bad
priests and lustful friars, of fascinating women whose love
is a "dream of lies and inconstancy," of fatuous nobles and,
at the top of the social pyramid, a royal family of half-
wits, sadists, Messalinas, and perjurers. The moral of it
all is summed up in the central plate of the *"Caprichos,"*
in which we see Goya himself, his head on his arms,

sprawled across his desk and fitfully sleeping, while the air above is peopled with the bats and owls of necromancy and just behind his chair lies an enormous witch's cat, malevolent as only Goya's cats can be, staring at the sleeper with baleful eyes. On the side of the desk are traced the words, "The dream of reason produces monsters." It is a caption that admits of more than one interpretation. When reason sleeps, the absurd and loathsome creatures of superstition wake and are active, goading their victim to an ignoble frenzy. But this is not all. Reason may also dream without sleeping, may intoxicate itself, as it did during the French Revolution, with the daydreams of inevitable progress, of liberty, equality, and fraternity imposed by violence, of human self-sufficiency and the ending of sorrow, not by the all too arduous method which alone offers any prospect of success, but by political rearrangements and a better technology. The *"Caprichos"* were published in the last year of the eighteenth century; in 1808 Goya and all Spain were given the opportunity of discovering the consequences of such daydreaming. Murat marched his troops into Madrid; the *"Desastres de la Guerra"* were about to begin.

Goya produced four main sets of etchings—the *"Caprichos,"* the *"Desastres de la Guerra,"* the *"Tauromaquia"* and the *"Disparates"* or *"Proverbios."* All of them are Later Works. The *"Caprichos"* were not published until he was fifty-three; the plates of the *"Desastres"* were etched between the ages of sixty-five and seventy-five; the *"Tauromaquia"* series first saw the light when he was sixty-nine (and at the age of almost eighty he learned the brand-new technique of lithography in order to be able to do justice to his beloved bulls in yet another medium); the *"Disparates"* were finished when he was seventy-three.

For the non-Spaniard the plates of the *"Tauromaquia"* series will probably seem the least interesting of Goya's etchings. They are brilliant records of the exploits of the bull ring; but unfortunately, or fortunately, most of us know very little about bullfighting. Consequently, we miss the finer shades of the significance of these little masterpieces of documentary art. Moreover, being documentary, the etchings of the *"Tauromaquia"* do not lend themselves to being executed with that splendid audacity, that dramatic breadth of treatment, which delights us in the later paintings and the etchings of the other three series. True, we find in this collection a few plates that are as fine as anything Goya ever produced—for example, that wonderful etching of the bull which has broken out of the arena and stands triumphant, a corpse hanging limp across its horns, among the spectators' benches. But by and large it is not to the *"Tauromaquia"* that we turn for the very best specimens of Goya's work in black and white, or for the most characteristic expressions of his mature personality. The nature of the subject matter makes it impossible for him, in these plates to reveal himself fully either as a man or as an artist.

Of the three other sets of etchings two, the *"Caprichos"* and *"Disparates,"* are fantastic and allegorical in subject matter, while the third, the *"Desastres,"* though for the most part it represents real happenings under the Napoleonic terror, represents them in a way which, being generalized and symbolical rather than directly documentary, permits of, and indeed demands, a treatment no less broad and dramatic than is given to the fantasies of the other collections.

War always weakens and often completely shatters the crust of customary decency which constitutes a civilization. It is a thin crust at the best of times, and beneath it lies—what? Look through Goya's *"Desastres"* and find out. The abyss of bestiality and diabolism and suffering seems almost bottomless. There is practically nothing of which human beings are not capable when war or revolution or anarchy gives them the necessary opportunity and excuse; and to their pain death alone imposes a limit.

Goya's record of disaster has a number of recurrent themes. There are those shadowy archways, for example, more sinister than those even of Piranesi's "Prisons," where women are violated, captives squat in a hopeless stupor, corpses lie rotting, emaciated children starve to death. Then there are the vague street corners at which the famine-stricken hold out their hands; but the whiskered French hussars and carabiniers look on without pity, and even the rich Spaniards pass by indifferently, as though they were "of another lineage." Of still more frequent occurrence in the series are the crests of those naked hillocks on which lie the dead, like so much garbage. Or else, in dramatic silhouette against the sky above those same hilltops, we see the hideous butchery of Spanish

men and women, and the no less hideous vengeance
meted out by infuriated Spaniards upon their tormentors.
Often the hillock sprouts a single tree, always low, sometimes maimed by gunfire. Upon its branches are impaled,
like the beetles and caterpillars in a butcher bird's larder,
whole naked torsos, sometimes decapitated, sometimes
without arms, or else a pair of amputated legs, or a
severed head—warnings, set there by the conquerors, of
the fate awaiting those who dare oppose the Emperor.
At other times the tree is used as a gallows—a less efficient gallows, indeed, than that majestic oak which, in
Callot's *"Misères de la Guerre,"* is fruited with more than
a score of swinging corpses, but good enough for a couple
of executions *en passant*, except, of course, in the case
recorded in one of Goya's most hair-raising plates, in
which the tree is too stumpy to permit of a man's hanging
clear of the ground. But the rope is fixed, none the less,
and to tighten the noose around their victim's neck, two
French soldiers tug at the legs, while with his foot a third
man thrusts with all his strength against the shoulders.

And so the record proceeds, horror after horror, unalle-
viated by any of the splendors which other painters have
been able to discover in war; for, significantly, Goya never
illustrates an engagement, never shows us impressive masses
of troops marching in column or deployed in the order of
battle. His concern is exclusively with war as it affects the
civilian population, with armies disintegrated into individual thieves and ravishers, tormentors and executioners—
and occasionally, when the *guerilleros* have won a skir-
mish, into individual victims tortured in their turn and
savagely done to death by the avengers of their own
earlier atrocities. All he shows us is war's disasters and
squalors, without any of the glory or even picturesqueness.

In the two remaining series of etchings we pass from
tragedy to satire and from historical fact to allegory and
pictorial metaphor and pure fantasy. Twenty years separate the *"Caprichos"* from the *"Disparates,"* and the later
collection is at once more somber and more enigmatic than
the earlier. Much of the satire of the *"Caprichos"* is
merely Goya's sharper version of what may be called
standard eighteenth-century humor. A plate such as
"Hasta la Muerte," showing the old hag before her mirror,
coquettishly trying on a new headdress, is just Rowland-
son-with-a-difference. But in certain other etchings a

stranger and more disquieting note is struck. Goya's handling of his material is such that standard eighteenth-century humor often undergoes a sea change into something darker and queerer, something that goes below the anecdotal surface of life into what lies beneath—the unplumbed depths of original sin and original stupidity. And in the second half of the series the subject matter reinforces the effect of the powerful and dramatically sinister treatment; for here the theme of almost all the plates is basely supernatural. We are in a world of demons, witches, and familiars, half horrible, half comic, but wholly disquieting inasmuch as it reveals the sort of thing that goes on in the squalid catacombs of the human mind.

In the *"Disparates"* the satire is on the whole less direct than in the *"Caprichos,"* the allegories are more general and more mysterious. Consider, for example, the technically astonishing plate, which shows a large family of three generations perched like huddling birds along a huge dead branch that projects into the utter vacancy of a dark sky. Obviously, much more is meant than meets the eye. But what? The question is one upon which the commentators have spent a great deal of ingenuity—spent it, one may suspect, in vain. For the satire, it would seem, is not directed against this particular social evil or that political mistake, but rather against unregenerate human nature as such. It is a statement, in the form of an image, about life in general. Literature and the scriptures of all the great religions abound in such brief metaphorical verdicts on human destiny. Man turns the wheel of sorrow, burns in the fire of craving, travels through a vale of tears, leads a life that is no better than a tale told by an idiot signifying nothing.

> Poor man, what Art? A tennis ball of error,
> A ship of glass tossed in a sea of terror:
> Issuing in blood and sorrow from the womb,
> Crawling in tears and mourning to the tomb.
> How slippery are thy paths, how sure thy fall!
> How art thou nothing, when thou art most of all!

And so on. Good, bad, and indifferent the quotations could be multiplied almost indefinitely. In the language of the plastic arts, Goya has added a score of memorable contributions to the stock of humanity's gnomic wisdom.

The *"Disparates"* of the dead branch is relatively easy to understand. So is the comment on Fear contained in the plate which shows soldiers running in terror from a gigantic cowled figure, spectral against a jet black sky. So is the etching of the ecstatically smiling woman riding a stallion that turns its head and, seizing her skirts between its teeth, tries to drag her from her seat. The allegorical use of the horse, as a symbol of the senses and the passions, and of the rational rider or charioteer who is at liberty to direct or be run away with, is at least as old as Plato.

But there are other plates in which the symbolism is less clear, the allegorical significance far from obvious. That horse on a tightrope, for example, with a woman dancing on its back; the men who fly with artificial wings against a sky of inky menace; the priests and the elephant; the old man wandering among phantoms: what is the meaning of these things? And perhaps the answer to that question is that they have no meaning in any ordinary sense of the word; that they refer to strictly private events taking place on the obscurer levels of their creator's mind. For us who look at them, it may be that their real point and significance consist precisely in the fact that they image forth so vividly, and yet, of necessity, so darkly and incomprehensibly, some 'at least of the unknown quantities that exist at the heart of every personality.

Goya once drew a picture of an ancient man tottering along under the burden of years, but with the accompanying caption, "I'm still learning." That old man was himself. To the end of a long life, he went on learning. As a very young man he paints like the feeble eclectics who were his masters. The first signs of power and freshness and originality appear in the cartoons for the tapestries, of which the earliest were executed when he was thirty. As a portraitist, however, he achieves nothing of outstanding interest until he is almost forty. But by that time he really knows what he's after, and during the second forty years of his life he moves steadily forward toward the consummate technical achievements, in oils, of the *"Pinturas Negras,"* and, in etching, of the *"Desastres"* and the *"Disparates."* Goya's is a stylistic growth away from restraint and into freedom, away from timidity and into expressive boldness.

From the technical point of view the most striking fact about almost all Goya's successful paintings and etchings is that they are composed in terms of one or more clearly delimited masses standing out from the background—often indeed, silhouetted against the sky. When he attempts what may be called an "allover" composition, the essay is rarely successful. For he lacks almost completely the power which Rubens so conspicuously possessed—the power of filling the entire canvas with figures or details of landscape, and upon that *plenum* imposing a clear and yet exquisitely subtle three-dimensional order. The lack of this power is already conspicuous in the tapestry cartoons, of which the best are invariably those in which Goya does his composing in terms of silhouetted masses and the worst those in which he attempts to organize a collection of figures distributed all over the canvas. And compare, from this point of view, the two paintings of the *Dos de Mayo*—the mamelukes cutting down the crowd in the Puerta del Sol, and the firing squads at work in the suburbs, after dark. The first is an attempt to do what Rubens would have done with an almost excessive facility —to impose a formally beautiful and dramatically significant order upon a crowd of human and animal figures covering the greater part of the canvas. The attempt is not successful, and in spite of its power and the beauty of its component parts, the picture as a whole is less satisfying as a composition, and for that reason less moving as a story, than is the companion piece, in which Goya arranges his figures in a series of sharply delimited balancing groups, dramatically contrasted with one another and the background. In this picture the artist is speaking his native language, and he is therefore able to express what he wants to say with the maximum force and clarity. This is not the case with the picture of the mamelukes. Here, the formal language is not truly his own, and consequently his eloquence lacks the moving power it possesses when he lets himself go in the genuine Goyescan idiom.

Fortunately, in the etchings, Goya is very seldom tempted to talk in anything else. Here he composes almost exclusively in terms of bold separate masses, silhouetted in luminous grays and whites against a darkness that ranges from stippled pepper-and-salt to intense black, or in blacks and heavily shaded grays against the whiteness of virgin paper. Sometimes there is only one mass, sometimes several, balanced and contrasted. Hardly ever does he make the, for him, almost fatal mistake of trying to organize his material in an allover composition.

With the *"Desastres"* and the *"Disparates"* his mastery of this, his predestined method of composition, becomes, one might say, absolute. It is not, of course, the only method of composition. Indeed, the nature of this particular artistic idiom is such that there are probably certain things that can never be expressed in it—things which Rembrandt, for example, was able to say in his supremely beautiful and subtle illustrations to the Bible. But within the field that he chose to cultivate—that the idiosyncrasies of his temperament and the quality of his artistic sensibilities compelled him to choose—Goya remains incomparable.

In 1541, when Domenico Theotokopoulos was born, his native island of Crete had been for more than three centuries under Venetian rule. Trade had followed the imperial flag, but not culture. In language, in thought, in art, the island remained what it had been ever since the People of the Sea finally broke the Minoan power—a part of Greece. In the Cretan schools young men studied the philosophers of ancient Athens and the theologians of Christian Byzantium; Byzantine paintings and Byzantine mosaics adorned the churches, and even in the revolutionary sixteenth century, the Cretan artists went their traditional way without paying the smallest attention to what had been happening in nearby Italy. Their pictures were two-dimensional, nonrealistic, innocent of perspective and chiaroscuro. So far as they were concerned, Giotto and Masaccio, to say nothing of Raphael and Michelangelo and Titian, might never have existed.

Young Domenico received a sound Greek education and studied painting under the best masters of the island. Not, however, for very long. In Candia one could see, along with the other importations from the mainland, examples of Venetian painting. The orthodox might shake their heads. What a way to treat the Mother of God! And

• From *Themes and Variations*, 1950.

that indecently human personage—was that supposed to be the Pantocrator? But to a young man of original and inquiring mind, their very unorthodoxy must have seemed attractive. They were tokens from a world where the artist was his own master, where too he might make technical experiments, where he was free to see and represent all the things which, for the Byzantines, simply didn't exist. Moreover, this world of artistic liberty was also a world where a man could make his fortune. Venice was rich; Crete, miserably poor. There was no future for a man in Candia; but on the mainland, on the mainland . . .

In the early 1560's, when the young immigrant from Crete first stepped ashore, Venice was at the height of her artistic glory. Titian was a very old man, but painting as well as, or indeed better than, he had ever done in his youth. Tintoretto, his junior by forty years, was hard at work, transforming the principles of High Renaissance composition into those of the baroque. Still in his youthful prime, Veronese was effortlessly turning out enormous masterpieces of decorative art. "Bliss was it in that dawn to be alive." But all dawns—the artistic no less than the political, the religious, the sexual—give place to mornings, afternoons, and nights. After having worked for several years as "a disciple of Titian" (to use the phrase by which he was later to be described) Domenico came to be profoundly dissatisfied with Venetian art. It could hardly have been otherwise. By nature introspective, by nurture a Christian Neoplatonist and a student of Byzantine art, the young man might admire Venetian technique, but could never approve the uses to which that technique was put. For his taste Venetian art was too pagan, too voluptuous, too decorative, too much concerned with appearances, insufficiently inward and serious. In search of an art more comformable to his own nature and ideals, Domenico migrated in 1570 to Rome. But Rome, alas, proved to be no less disappointing than Venice. The great masters of the High Renaissance were all dead, and their successors were second-rate mannerists, incapable of creating anything new and living parasitically upon the achievements of the past. For Domenico, the living were without interest, and even the mighty dead were not the masters he had been looking for. Of Michelangelo, for example, he complained that the man did not know how to paint—which is a rather violent way of expressing the unquestionable truth that Michelangelo was primarily a sculptor and that his paintings are in some sort translations of sculpture into a language which was not the artist's native tongue. To a young man whose vocation was to express himself, not in marble, not in transcriptions of sculpture, but in color and the rich texture of oil pigments, the frescoes of the Sistine Chapel were not very instructive.

The artist's stay in Rome lasted for several years. Then, at some date prior to 1577, he undertook yet another migration, this time to Spain. Why to Spain? As usual, we do not know. And when, some years later, during a lawsuit, the same question was put to El Greco himself, he declined to answer. Evidently he was of the opinion that people should mind their own business.

The Cretan's wanderings were now at an end. He settled in Toledo, and there with his wife, Jeronima de las Cuevas, and his son, Jorge Manuel, he remained until his death in 1614. Of his life in Spain we know only a very little more than we know of his life in Crete and Italy— that is to say, next to nothing. Here are some of the scanty odds and ends of information that have come down to us.

Professionally, El Greco was successful. Many commissions came his way and he was well paid for his work. On several occasions he went to law with his ecclesiastical patrons in order to get his price. He had the reputation of spending his money with a lordly extravagance, and it was said that he paid an orchestra to make music while he ate his meals. His apartment on the verge of the great canyon of the Tagus contained twenty-four rooms, most of which, however, were left almost completely unfurnished. Of his own genius he had no doubts. He knew that he painted superlatively well and he was quite ready to say so in public. Moreover, when Philip II and certain of the clergy objected to his pictures on the ground that they did not respect the norms of ecclesiastical art, he steadfastly refused to compromise and went on painting exactly as he thought fit. Like Tintoretto, he modeled small clay figures, with the aid of which he studied effects of lighting and foreshortening. Pacheco, the father-in-law of Velasquez, saw a whole cupboardful of these figures when he visited El Greco shortly before the latter's death. Needless to say, they have all disappeared, and along with them has gone the treatise which El Greco wrote on painting.

Among the painter's friends were poets, men of learning,
eminent ecclesiastics. His library, as we know from the in-
ventory which was made after his death, contained,
among other Greek works, the famous *Mystical Theology*
of Dionysius the Areopagite, together with more recent
Italian Neoplatonic books on Neoplatonic philosophy. In
the light of this fact, a curious anecdote recorded by
Giulio Clovio, one of El Greco's Roman friends, takes on
a special significance. "Yesterday," wrote Clovio in a letter
which is still extant, "I called at his [El Greco's] lodgings
to take him for a walk through the city. The weather was
very fine. . . . But on entering the studio I was amazed
to find the curtains so closely drawn it was hardly possible to see anything. The painter was sitting in a chair,
neither working nor sleeping, and declined to go out with
me on the ground that the light of day disturbed his inward light." From this it would appear that El Greco took
more than a theoretical interest in the mystical states
described by Dionysius and the Neoplatonists; he also
practiced some form of meditation.

Of El Greco's personal appearance we know nothing
for certain. The so-called "self-portrait" may perhaps represent the painter's features; or, on the other hand, it may
not. The evidence is inconclusive. At every turn the man
eludes us. Only his work remains.

A representational picture is one that "tells a story"—
the story, for example, of the Nativity, the story of Mars
and Venus, the story of a certain landscape or a certain
person as they appeared at a certain moment of time. But
this story is never the whole story. A picture always expresses more than is implicit in its subject. Every painter
who tells a story tells it in his own manner, and that manner tells another story superimposed, as it were, upon the
first—a story about the painter himself, a story about the
way in which one highly gifted individual reacted to his
experience of our universe. The first story is told deliberately; the second tells itself independently of the artist's
conscious will. He cannot help telling it, for it is the expression of his own intimate being—of the temperament
with which he was born, the character which he himself
has forged and the unconscious tendencies formed by the
interaction of temperament, character, and outward circumstances.

Like most of his predecessors and contemporaries, El

Greco was mainly a religious painter, a teller of old familiar stories, from the Gospels and the legends of the saints. But he told them in his own peculiar manner, and that manner tells another story, so enigmatic that we pore over it in fascinated bewilderment, trying to construe its meaning.

In looking at any of the great compositions of El Greco's maturity we must always remember that the intention of the artist was neither to imitate Nature nor to tell a story with dramatic verisimilitude. Like the postimpressionists three centuries later, El Greco used natural objects as the raw material out of which, by a process of calculated distortion, he might create his own world of pictorial forms in pictorial space under pictorial illumination. Within this private universe he situated his religious subject matter, using it as a vehicle for expressing what he wanted to say about life.

And what *did* El Greco want to say? The answer can only be inferred; but to me, at least, it seems sufficiently clear. Those faces with their uniformly rapturous expression, those hands clasped in devotion or lifted towards heaven, those figures stretched out to the point where the whole inordinately elongated anatomy becomes a living symbol of upward aspiration—all these bear witness to the artist's constant preoccupation with the ideas of mystical religion. His aim is to assert the soul's capacity to come, through effort and through grace, to ecstatic union with the divine Spirit. This idea of union is more and more emphatically stressed as the painter advances in years. The frontier between earth and heaven, which is clearly defined in such works as "The Burial of Count Orgaz" and "The Dream of Philip II," grows fainter and finally disappears. In the latest version of Christ's Baptism there is no separation of any kind. The forms and colors flow continuously from the bottom of the picture to the top. The two realms are totally fused.

Does this mean that El Greco actually found a perfect pictorial expression for what his contemporary, St. Teresa of Avila, called "the spiritual marriage"? I think not. For all their extraordinary beauty, these great paintings are strangely oppressive and disquieting. Consciously El Greco was telling two stories—a story from the Gospels or the legends of the saints, and a story about mystical union with the divine. But, unconsciously, he told yet another story, having little or nothing to do with the two he knew he was telling. All that is disquieting in El Greco pertains to this third story and is conveyed to the spectator by his highly individual manner of treating space and the forms by which that space is occupied.

In the Byzantine art, with which El Greco was familiar in his youth, there is no third dimension. The figures in the icons and mosaics are the inhabitants of a Flatland in which there is no question of perspective. And precisely because there is no perspective, these figures seem to exist in a celestial universe having implications of indefinite extension. From ancient and conservative Byzantium El Greco traveled through time as well as space to modern Venice. Here, in Titian's paintings, he found the realistic representation of a third dimension traveling back from the picture plane to faraway landscapes of blue mountains under majestic clouds. And in Tintoretto's compositions he could study those rocketing centrifugal movements that carry the spectator's mind beyond the picture frame and suggest the endless succession of things and spaces existing in the world outside.

The nature of El Greco's personality was such that he chose to combine Byzantium and Venice in the strangest possible way. His pictures are neither flat nor fully three-dimensional. There is depth in his private universe, but only a very little of it. From the picture plane to the remotest object in the background there is, in most cases, an apparent distance of only a few feet. On earth as in heaven there is hardly room to swing a cat. Moreover, unlike Tintoretto and the baroque artists of the seventeenth century, El Greco never hints at the boundlessness beyond the picture frame. His compositions are centripetal, turned inwards on themselves. He is the painter of movement in a narrow room, of agitation in prison. This effect of confinement is enhanced by the almost complete absence from his paintings of a landscape background. The whole picture space is tightly packed with figures, human and divine; and where any chink is left between body and body, we are shown only a confining wall of cloud as opaque as earth, or of earth as fluidly plastic as the clouds. So far as El Greco is concerned, the world of nonhuman Nature is practically nonexistent.

No less disquieting than the narrowness of El Greco's universe is the quality of the forms with which he filled it. Everything here is organic, but organic on a low level, organic at a point well below the limit of life's perfection. That is why there is no sensuality in these paintings, nothing of the voluptuous. In a work of art we are charmed and attracted by forms which represent or at least suggest the forms of such objects as we find attractive in Nature—flowers, for example, fruits, animals, human bodies in their youthful strength and beauty. In life we are not at all attracted by protoplasm in the raw or by individual organs separated from the organism as a whole. But it is with forms suggestive precisely of such objects that El Greco fills his pictures. Under his brush the human body, when it is naked, loses its bony framework and even its musculature, and becomes a thing of ectoplasm—beautifully appropriate in its strange pictorial context, but not a little uncanny when thought of in the context of real life. And when El Greco clothes his boneless creatures, their draperies become pure abstractions, having the form of something indeterminately physiological.

And here a brief parenthesis is in order. A painter or a sculptor can be simultaneously representational and non-representational. In their architectural backgrounds and, above all, in their draperies, many works even of the Renaissance and the baroque incorporate passages of almost unadulterated abstraction. These are often expressive in the highest degree. Indeed, the whole tone of a representational work may be established, and its inner meaning expressed, by those parts of it which are most nearly abstract. Thus, the pictures of Piero della Francesca leave upon us an impression of calm, of power, of intellectual objectivity and stoical detachment. From those of Cosimo Tura there emanates a sense of disquiet, even of anguish. When we analyze the purely pictorial reasons for our perception of a profound difference in the temperaments of the two artists, we find that a very important part is played by the least representational elements in their pictures—the draperies. In Piero's draperies there are large unbroken surfaces, and the folds are designed to emphasize the elementary solid-geometrical structure of the figures. In Tura's draperies the surfaces are broken up, and there is a profusion of sharp angles, of jagged and flamelike forms. Something analogous may be found in the work of two great painters of a later period, Poussin and Watteau. Watteau's draperies are broken into innumerable tiny folds and wrinkles, so that the color of a mantle or a doublet is never the same for half an inch together. The impression left upon the spectator is one of extreme sensibility and the most delicate refinement. Poussin's much broader treatment of these almost nonrepresentational accessories seems to express a more masculine temperament and a philosophy of life akin to Piero's noble stoicism.

In some works the nonrepresentational passages are actually more important than the representational. Thus, in many of Bernini's statues, only the hands, feet, and face are fully representational; all the rest is drapery—that is to say, a writhing and undulant abstraction. It is the same with El Greco's paintings. In some of them a third, a half, even as much as two thirds of the entire surface is occupied by low-level organic abstractions, to which, because of their representational context, we give the name of draperies, or clouds, or rocks. These abstractions are powerfully expressive, and it is through them that, to a considerable extent, El Greco tells the private story that underlies the official subject matter of his paintings.

At this point the pure abstractionist will come forward with a question. Seeing that the nonrepresentational passages in representational works are so expressive, why should anyone bother with representation? Why trouble to tell a high-level story about recognizable objects when the more important low-level story about the artist's temperament and reactions to life can be told in terms of pure abstractions? I myself have no objection to pure abstractions which, in the hands of a gifted artist, can achieve their own kind of aesthetic perfection. But this perfection, it seems to me, is a perfection within rather narrow limits. The Greeks called the circle "a perfect figure." And so it is—one cannot improve on it. And yet a composition consisting of a red circle inscribed within a black square would strike us, for all its perfection, as being a little dull. Even aesthetically the perfect figure of a circle is less interesting than the perfect figure of a young woman. This does not mean, of course, that the representation of the young woman by a bad artist will be more valuable, as a picture, than a composition of circles, squares, and triangles devised by a good one. But it does mean, I think, that Nature is a richer source of forms than any textbook of plane or solid geometry. Nature has evolved innumerable forms and, as we ourselves move from point to point, we see large numbers of these forms, grouped in an endless variety of ways and thus creating an endless variety of new forms, all of which may be used as the raw materials of works of art. What is given is incomparably richer than what we can invent. But the richness of Nature is, from our point of view, a chaos upon which we, as philosophers, men of science, technicians, and artists, must impose various kinds of unity. Now, I would say that, other things being equal, a work of art which imposes aesthetic unity upon a large number of formal and psychological elements is a greater and more interesting work than one in which unity is imposed upon only a few elements. In other words, there is a hierarchy of perfections. Bach's Two-Part Inventions are perfect in their way. But his *Chromatic Fantasia* is also perfect; and since its perfection involves the imposition of aesthetic unity upon a larger number of elements it is (as we all in fact recognize) a greater work. The old distinction between the Fine Arts and the crafts is based to some extent upon snobbery and other nonaesthetic considerations. But not entirely. In the hierarchy of perfections a perfect vase or a perfect carpet occupies a lower rank than that, say, of Giotto's frescoes at Padua, or Rembrandt's "Polish Rider," or the "Grande Jatte" of Georges Seurat. In these and a hundred other masterpieces of painting the pictorial whole embraces and unifies a repertory of forms much more numerous, varied, strange, and interesting than those which come together in the wholes organized by even the most gifted craftsmen. And, over and above this richer and subtler formal perfection, we are presented with the nonpictorial bonus of a story and, explicit or implicit, a criticism of life. At their best, nonrepresentational compositions achieve perfection; but it is a perfection nearer to that of the jug or rug than to that of the enormously complex and yet completely unified masterpieces of representational art—most of which, as we have seen, contain expressive passages of almost pure abstraction. At the present time it would seem that the most sensible and rewarding thing for a painter to do is (like Braque, for example) to make the best and the most of both worlds, representational as well as nonrepresentational.

Within his own Byzantine-Venetian tradition El Greco did precisely this, combining representation with abstraction in a manner which we are accustomed to regard as characteristically modern. His intention, as we have seen, was to use this powerful artistic instrument to express, in visual terms, man's capacity for union with the divine. But the artistic means he employed were such that it was not possible for him to carry out that intention. The existence of a spiritual reality transcendent and yet immanent, absolutely other and yet the sustaining essence of every being, has frequently been rendered in visual symbols—but not symbols of the kind employed by El Greco. The agitation of quasi-visceral forms in an overcrowded and almost spaceless world, from which nonhuman Nature has been banished, cannot, in the very nature of things, express man's union with the Spirit who must be worshipped in spirit.

Landscape and the human figure in repose—these are the symbols through which, in the past, the spiritual life has been most clearly and powerfully expressed. "Be still and know that I am God." Recollectedness is the indispensable means to the unitive knowledge of spiritual reality; and though recollectedness should, and by some actually can, be practiced in the midst of the most violent physical activity, it is most effectively symbolized by a body in repose and a face that expresses an inner serenity. The carved or painted Buddhas and Bodhisattvas of India and the Far East are perhaps the most perfect examples of such visual symbols of the spiritual life. Hardly less adequate are the majestic Byzantine figures of Christ, the Virgin, and the saints. It seems strange that El Greco, who received his first training from Byzantine masters, should not have recognized the symbolical value of repose, but should have preferred to represent or, though his accessory abstractions, to imply, an agitation wholly incompatible with the spiritual life of which he had read in the pages of Dionysius.

No less strange is the fact that a disciple of Titian should have ignored landscape and that a Neoplatonist should have failed to perceive that, in the aged master's religious pictures, the only hint of spirituality was to be found, not in the all too human figures, but in the backgrounds of Alpine foothills, peaks, and skies. Civilized man spends most of his life in a cozy little universe of material artifacts, of social conventions, and of verbalized ideas. Only rarely, if he is the inhabitant of a well-ordered city, does he come into direct contact with the mystery of the nonhuman world, does he become aware of modes of being incommensurable with his own, of vast, indefinite extensions, of durations all but everlasting. From time immemorial deity has been associated with the boundlessness of earth and sky, with the longevity of trees, rivers, and mountains, with Leviathan and the whirlwind, with sunshine and the lilies of the field. Space and time on the cosmic scale are symbols of the infinity and eternity of Spirit. Nonhuman Nature is the outward and visible expression of the mystery which confronts us when we look into the depths of our own being. The first artists to concern themselves with the spiritual significance of Nature were the Taoist landscape painters of China. "Cherishing the Way, a virtuous man responds to objects. Clarifying his mind, a wise man appreciates forms. As to landscapes, they exist in material substance and soar into the realm of spirit. . . . The virtuous man follows the Way by spiritual insight; the wise man takes the same approach. But the lovers of landscape are led into the Way by a sense of form. . . . The significance which is too subtle to be communicated by means of words of mouth may be grasped by the mind through books and writings. Then how much more so in my case, when I have wandered among the rocks and hills and carefully observed them with my own eyes! I render form by form and appearance by appearance. . . . The truth comprises the expression received through the eyes and recognized by the mind. If, in painting, therefore, the likeness of an object is skillfully portrayed, both the eye and the mind will approve. When the eyes respond and the mind agrees with the objects, the divine spirit may be felt and truth may be attained in the painting." So wrote Tsung Ping who was a contemporary of St. Augustine, in an *Introduction to Landscape Painting*, which has become a Chinese classic. When, twelve hundred years later, European artists discovered landscape, they developed no philosophy to explain and justify what they were doing. That was left to the poets—to Wordsworth, to Shelley, to Whitman. The Presence which they found in Nature, "the Spirit of each spot," is identical with Hsuan P'in, the mysterious Valley Spirit of the Tao Te Ching, who reveals herself to the landscape painter and, by him, is revealed to others in his pictures. But the lack of an explanatory

philosophy did not prevent the best of the European
landscape painters from making manifest that

> something far more deeply interfused,
> Whose dwelling is the light of setting suns,
> And the round ocean, and the living air,
> And the blue sky, and in the mind of man.

"This is not drawing," Blake exclaimed, when he was
shown one of Constable's sketches, "this is inspiration."
And though Constable himself protested that it was only
drawing, the fact remains that the best of his landscapes
are powerful and convincing renderings of the spiritual
reality in which all things have their being. Indeed, they
are much more adequate as symbols of spiritual life than
the majority of the works in which Blake consciously tried
to express his spiritualist philosophy. Much less gifted as
painter than as poet, and brought up in a deplorable
artistic tradition, Blake rarely produced a picture that
"comes off" to the extent of expressing what he says so
perfectly in his lyrics and in isolated passages of the *Prophetic Books*. Constable, on the other hand, is a great
Nature mystic without knowing or intending it. In this he
reminds us of Seurat. "They see poetry in what I do,"
complained that consummate master of landscape. "No; I
apply my method and that is all there is to it." But the
method was applied by a painter who combined the most
exquisite sensibility with intellectual powers of the first
order. Consequently what Seurat supposed to be merely
pointillisme was in fact inspiration—a vision of the world
in which material reality is the symbol and, one might
say, the incarnation of an all-embracing spiritual reality.
The famous method was the means whereby he told this
Taoistic and Wordsworthian story; *pointillisme,* as he used
it, permitted him to render empty space as no other painter
has ever done, and to impose, through color, an unprecedented degree of unity upon his composition. In Seurat's
paintings the near and the far are separate and yet are
one. The emptiness which is the symbol of infinity is of
the same substance as the finite forms it contains. The
transient participates in the eternal, *samsara* and *nirvana*
are one and the same. Such is the poetry with which, in
spite of himself, Seurat filled those wonderful landscapes
of Honfleur and Gravelines and the Seine. And such is the
poetry which El Greco, in spite of what seems to have been

a conscious desire to imply it, was forced by the nature of his artistic instrument to exclude from every picture he painted. His peculiar treatment of space and form tells a story of obscure happenings in the subconscious mind— of some haunting fear of wide vistas and the open air, some dream of security in the imagined equivalent of a womb. The conscious aspiration towards union with, and perfect freedom in, the divine Spirit is overridden by a subconscious longing for the consolations of some ineffable uterine state.

When we think of it in relation to the great world of human experience, El Greco's universe of swallowed spirit and visceral rapture seems, as I have said, curiously oppressive and disquieting. But considered as an isolated artistic system, how strong and coherent it seems, how perfectly unified, how fascinatingly beautiful! And because of this inner harmony and coherence, it asserts in one way all that it had denied in another. El Greco's conscious purpose was to affirm man's capacity for union with the divine. Unconsciously, by his choice of forms and his peculiar treatment of space, he proclaimed the triumph of the organic and the incapacity of spirit, so far as he personally was concerned, to transfigure the matter with which it is associated. But at the same time he was a painter of genius. Out of the visceral forms and cramped spaces, imposed upon him by a part of his being beyond his voluntary control, he was able to create a new kind of order and perfection and, through this order and perfection, to reaffirm the possibility of man's union with the Spirit—a possibility which the raw materials of his pictures had seemed to rule out.

There is no question here of a dialectical process of thesis, antithesis, and synthesis. A work of art is not a becoming, but a multiple being. It exists and has significance on several levels at once. In most cases these significances are of the same kind and harmoniusly reinforce one another. Not always, however. Occasionally it happens that each of the meanings is logically exclusive of all the rest. There is then a happy marriage of incompatibles, a perfect fusion of contradictions. It is one of those states which, though inconceivable, actually occur. Such things cannot be; and yet, when you enter the Prado, when you visit Toledo, there they actually are.

5

Variations on "The Prisons"●

At the top of the main staircase in University College, London, there stands a boxlike structure of varnished wood, somewhat larger than a telephone booth, somewhat smaller than an outdoor privy. When the door of this miniature house is opened, a light goes on inside, and those who stand upon the threshold find themselves confronted by a little old gentleman sitting bolt upright in a chair and smiling benevolently into space. His hair is gray and hangs almost to his shoulders; his wide-brimmed straw hat is like something out of the illustrations to an early edition of *Paul et Virginie;* he wears a cutaway coat (green, if I remember rightly, with metal buttons) and pantaloons of white cotton, discreetly striped. This little old gentleman is Jeremy Bentham, or at least what remains of Jeremy Bentham after the dissection ordered in his will—a skeleton with hands and face of wax, dressed in the clothes which once belonged to the author of *The Principles of Morals and Legislation.*

To this odd shrine (so characteristic, in its excessive unpretentiousness, of "that nook-shotten isle of Albion") I paid my visit of curiosity in the company of one of the most extraordinary, one of the most admirable men of our time, Dr. Albert Schweitzer. Many years have passed

● From *Themes and Variations,* 1950.

since then; but I remember very clearly the expression of affectionate amusement which appeared on Schweitzer's face as he looked at the mummy. "Dear Bentham," he said at last, "dear Bentham! I like him so much better than Hegel. He was responsible for so much less harm."

The comment was unexpected, but true and, in our twentieth-century context, painfully to the point. The German philosopher was proud of being *tief*, but lacked completely the humility which is the necessary condition of the ultimate profundity. That was why he ended up as the idolater of the Prussian state and the spiritual father of those Marxian theories of history, in terms of which it is possible to justify every atrocity on the part of true believers and to condemn every good or reasonable act performed by infidels. Bentham, on the contrary, made no claims to *tief*-ness. Shallow with the kindly, sensible shallowness of the eighteenth century, he thought of individuals as real people, not as mere cells in the brawn and bone of a social organism whose soul is the State. From Hegel's depths have sprung tyranny, war, and persecutions; from the shallows of Bentham, a host of unpretentious but real benefits—the repeal of antiquated laws, the introduction of sewage systems, the reform of municipal government, almost everything sensible and humane in the civilization of the nineteenth century. Only in one field did Bentham ever sow the teeth of dragons. He had the logician's passion for order and consistency; and he wanted to impose his ideas of tidiness, not only upon thoughts and words, but also upon things and institutions. Now tidiness is undeniably a good—but a good of which it is easily possible to have too much and at too high a price. The love of tidiness has often figured, along with the love of power, as an incitement to tyranny. In human affairs the extreme of messiness is anarchy; the extreme of tidiness, an army or a penitentiary. Anarchy is the enemy of liberty and so, at its highest pitch, is mechanical efficiency. The good life can be lived only in a society where tidiness is preached and practiced, but not too fanatically, and where efficiency is always haloed, as it were, by a tolerated aura of mess. Bentham himself was no tyrant and no worshipper of the all-efficient, ubiquitous, and providential State. But he loved tidiness and inculcated that kind of social efficiency which has been and is being made an excuse for the concentration of power in the hands of a few experts and the regimentation of the masses. And meanwhile we have to remember the strange and rather alarming fact that Bentham devoted about twenty-five years of his long life to the elaboration in minutest detail of plans for a perfectly efficient prison. The Panopticon, as he called it, was to be a circular building so constructed that every convict should pass his life in perpetual solitude while remaining under the perpetual surveillance of a warder posted at the center. (Significantly enough, Jeremy Bentham borrowed the idea of the Panopticon from his brother, Sir Samuel, the naval architect, who, while employed by Catherine the Great to build warships for Russia, had designed a factory along panoptical lines, for the purpose of getting more work out of the newly industrialized moujiks.) Bentham's plan for a totalitarian housing project was never carried out. To console him for his disappointment, the philosopher was granted, by Act of Parliament, twenty-three thousand pounds from the public funds.

The architecture of modern prisons lacks the logical perfection of the Panopticon; but its inspiration is that same passion for a more than human tidiness which moved the Bentham brothers and which has been, time out of mind, characteristic of martinets and dictators. Before the days of Howard and Bentham and the Philadelphia Quakers, nobody, for some odd reason, seems ever to have thought of making prisons orderly and efficient. The jails to which Elizabeth Fry brought her inexhaustible treasures of charity and common sense were like the embodiments of some criminal delirium. Passing those doors, the prisoner found himself condemned to an existence resembling that of Hobbes's theoretical State of Nature. Behind the façade of Newgate—a façade which its architect, uninhibited by the tiresome necessity of finding a place for windows, had been able to make consummately elegant—there existed, not a world of men and women, not even a world of beasts, but a chaos, a pandemonium.

The artist whose work most faithfully reflects the nature of this hell is Hogarth—not the Hogarth of the harmoniously colored paintings, but he of the engravings, he of the hard insensitive line, the ruthless delineator of senseless evil and chaotic misery, as well within the Fleet and Newgate and Bedlam as outside, in those other prisons, those other asylums, the dram shops of Gin Alley, the brothels and gaming rooms of Covent Garden, the suburban playgrounds, where children torment their dogs and birds with scarcely imaginable refinements of cruelty and obscenity.

Within a space of thirty or forty years the Prison Discipline Society accomplished an extraordinary reformation. From being subhumanly anarchical, prisons became subhumanly mechanical. Ever since Sir Joshua Jebb erected his model jail at Pentonville, the consciousness of being inside a machine, inside a realized idea of absolute tidiness and perfect regimentation, has been a principal part of the punishment of convicts. In the Nazi concentration camps hell on earth was not of the old Hogarthian kind, but neat, tidy, thoroughly scientific. Seen from the air, Belsen is said to have looked like an atomic research laboratory or a well-designed motion picture studio. The Bentham brothers have been dead these hundred years and more; but the spirit of the Panopticon, the spirit of Sir Samuel's moujik-compelling workhouse, has gone marching on to strange and terrible destinations.

Today every efficient office, every up-to-date factory is a panoptical prison, in which the worker suffers (more or less, according to the character of the warders and the degree of his own sensibility) from the consciousness of being inside a machine. It is, I think, only in literature that there has been an adequate artistic rendering of this consciousness. De Vigny, for example, has said fine and penetrating things about the soldier's enslavement to an ideal of absolute tidiness; and in *War and Peace* there is a memorable chapter on the way in which the impersonal forces of Orders from Above, of High Policy expressing itself through the workings of a system, transforms Pierre's kindly French jailers into insensitive and pitiless automata. But in the twentieth century an army is only one among many Panopticons. There are also the regiments of industry, the regiments of bookkeeping and administration. These have evoked a good deal of plaintive or truculent writing, but not much, and nothing very satisfactory, in the way of pictorial art. There were, it is true, certain Cubists who liked to paint machines or to represent human figures as though they were parts of machines. But a machine, after all, is itself a work of art, much more subtle, much more interesting from a formal point of view, than any representation of a machine can be. In other words, a machine is its own highest artistic expression and merely loses by being simplified and quintessentialized in a symbolic representation. As for the representation of human beings in mechanomorphic guise—this is effective only to a certain point. For the real horror of the situation in an industrial or administrative Panopticon is not that human beings are transformed into machines (if they could be so transformed, they would be perfectly happy in their prisons); no, the horror consists precisely in the fact that they are not machines, but 'freedom-loving animals, far-ranging minds, and godlike spirits, who find themselves subordinated to machines and constrained to live within the issueless tunnel of an arbitrary and inhuman system.

Beyond the real historical prisons of too much tidiness and those where anarchy engenders the hell of physical and moral chaos, there lie yet other prisons, no less terrible for being fantastic and unembodied—the metaphysical prisons, whose seat is within the mind, whose walls are made of nightmare and incomprehension, whose chains are anxiety and their racks a sense of personal and even generic guilt. De Quincey's Oxford Street and the road on which he had his vision of sudden death were prisons of this kind. So was the luxurious inferno described by Beckford in *Vathek*. So were the castles, the courtrooms, the penal colonies inhabited by the personages of Kafka's novels. And, passing from the world of words to that of forms, we find these same metaphysical prisons delineated with incomparable force in the strangest and, in many ways the most beautiful, of Piranesi's etchings.

Historical generalizations are delightful to make and thrilling to read. But how much, I wonder, do they contribute to our understanding of the human enigma? The question is one which I will not venture to answer, except with a series of other questions. For example, if, as we are told, the art of a period reflects the social history of that period, in what way precisely do Perugino's paintings express the age whose history is written in *The Prince* of Machiavelli? Again, modern historians assure us that the thirteenth century was the Age of Faith and a period of Progress. Then why should all the moralists who actually lived during the thirteenth century have regarded it as an age of decadence, and why should its liveliest chronicler,

Salimbene, depict for us a society that behaves as though it had never even heard of Christian morals? Or consider the fourth century in Constantinople. At this time and place, we are assured by certain historians, men were wholly preoccupied with problems of theology. If this is the case, why do the writers who were contemporary with those men complain that they lived only for the chariot races? And finally, why should Voltaire and Hume be regarded as more typical of the eighteenth century than Bach and Wesley? Why have I myself, in an earlier paragraph, spoken of the kindly, sensible shallowness of the eighteenth century, when that century gave birth to such men as William Law and Saint-Martin, to the author of the *Songs of Experience* and the engraver of "The Prisons." . . . The truth is, of course, that every variety of human being exists at every period. In religion, for example, every generation has its fetishists, its revivalists, its legalists, its rationalists, and its mystics. And, whatever the prevailing fashion in art may happen to be, every age has its congenital romantics and its natural classicists. True, at any period the prevailing fashions in art, in religion, in modes of thought and feeling are more or less rigid. Consequently it is always more or less hard for those whose temperaments are at odds with the fashion to express themselves. Any given work of art may be represented as the diagonal in a parallelogram of forces—a parallelogram of which the base is the prevailing tradition and the socially important events of the time, and in which the upright is the artist's temperament and his private life. In some works the base is longer than the upright; in others the upright is longer than the base.

Piranesi's "Prisons" are creations of the second kind. In them the personal, private, and therefore universal and everlasting upright is notably longer than the merely historical and therefore transient and local base. The proof of this is to be found in the fact that these extraordinary etchings have continued, during two centuries, to seem completely relevant and modern, not merely in their formal aspects, but also as expressions of obscure psychological turths. To use a once popular religious phrase, they "spoke to the condition" of Coleridge and De Quincey and they speak no less eloquently to ours. That which Piranesi expressed is not subject to historical change. He is not, like Hogarth, recording the facts of contemporary social life. Nor is he, like Bentham, trying to design a mechanism that shall change the nature of such facts. His concern is with states of the soul—states that are largely independent of external circumstances, states that recur whenever Nature, at her everlasting game of chance, combines the hereditary factors of physique and temperament in certain patterns.

In the past psychology was generally treated as a branch of ethics or theology. Thus, for St. Augustine, the problem of human differences was the same as the problem of Grace and the mystery of God's Good Pleasure. And it is only in quite recent times that men have learned to talk about the idiosyncrasies of personal behavior in any terms but those of sin and virtue. The metaphysical prisons delineated by Piranesi, and described by so many modern poets and novelists, were well known to our ancestors— but well known, not as symptoms of disease or of some temperamental peculiarity, not as states to be analyzed and expressed by lyric poets, but rather as moral imperfections, as criminal rebellions against God, as obstacles in the way of enlightenment. Thus the *Weltschmerz,* of which the German Romantics were so proud, the *ennui, fruit de la morne incuriosité,* which was the theme of so many of Baudelaire's most splendid verses, is nothing else than that *acedia,* for indulging in which the constitutionally bored and melancholy were plunged head over ears in the black mud of hell's third circle. And this is what St. Catherine of Siena had to say about the state of mind which is the very climate and atmosphere of all Kafka's novels: "Confusion is a leprosy that dries up body and soul, and binds the arms of holy desire. It makes the soul unendurable to itself, disposing the mind to conflicts and fantasies. It robs the soul of supernatural light and darkens its natural light. Let the demons of confusion be vanquished by living faith and holy desire." To someone like St. Catherine, whose primary concern is union with God and the salvation of souls, even to someone whose preoccupation with Christianity was, like Dante's, rather that of a philosopher than of a theocentric saint, the idea of treating spiritual confusion or *acedia* or any other kind of metaphysical prison as merely a subject for scientific research or artistic manipulation would have seemed a kind of criminal imbecility. The historical base, upon which medieval thinkers and artists erected their personal uprights, was so long and so deeply rooted in traditional theology and ethics that it proved impossible even for Boccaccio—born storyteller and passionate humanist though he was—to pay more than the most perfunctory attention to psychology. In the Decameron even the outward appearance of the personages is hardly described; and the characterization is confined to simple adjectives, such as "gentle," "courtly," "avaricious," "amorous," and the like. It required a greater genius and a profounder skepticism than Boccaccio's to invent a psychology independent of theology and ethics. And let us remember that Chaucer—the Chaucer of the later *Canterbury Tales*—remained without any rival until the time of Shakespeare. In relation to its traditional base, his personal upright is the tallest in all medieval literature. The resulting diagonal represents a work of truly astounding originality.

On their much smaller scale "The Prisons" of Piranesi are also astonishingly original. No previous painter or draftsman had ever done anything at all like them. There had, of course, been plenty of fantasists before the days of Piranesi—even fantasists who expressed themselves in terms of architectural design, like the Bibienas. But the Bibienas were men of the theater and their architectural inventions were intended primarily to astonish the groundlings, to express, not the subterranean workings of a tormented soul, but those thoroughly vulgar aspirations towards grandiosity which, throughout the seventeenth and eighteenth centuries, tormented the great ones of the earth, together with all who snobbishly wanted to be like them. Another, more celebrated fantasist was Salvator Rosa—a man who, for reasons which are now incomprehensible, was regarded by the critics of four and five generations ago as one of the world's greatest artists. But Salvator Rosa's romantic fantasies are pretty cheap and obvious. He is a melodramatist who never penetrates beneath the surface. If he were alive today, he would be known, most probably, as the indefatigable author of one of the more bloodthirsty and uninhibited comic strips. Much more talented was Magnasco, whose speciality was monks by candlelight in a state of Gothic or Greco-esque elongation. His inventions are always pleasing, but always, one feels, without any deep or abiding significance —things created arbitrarily on one of the higher levels of consciousness, somewhere near the top of a very whimsical and accomplished head. The fantasy displayed in "The Prisons" is altogether of a different order. It is a fantasy without precedent, based upon facts, which Piranesi was the first to describe in pictorial terms. All the plates in the series are self-evidently variations on a single symbol, whose reference is to things existing in the physical and metaphysical depths of human souls and bodies—to *acedia* and confusion, to nightmare and *angst*, to incomprehension and panic bewilderment.

The most disquietingly obvious fact about all these dungeons is the perfect pointlessness which reigns throughout. Their architecture is colossal and magnificent. One is made to feel that the genius of great artists and the labor of innumerable slaves have gone into the creation of these monuments, every detail of which is completely without a purpose. Yes, without a purpose; for the staircases lead nowhere, the vaults support nothing but their own weight and enclose vast spaces that are never truly rooms but only anterooms, lumber rooms, vestibules, outhouses. And this magnificence of cyclopean stone is everywhere made squalid by wooden ladders, by flimsy gangways and catwalks. And the squalor is for squalor's sake, since all these rickety roads through space are manifestly without destination. Below them, on the floor, stand great machines incapable of doing anything in particular, and from the arches overhead hang ropes that carry nothing except a sickening suggestion of torture. Some of the prisons are lighted only by narrow windows. Others are half open to the sky, with hints of yet other vaults and walls in the distance. But even where the enclosure is more or less complete, Piranesi always contrives to give the impression that this colossal pointlessness goes on indefinitely and is coextensive with the universe. Engaged in no recognizable activity, paying no attention to one another, a few small faceless figures haunt the shadows. Their insignificant presence merely emphasizes the fact that there is nobody at home.

Physically, every human being is always alone, suffering in solitude, enjoying in solitude, incapable of participating in the vital processes of his fellows. But, though self-contained, this island-organism is never self-sufficient. Each living solitude is dependent upon other living solitudes and, more completely still, upon the ocean of being from which it lifts its tiny reef of individuality. The realization of this paradox of solitude in the midst of dependence, of isolation accompanied by insufficiency, is one of the principal causes of confusion and *acedia* and anxiety. And in their turn, of course, confusion and *acedia* and anxiety intensify the sense of loneliness and make the human paradox seem yet more tragic. The occupants of these metaphysical prisons are the hopeless spectators of "this pomp of worlds, this pain of birth"—of a magnificence without meaning, a misery without end and beyond the power of unaided man to understand or to bear.

It is said that the first idea of "The Prisons" came to Piranesi in the delirium of fever. What is certain, however, is that this first idea was not the last; for some of the etchings exist in early states, in which many of the most characteristic and most disquieting details of "The Prisons," as we now know them, are lacking. From this it is to be inferred that the state of mind expressed in these etchings was, for Piranesi, chronic and in some sort normal. Fever may have originally suggested "The Prisons"; but in the years which elapsed between Piranesi's first essays and the final publication of the plates, recurrent moods of confusion and *acedia* and *angst* must have been responsible for such obscure but, as we now see, indispensable symbols as the ropes, the aimless engines, the makeshift wooden stairs and bridges.

The plates of "The Prisons" were published while their author was still a young man, and during the remainder of his fairly long life Piranesi never returned to the theme which, in them, he had handled with such consummate mastery. Most of his work, thenceforward, was topographical and archaeological. His theme was always Rome; and this was true even when he abandoned the facts of ruins and baroque churches to undertake excursions into the realm of fantasy. For what he liked to imagine was still Rome—Rome as it ought to have been, as it might have been, if Augustus and his successors had possessed an inexhaustible treasury and an inexhaustible supply of man power. It is fortunate that their resources were limited; for the hypothetical Rome of Piranesi's fancy and the imperial dream is a nightmare of pretentiousness and grandiose vulgarity.

St. Catherine held that the demons of confusion are to be vanquished only by holy desire and faith in the Christian revelation. But actually any sustained desire and any intense faith will win the battle. Piranesi seems to have been without any profound religious conviction or mystical aspiration. His faith was that of a humanist, his god was Roman antiquity, and his motivating desire was a mixture of the artist's will to beauty, the archaeologist's will to historical truth, and the poor man's will to make a living for his family. These, apparently, were sufficient antidotes to *acedia* and spiritual confusion. At any rate he never gave a second expression to the state of mind which inspired "The Prisons."

Considered from a purely formal point of view, "The Prisons" are remarkable as being the nearest eighteenth-century approach to a purely abstract art. The raw material of Piranesi's designs consists of architectural forms; but, because "The Prisons" are images of confusion, because their essence is pointlessness, the combinations of architectural forms never add up to an architectural drawing, but remain free designs, untrammeled by any considerations of utility or even of possibility, and limited only by the necessity of evoking the general idea of a building. In other words, Piranesi uses architectural forms to produce a series of beautifully intricate designs, which resemble the abstractions of the Cubists in being composed of geometrical elements, but which have the advantage of combining pure geometry with enough subject matter, enough literature, to express, more forcibly than a mere pattern can do, the obscure and terrible states of spiritual confusion and *acedia*.

Of natural as opposed to geometrical, forms Piranesi, in "The Prisons," makes hardly any use. There is not a leaf or a blade of grass in the whole series, not a bird or an animal. Here and there, irrelevantly alive in the midst of the stony abstractions, stand a few human figures, darkly cloaked, featureless and impassive.

In the topographical etchings things are very different. Here Piranesi uses natural forms as a romantically decorative foil to the pure geometry of the monuments. The trees have an unkempt wildness; the personages in the foreground are either beggars inconceivably ragged, or else fine ladies and gentlemen no less inconceivably beribboned and bewigged, sometimes on foot, sometimes in rococo coaches, carved into the likeness of wedding cakes or merry-go-rounds. Everywhere the purpose is to set off the smoothness and solidity of hewn stone by juxtaposing the wavering, flamelike forms of plants and human beings. At the same time the figures serve another purpose, which is to make the monuments seem larger than in fact they are. Men and women are reduced to the stature of children; horses become as small as mastiffs. Inside the basilicas the pious reach up to the holy water fonts and, even on tiptoe, can hardly wet their fingers. Peopled by dwarfs, the most modest of baroque buildings assumes heroic proportions; a little piece of classicism by Piero da Cortona seems gravely portentous, and the delightful gimcrack of Borromini takes on the quality of something Cyclopean. This trick of increasing the apparent size of buildings by diminishing the known yardstick of the human figure was a favorite device among eighteenth-century artists. It was reduced to its final absurdity in such pictures as the "Belshazzar's Feast" of John Martin, where the antlike king and his courtiers sit down to dinner in a hall about two miles long and fifteen hundred feet high.

In "The Prisons" there is no hint of this ingenuous and simple-minded theatricality. Such prisoners as we are shown exist for the purpose of emphasizing, not the superhuman grandeur of the buildings, but their inhuman vacancy, their subhuman pointlessness. They are, quite literally, lost souls, wandering—or not even wandering, standing about—in a labyrinthine emptiness. It is interesting to compare them with the personages in Blake's illustrations to the *Inferno* of Dante. These damned souls are so far from being lost that they seem to be perfectly at home among their flames and crags and morasses. In all the circles of hell everybody is vaguely heroic in the corrupt classical manner of the late eighteenth century, and everybody appears to take the liveliest interest in his fellows. In "The Prisons" there are no Michelangelesque muscles, no exhibitionism of athletic extroverts, no trace of social life, and no hint that such a thing is even possible. Every man is muffled up, furtive and, even when in company, completely alone. Blake's drawings are curious and sometimes beautiful, but never for a moment can we take them seriously as symbols of extremest suffering. Piranesi's prisoners, on the contrary, are the inhabitants of a hell which, though but one out of the many worst of all possible worlds, is completely credible and bears the stamp of self-evident authenticity.

6

Doodles in a Dictionary●

In only one respect do I resemble Shakespeare: I know little Latin and less Greek. Once, long ago, I knew quite a lot of both. I had to; for I was brought up in what it is now fashionable to call the Western Tradition, the educational system which equated wisdom with a knowledge of the classical authors in the original and defined culture as an ability to write grammatically correct Greek and Latin prose. And not merely prose; for at Eton, in my day, we strictly meditated the thankless Muse. The whole of every Tuesday, from seven in the morning until ten at night, was devoted to the exhausting and preposterous task of translating thirty or forty lines of English poetry into Latin or, on great occasions, Greek verses. For those who were most successful in producing pastiches of Ovid or Horace or Euripides, there were handsome prizes. I still have a Matthew Arnold in crimson morocco, a Shelley in half-calf, to testify to my onetime prowess in these odd fields of endeavor. Today I could no more write a copy of Greek iambics, or even of Latin hexameters, than I could fly. All I can remember of these once indispensable arts is the intense boredom by which the practice of them was accompanied. Even today the sight of Dr. Smith's *Shorter Latin Dictionary*, or of Liddell's and Scott's *Greek*

● From *Tomorrow and Tomorrow and Tomorrow*, 1956.

Lexicon, has power to recall that ancient ennui. What dreary hours I have spent frantically turning those pages in search of a word for "cow" that could be scanned as a dactyl, or to make sure that my memory of the irregular verbs and the Greek accents was not at fault! I hate to think of all that wasted time. And yet, in view of the fact that most human beings are destined to pass most of their lives at jobs in which it is impossible for them to take the slightest interest, this old-fashioned training with the dictionary may have been extremely salutary. At least it taught one to know and expect the worst of life. Whereas the pupil in a progressive school, where everything is made to seem entertaining and significant, lives in a fool's paradise. As a preparation for life, not as it ought to be, but as it actually is, the horrors of Greek grammar and the systematic idiocy of Latin verses were perfectly appropriate. On the other hand, it must be admitted that they tended to leave their victims with a quite irrational distaste for poor dear Dr. Smith.

Not long ago, for example, I had an urgent call from my friend Jake Zeitlin, the bookseller. "I have something to show you," he said, "something very exciting." I walked over to his shop without delay. But when, triumphantly, he held up a small Latin dictionary, my heart sank and I found myself feeling—such is the force of the conditioned reflex—some of the weariness of spirit which such objects had evoked during my school days, nearly half a century ago. True, this particular dictionary was the work of an *Agrégé des Classes de Grammaire des Lycées,* and the equivalents of the Latin words were in French. But the resemblance to Dr. Smith was sufficiently close to trigger my customary reaction. Looking at it, I felt all of a sudden like one who has just inhaled a lungful of stale air at the entrance to a subway station. But then the book was opened and reverently laid before me. On the almost blank flyleaf was an exquisite pen-and-ink drawing of three horses in tandem straining on the traces of a heavy two-wheeled cart. It was a marvel of expressiveness, of truth to nature, of economy of means. How had this lovely thing found its way into the dismal counterpart of Shorter Smith? The answer, when it came, was as simple as it was surprising. This dictionary had belonged, in the late seventies and earliest eighties of the last century, to a boy called Henri de Toulouse-Lautrec.

In 1880, when most of these drawings were made, Toulouse-Lautrec was sixteen. The first of the two accidents which were to transform a merely delicate child into a grotesquely deformed cripple had taken place in the spring of 1878; the second, fifteen months later, in the late summer of 1879. By 1880 the broken thighbones had mended, more or less; and he still believed—to judge from the pictures he drew of himself at this time—that his legs would start growing again. He was mistaken. His trunk developed normally and became in due course the torso of an adult man; the legs remained what they had been at the time of his first fall, the short, spindly shanks of a boy of fourteen. Meanwhile life had to be lived; and in spite of pain, in spite of enforced inactivity, in spite of the suspicion and then the certainty that henceforward he had to face the world as a dwarfish monster, Lautrec lived it with unfailing courage and irrepressible high spirits. His education, interrupted after less than three years at the *lycée*, was carried on under private tutors, and in 1880 he sat for his baccalaureate examination, failed, took the test again in 1881 and came through with flying colors. It was in the interval between the two examinations that he decorated the margins of his dictionary with the drawings at which I was now looking, entranced, in Jake Zeitlin's shop.

Up to the age of ten (provided of course that his teachers don't interfere) practically every child paints like a genius. Fifteen years later the chances of his still painting like a genius are about four hundred thousand to one. Why this infinitesimal minority should fulfill the promise of childhood, while all the rest either dwindle into mediocrity or forget the very existence of the art they once practiced (within the limits of childish capacity) with such amazing skill and originality, is an unsolved riddle. When we have learned its answer, we may be able to transform education from the sadly disappointing affair it now is into the instrument of social and individual reconstruction which it ought to be. Meanwhile we can only record the facts without understanding them. For some as yet entirely mysterious reason, Lautrec was one of the infinitesimal minority. His interest in painting began very early and along with it, presumably, went the ordinary childish genius. At three, it is recorded, he asked to be allowed to sign the parish register on the occasion of his baby brother's christening. It was objected, not unreasonably, that he didn't know how to write. "Very well," he answered, "I will draw an ox." Throughout his childhood oxen remained a favorite subject; and along with oxen, dogs, poultry, falcons (his father, Count Alphonse de Toulouse-Lautrec, was a passionate falconer), and above all horses. He would spend long hours in the barnyard of one or other of the family châteaux, gazing intently at the birds and animals. And what he saw he remembered, not vaguely and imprecisely as the rest of us remember things, but in all its detail. And later, when the imaginative and symbolic art of childhood gave place to his first adolescent essays in representation, he was able to reproduce these memories with amazing precision. Later, as a mature artist, he seldom used models; he preferred to rely on a memory which could supply him with everything he needed. Is this kind of memory inborn, or can it be acquired by suitable training Are we all capable of accurate recall, and do we fail to realize our innate potentialities because of some improper use of our minds and bodies? Here is another riddle which educators might profitably investigate.

Lautrec was good at Latin and in the course of his three years at school carried off several prizes for composition and translation. But proficiency did not exclude boredom, and when the learned foolery of grammar and versification became unbearable, he would open the equivalent of Shorter Smith, dip his pen in the ink and draw a tiny masterpiece. "Dictionnaire Latin-Français." Above the words is a cavalryman galloping to the left, a jockey walking his horse towards the right. We open the book at random and find "Prophetice, Propheticus," with a falcon alighting on them. "Coetus" and "Cohaerentia" are topped by a pair of horse's hoofs, glimpsed from the back as the animal canters past. Two pages of the preface are made beautiful, the first by an unusually large drawing of a tired old nag, the second by a no less powerful version of the three horses in tandem which adorned the flyleaf.

The draftsman was only sixteen; but these furtive doodlings, while his tutor's back was turned, are the works of an already mature artist, and exhibit an easy mastery of the medium and an understanding of the subject matter which, in the case even of men of outstanding talent, are

ordinarily the fruit of long experience and constant practice. Lautrec's master, the academician and fashionable
portrait painter, Bonnat, was of another opinion. "Perhaps
you are curious to know," the boy wrote in a letter to his
Uncle Charles, "what sort of encouragement I am getting
from Bonnat. He tells me: 'Your painting isn't bad; it's
clever, but still it isn't bad. But your drawing is simply
atrocious.'" This to a pupil who could scribble from
memory little things of which even the greatest master
would not feel ashamed! The reason for Bonnat's disap-
proval becomes clear when we read what a fellow student
wrote of Lautrec in the life class. "He made a great effort to copy the model exactly; but in spite of himself he
exaggerated certain typical details, sometimes the general
character, so that he distorted without trying to or even
wanting to. I have seen him forcing himself to 'prettify' his
study of a model—in my opinion, without success. The
expression *'se forcer à faire joli'* is his own."

The word "fact" is derived from *"factum,"* something
made. And in fact, a fact is never as we like to suppose, a
wholly independent, given thing, but always what we
choose to make of that given thing. A fact is that particular version of the given which, in any particular context,
we find useful. The same event, say the explosion of an
H-bomb, is simultaneously a fact in the sphere of physics
and chemistry, a fact in physiology, medicine, and genet-
ics, a psychological fact, a political fact, an economic
fact, an ethical fact, even an aesthetic fact—for the atomic
cloud is wonderfully beautiful. A great representational artist, such as Lautrec or Goya, as Degas or Rembrandt,
is interested in several aspects of experience—the aesthetic,
the biological, the psychological, and sometimes, the
ethical—and the facts which he sets down on paper or canvas are forms which he extracts from given reality, which
he *makes,* for the purpose of expressing and communicat-
ing his own special preoccupations. For this reason he
finds no incompatibility between truth to nature and distortion. Indeed, if there is to be truth to the particular
aspects of nature in which he is interested, there must
be a certain amount of distortion. Sometimes the distortion is mainly a matter of omission. (Few even of the
most realistic painters portray *every* eyelash.) Sometimes
it is due to an exaggeration of that which, in the given, reveals most clearly the side of Nature to which the artist

aspires to be true. Hsieh Ho, the fifth-century Chinese artist who formulated the famous Six Principles of Chinese painting, expresses the same truth in another way. "The first principle is that, through a vitalizing spirit, a painting should possess the movement of life." A number of other renderings of the First Principle have been suggested, such as "a painting should possess rhythmic vitality"; "a painting should express the life movement of the spirit through the rhythm of things"; "a painting should manifest the fusion of the rhythm of the spirit with the movement of living things." But, however the renderings may vary, "it is quite evident," in the words of the great Sinologist, Osvald Sirén, "that the First Principle refers to something beyond the material form, call it character, soul, or expression. It depends on the operation of the spirit, or the mysterious breath of life, by which the figures may become as though they were moving or breathing." It is to this rhythm of the spirit manifested by the movement of given events that the artist pays attention; and in order to render this spiritual essence of things, he may be compelled to distort appearances, to refrain both from exactly copying or conventionally prettifying. In his own way Lautrec was a faithful exponent of Hsieh Ho's First Principle. Even as a boy, as yet completely ignorant of the masters under whose influence his mature style was to be formed, Hokusai, Degas, Goya, even in the margins of his Latin dictionary he was making manifest the vitalizing spirit in the movements of life.

The horse is now an almost extinct animal and in a few years, I suppose, will be seen only in zoos and, perhaps, on race tracks and in the parks of Texas oil millionaires. For the man in the street—a street now blessedly undefiled by the mountains of dung which, in my childhood used to make of every metropolis an Augean stable—the disappearance of the horse is a blessing. For the budding artist, it is a disaster. The Percheron, the thoroughbred hunter, the sleek cob, the splendid creatures that drew the rich man's carriage, even the miserable hacks in the shafts of cabs and omnibuses—each in its own way manifestly embodied the rhythm of the spirit in the movement of its equine life. Today, in the great cities of Europe and America, the movement of life is confined to human beings, most of whom are incredibly graceless, and to a few dogs, cats, and starlings. Communications are assured (and at the same time obstructed) by automobiles. But automobiles completely lack the movement of life. They are static objects fitted with a motor. To make them look as though they had the movement of life, their manufacturers give them inconvenient shapes and decorate them with arrowy strips of chromium. But it is all in vain. The most rakish sports car remains, even at a hundred miles an hour, essentially undynamic. Whereas even at five miles an hour, even a cab horse is a manifestation of life movement, an embodiment of the rhythm of the spirit. In the past, the horse was ubiquitous. Wherever he turned the young artist saw life movement. Walking or trotting, cantering or galloping, it challenged his powers of representation and expression, it spurred him to explore the underlying mystery of the spirit which lives and moves in forms. What amazing works of art have owed their existence to the horse! In ancient Mesopotamia, in Greece, in China and Japan, among the Etruscans and at Rome, in the battle pictures of the Renaissance, in scores of paintings by Rubens, by Velázquez, by Géricault, by Delacroix— what a cavalcade! The invention of the internal-combustion engine has deprived the painters and sculptors of the twentieth century of one of the richest sources of artistic inspiration. Along with Degas, Lautrec was almost the last of the great portrayers of horses. Indeed, if Count Alphonse had had his way, Henri would never have painted anything else. "This little book," wrote the count on the flyleaf of a manual of falconry presented to his son when he was eleven, "will teach you to enjoy the life of the great outdoors, and if one day you should experience the bitterness of life, dogs and falcons and, above all, horses will be your faithful companions and will help you to forget a little." And it is not only the bitterness of human life, it is also its appalling vulgarity that dogs and falcons and horses will help us forget. This, surely, is why Disney's nature films have achieved so wide a popularity. After an overdose of all too human hams, what an enormous relief to see even a tarantula, even a pair of scorpions! But, alas, life in the great outdoors was not the life which fate had prepared for Henri de Toulouse-Lautrec. His accident debarred him from participation in any form of sport or country exercise. And although he still loved horses and was never tired of studying their life movements at the circus and on the race track, he loved Montmartre and alcohol, cabaret singers and prostitutes with an even intenser passion. "Any curiosity," wrote one of his friends, "delighted him, stirred him to joyful enthusiasm. He would fish out such odds and ends as a Japanese wig, a ballet slipper, a peculiar hat, a shoe with an exaggeratedly high heel and show them to you with the most amusing remarks; or else he would unexpectedly turn up, in the pile of debris, a fine Hokusai print, a letter written by a pimp to his mistress, a set of photographs of such splendid masterpieces of painting as Uccello's 'Battle' in the National Gallery or Carpaccio's 'Courtesans Playing with Animals' in the Correr Museum, all of which he accompanied by enthusiastic exclamations and sensitive or explosive comments." The drunks and tarts, the lecherous gentlemen in top hats, the sensation-hunting ladies in feather boas, the stable boys, the Lesbians, the bearded surgeons performing operations with a horrifying disregard of the first principles of asepsis—these also were curiosities, more remarkable even than Japanese wigs, and these became the subject matter of most of Lautrec's pictures, the environment in which he liked to live. He portrayed them simply as curiosities, passing no moral judgment, merely rendering the intrinsic oddity of what he saw around him. It was in this spirit of the curiosity hunter, the collector of odds and ends, that he visited the theater. Plays as such did not interest him. Good or bad, they were merely strings of words. What he liked in a theater was not the literature, but the actors—the way they grimaced and gesticulated, the curious effects produced by the lights from above and beneath, the garish costumes moving against preposterously romantic backgrounds of painted canvas. The first beginnings of this interest in the theater are visible in Lautrec's dictionary. Above *"pugillus,"* there is a diminutive jester in cap and bells—a memory, presumably, of some figure seen during the carnival at Nice. And encroaching upon *"Quamprimum, Quamquam, Quamvis"* and *"Quanam"* is a personage whose attitude and vaguely medieval costume would seem to be those of an actor in one of the touring companies which Henri may have seen on the Riviera. And finally, opposite *"Naenia"* (the word for "funeral chant") there is a beautiful sketch of a young actress dressed as a page in tights (for legs were not bared until well after the first World War), the briefest of trunk hose, and a doublet. There is no effort in this or any other drawing by the youthful Lautrec to stress the femininity of his model. Our current obsession with the bosom is conspicuously absent. Generally speaking, hope springs eternal in the male breast in regard to the female breast. Here there is no undue optimism. In Lautrec, the clearsighted artist is stronger than the yearning adolescent, as it was to be stronger, later on, than the frequenter of brothels. There is never anything sexy about Lautrec's art; but there also is never anything deliberately, sarcastically antifeminist in it. Degas, it is evident, took pleasure in posing his models in the most unalluring postures. A lady who had visited an exhibition of his works once asked him why he chose to make all his women look so ugly. "Madame," the painter replied, "because women generally *are* ugly." Unlike Degas, Lautrec never set out to prove that they were either ugly or attractive. He just looked at them, as he had looked from his earliest childhood at oxen, horses, falcons, dogs; then, from memory and with appropriate distortions, rendered their life movement, now graceful, now grotesque, and the underlying rhythm of the mysterious spirit that manifests itself in every aspect of our beautiful, frightful, unutterably odd and adorable universe.

7

On the Absence of Painters in the Tropics•

No good pictures have ever been painted, so far as I am aware, of tropical landscapes. Here are two good reasons for this, of which the first is that no good painters have ever worked in the tropics. True, the temples of Ceylon, the ghats at Benares, Penang harbor, the palms and fantastic volcanoes of Java are annually reproduced in fifty thousand water colors. But they are the water colors of amateurs. We have all seen them. They are the stuff that oleographs are made of. If it were not for the fact that they kept their creators harmlessly busy and contented, they ought to be put down by law. The tropics and the East are given over to amateurs. Practically every tourist who travels through them carries a paintbox. But how few serious and competent professionals ever accompany these tourists. It is difficult indeed to think of any who have ever crossed the Line. Professional painters of merit are generally poor, and their absence from the tropics may be due in part to their poverty. But poverty is not an insuperable barrier to a determined artist, and the real reason, I believe, why painters avoid the tropics is that they know them to be unpaintable. In this intrinsic unpaintableness consists the second and most adequate reason for the nonexistence of decent pictures of tropical scenery.

• From *Jesting Pilate* ("Labuan"), 1926.

It is a significant fact that the scenery which the enthusiastic amateur finds most picturesque, most richly "paintable"—it is a favorite word of water-coloring spinsters —is the scenery most carefully avoided by serious professionals. Turner is one of the few great landscape painters who ever chose to represent picturesque subjects. The rest have always preferred to meditate before more ordinary, less spectacular scenes. Italy offers extravagant beauties; but the English have obstinately gone on painting in the placid home countries of their own islands; the French have never wandered further than to the bare hills of Provence; the Flemings have found their subjects within a hundred miles of Antwerp; the Dutch have stuck to their polders and estuaries. Strange at first sight, the phenomenon is easily explained. A picturesque landscape (which is, by definition, a landscape naturally possessing some of the qualities of a man-made picture) is one which inevitably imposes itself on the painter. In the face of its overwhelming grandiosities, its naturally dramatic character, its ready-made composition, he finds himself being reduced to the role of a merely passive recording instrument. That is all very well for the amateurs. A picturesque landscape excuses them from making any creative gesture of their own; all they have to do is to sit down and faithfully copy. But the serious painter does not want to be imposed upon by his subject; he wants to impose himself on it. He does not want to be excused from making an effort of his own. On the contrary, he feels impelled by his talent to make the creative gesture which molds the chaos of the world into an ordered and human cosmos—which turns nature into art. That is why he avoids the rich, the picturesque, the imposing, the dramatic. He wants a plain, and almost neutral subject, on which he can impress his own human ideas of composition and harmony, his own conception of the grand and the dramatic. The quiet English downland is less definitely formed than the prodigious landscapes of the Alban Hills; Flanders and the lower Seine are more malleable, so to speak, more amenable to artistic treatment, than the Bay of Naples; Delft is more easily digested by the intellect than Tivoli. Turner, it is true, could swallow Italy and turn it into art; but then he was a kind of spiritual ostrich. Most painters prefer a lighter diet.

What is true of Italian is true, *a fortiori*, of tropical landscape. The picturesqueness of the most "paintable" parts of the tropical Orient is so excessive, that the serious artist must feel, when confronted with them, as though he were being bullied, robbed of his initiative, dictated to. He might enjoy looking at Java or Borneo; but he would never dream of painting there. If he wanted subjects to paint he would go back to Essex or Normandy.

Tropical landscapes besides being too picturesque to be turned into good pictures, are also too rich. Things in this part of the world have a way of being unmanageably thick on the ground. There is no room in a painting for the profusion that exists in tropical reality. The painter of the average tropical scene would have to begin by leaving nine tenths of reality out of his picture. That was what Gauguin, one of the few good painters who ever practiced in the tropics, habitually did. If he had not, there would have been no seeing the wood for the inordinate quantity of the trees.

The various aspects of the tropical world still await their interpreters. A hundred admirable painters have taught us to know what European landscapes really look like. But the artistic essence of the tropical Orient remains to be distilled. Java awaits its Gainsborough and its Constable; Benares its Caneletto. Sportsmen are plentiful in the Malayan forests, and sometimes they carry sketchbooks as well as rifles. But the Corot who will tell us how those forests should be seen has not yet walked among their green and leech-infested shadows. We are compelled to see the tropics either in terms of the snapshot, the amateur's imitation of the oleograph, or of the steamship company's poster. Palm trees, Reckitt's blue sky and ocean, purple mountains, silver or golden sands —as far as it goes, the steamship poster (which is at least the work of a professional) is remarkably truthful. When I saw the immense *Laconia* steaming into the harbor of Labuan, I could have believed myself in a London tube station, looking at the advertisements of winter cruises in the South Seas. But there is something more subtly and essentially real to be got out of the tropics than the amateur's water color and the steamship poster—something which we can all dimly recognize, but to which no professional seer has yet taught us to give a definite outline. English landscapes were beautiful before Gainsborough was born, and men were moved by the contemplation of their beauty; but it was Gainsborough who made the loveliness clearly visible, who gave it a name and a definition.

The best pictures of the tropics are in books. There is more of the essence and the inward reality of the tropics in a book by Conrad or Herman Melville, more in a good passage by H. M. Tomlinson, more even in the rather maudlin Pierre Loti than in any existing painting of the places they describe. But description, even the description of the most accomplished writers, is very unsatisfying and inadequate. And it is no use practicing symbolical evocations on those who have never seen the realities which it is desired to evoke. For those who have eaten a mutton pie, it is all very well to speak of "dreams of fleecy flocks, pent in a wheaten cell." But we may be quite sure that the congenital vegetarian would never succeed, with the help of only this recipe, in preparing the homely dish. The art of evocation is an admirable one; but when there is nothing in the reader's mind to be evoked, it is practiced in vain. It is no use whistling to a dog which isn't there. Symbolical evocation will never create a true picture of the tropics in the minds of those who have passed their lives in Bayswater. No, the only way of explaining to those who have never been there— as well as to those who have—what the tropics are really like, would be to distill them into pictures. The thing has never been done, and it seems to me quite probable, for the reasons I have already given, that it never will be.

8

Indian Water Colors•

The Lahore Museum is rich in Indo-Persian water colors of the Mogul period. A few of them are genuinely good. But all are in the highest degree "amusing" (and in these days, after all, it is to the amusing rather than to the good in art that we pay our tribute of admiration).

The subjects of these paintings are mostly scenes of domestic and courtly life, as it was lived in the great Imperial days. If we may judge by these representations, the distractions of the Moguls were remarkably simple, simpler even than those in vogue among the grandees of Europe at the same period. Hunting, war, and love-making, from time immemorial the sports of kings, were practiced as copiously and patronized as freely by Western potentates as by their Oriental cousins. But the amusement of "looking at the clouds" was never, so far as I am aware, a favorite pastime among the great of Europe. In India, on the contrary, it seems to have been one of the principal occupations of kings and queens. So ordinary was the pastime that the Mogul artists found it necessary to invent a special pictorial convention to represent it. These cloud-gazers, of whom quite a surprising number are portrayed in the pictures of the Lahore collection, are represented as standing or reclining on the roofs of their

• From *Jesting Pilate* (Lahore), 1926.

palaces looking up at a sky full of pitch-black vapors, against which a flight of somewhat heraldic swans stands out with a peculiar brilliance.

Innocent pleasures! The capacity to enjoy them is perhaps a sign of the superiority of Oriental civilization to our own. To Europeans, I am afraid, this "looking at the clouds" would seem a little tedious. But then, we are barbarians and entirely ignorant of the art of living. One of the choicest inventions in the field of this epicurean art, of which we hurried Westerners know so little, is frequently represented in these pictures. It is shown in almost all the numerous love scenes between black-bearded nawabs and fawn-eyed, trousered beauties, which form the nucleus of this delightful collection. Any fool, any savage can make love—of a kind. But it needs a *viveur* of genius to think of combining amorous dalliance—on carpets, be it added, of the most exquisite Persian design—with the leisured smoking of a silver and crystal hookah. That, surely, is true art.

Rimini was honored, that morning, by the presence of three distinguished visitors—ourselves and the Thaumaturgical Arm of St. Francis Xavier. Divorced from the rest of the saint's remains, whose home is a jewelled tabernacle in the church of Jesus at Old Goa, the Arm, like ourselves, was making an Italian tour. But while we poor common tourists were spending money on the way, the Thaumaturgical Arm—and this was perhaps its most miraculous achievement—was raking it in. It had only to show itself through the crystal window of the reliquary in which it traveled—a skeleton arm, with a huge amethyst ring still glittering on one of the fingers of its bony hand—to command the veneration of all beholders and a copper collection, thinly interspersed with nickel and the smallest paper The copper collection went to the foreign missions; what happened to the veneration, I do not venture to guess. It was set down, no doubt, with their offered pence, to the credit of those who felt it, in the recording angel's book.

I felt rather sorry for St. Francis Xavier's arm. The body of the saint, after translation from China to Malacca and from Malacca to India, now reposes, as I have said, in the gaudy shrine at Goa. After a life so extraordinarily strenuous as was his, the great missionary deserves to rest

• From *Essays New and Old*, 1927.

in peace. And so he does, most of him. But his right arm
has had to forgo its secular quiet; its missionary voyages
are not yet over. In its gold and crystal box it travels in-
defatigably through Catholic Christendom collecting pence
—"for spoiling Indian innocence," as Mr. Matthew Green
tersely and rather tartly put it, two hundred years ago.
Poor Arm!

We found it, that morning, in the church of San
Francesco at Rimini. A crowd of adorers filled the building
and overflowed into the street outside. The people seemed
to be waiting rather vaguely in the hope of something
thaumaturgical happening. Within the church, a long
queue of men and women shuffled slowly up into the
choir to kiss the jewelled bone-box and deposit their
soldi. Outside, among the crowd at the door of the
church, stood a number of hawkers, selling picture post
cards of the Thaumaturgical Arm and brief but fabulous
biographies of its owner. We got into conversation with
one of them, who told us that he followed the Arm from
town to town, selling his wares wherever it stopped to
show itself. The business seemed a tolerably profitable
one; it enabled him, at any rate, to keep a wife and
family living in comfort at Milan. He showed us their
photographs; mother and children—they all looked well
nourished. But, poor fellow! his business kept him almost uninterruptedly away from home. "What does one
marry for?" he said as he put the photographs back
into his pocket. "What?" He sighed and shook his head.
If only the Arm could be induced to settle down for a
little!

During the lunch hour the Arm was taken for a drive
round Rimini. Red and yellow counterpanes were hung
out of all the windows in its honor; the faithful waited
impatiently. And at last it came, driving in a very large,
very noisy and dirty old Fiat, accompanied, not, as one
might have expected, by the ecclesiastical dignitaries of
the city, but by seven or eight very secular young men in
black shirts, with frizzy hair, their trouser pockets bulging with automatic pistols—the committee of the local
Fascio, no doubt.

The Arm occupied the front seat, next the driver; the
Fascists lolled behind. As the car passed, the faithful did
a very curious thing; mingling the gestures of reverence
and applause, they fell on their knees and clapped their
hands. The Arm was treated as though it were a com-

bination of Jackie Coogan and the Host. After lunch, it was driven rapidly away to Bologna. The vendors of sacred pictures followed as fast as the Italian trains would take them, the crowd dispersed, and the church of San Francesco reverted to its habitual silence.

For this we were rather glad; for it was not to see a fragment of St. Francis Xavier that we had come to Rimini; it was to look at the church of St. Francis of Assisi. Sight-seeing, so long as the Arm was there, had been impossible; its departure left us free to look round at our ease. Still, I was very glad that we had seen the peripatetic relic and its adorers in San Francesco. In this strange church which Malatesta found a Christian temple, rebuilt in pagan form and rededicated to himself, his mistress, and the humanities, the scenes we had just witnessed possessed a certain piercing incongruousness that provoked—the wit of circumstances—a kind of meditative mirth. I tried to imagine what the first St. Francis would have thought of Sigismondo Malatesta, what Sigismondo thought of him, and how he would have regarded the descration of his Nietzschean temple by this posthumous visit of a bit of the second St. Francis. One can imagine a pleasant little Gobinesque or Lucianic dialogue between the four of them in the Elysian fields, a light and airy skating over the most fearful depths of the spirit. And for those who have ears to hear there is eloquence in the dumb disputation of the stones. The Gothic arches of the interior protest against the Roman shell with which Alberti enclosed St. Francis's church; protest aginst Matteo de Pasti's pagan decorations and Malatesta's blasphemous self-exaltation; protest, while they commend the missionary's untiring disinterestedness, against the excessive richness of his Jesuit reliquary. Grave, restrained, and intellectual, Alberti's classical façade seems to deplore the *naïveté* of the first St. Francis and the intolerant enthusiasms of the second, and, praising Malatesta's intelligence, to rebuke him for his lusts and excesses. Malatesta, meanwhile, laughs cynically at all of them. Power, pleasure, and Isotta—these, he announces, through the scheme of decorations which he made Matteo de Pasti carry out, these are the only things that matter.

The exterior of the church is entirely Alberti's. Neither St. Francis nor Malatesta are allowed to disturb its solemn and harmonious beauty. Its façade is a triumphal arch, a nobler version of that arch of Augustus which spans the

street at the other end of Rimini. In the colossal thickness
of the southern wall, Alberti has pierced a series of deep
arched niches. Recessed shadow alternates harmoniously
down a long perspective with smooth sunlit stone; and in
every niche, plain and severe like the character of an
early Roman in the pages of Plutarch, stands the sarcophagus of a scholar or a philosopher. There is nothing
here of St. Francis's prelapsarian ingenuousness. Alberti
is an entirely conscious adult; he worships, but worships
reason, rationally. The whole building is a hymn to intellectual beauty, an exaltation of reason as the only source
of human greatness. Its form is Roman; for Rome was
the retrospective Utopia in which such men as Alberti,
from the time of the Renaissance down to a much later
date, saw the fulfillment of their ideals. The Roman myth
dies hard, the Greek harder still; there are certain victims
of a classical education who still regard the Republic as
the home of all virtues and see in Periclean Athens the
unique repository of human intelligence.

Malatesta would have got a better personal apotheosis
if he had lived in a later century. Alberti was too severe
and stoical an artist to condescend to mere theatrical
grandiosity. Nor, indeed, was the art of being grandiose
really understood till the seventeenth century, the age of
baroque, of kingly and clerical display. The hard-working
missionary, whose arm we had seen that morning in Malatesta's temple, reposes at Goa in the sort of surroundings
that would be perfectly suitable in a tyrant's self-raised
shrine. Alberti's monument, on the contrary, is a tribute
to intellectual greatness. As a memorial to a particularly
cunning and murderous ruffian it is absurd.

In the interior of the church, it is true, Malatesta had
things all his own way. Alberti was not there to interfere
in his scheme of decoration, so that Sigismondo was able
to dictate to Matteo de Pasti and his colleagues all the
themes of their carving. The interior is consequently one
vast personal tribute to Malatesta and Isotta, with an occasional good word in favor of the pagan gods, of literature, art, and science. The too expressive theatrical gesture
of the baroque architects and decorators had not yet
been invented; Sigismondo's vulgar tyranny is consequently
celebrated in the most perfect taste and in terms of a
delicate and learned fantasy. Sigismondo got better than
his deserts; he deserved Borromini, the Cavaliere Arpino
and a tenth-rate imitator of Bernini. What he actually got,

owing to the accident of his date, was Matteo de Pasti, Piero della Francesca, and Leon Battista Alberti.

Alberti's share in the monument, then, is a kind of hymn to intellectual beauty, a paean in praise of civilization, couched in the language of Rome—but freely and not pedantically employed, as the philosophers and the poets of the age employed the Latin idiom. To my mind, he was almost the noblest Roman of them all. The exterior of San Francesco at Rimini, the interior of Sant' Andrea at Mantua (sadly daubed about by later decorators and with Juvara's absurd high-drummed cupola in the midst instead of the saucer dome designed by Alberti himself), are as fine as anything in the whole range of Renaissance architecture. What renders them the more remarkable is that they were without precedent in his age. Alberti was one of the reinventors of the style. Of his particular Roman manner, indeed (the manner which became the current idiom of the later Renaissance), he was the sole rediscoverer. The other early Renaissance manner, based, like Alberti's, on the classics—the manner of Brunelleschi —was doomed, so far at any rate as ecclesiastical architecture was concerned, to extinction. Sant' Andrea at Mantua is the model from which the typical churches of the later Renaissance were imitated, not Brunelleschi's Florentine San Lorenzo or Santo Spirito.

A comparison between these nearly contemporary architects—Brunelleschi was born some twenty-five years before Alberti—is extremely interesting and instructive. Both were enthusiastic students of the antique, both knew their Rome, both employed in their buildings the characteristic elements of classical architecture. And yet it would be difficult to discover two architects whose work is more completely dissimilar. Compare the interiors of Brunelleschi's two Florentine churches with that of Alberti's Sant' Andrea. Brunelleschi's churches are divided into a nave and aisles by rows of tall slender pillars supporting round arches. The details are classical and so correct that they might have been executed by Roman workmen. But the general design is not Roman, but Romanesque. His churches are simply more spidery versions of eleventh-century basilicas, with "purer" details. All is airiness and lightness; there is even a certain air of insecurity about these church interiors, so slender are the pillars, so much free space is to be seen.

What a contrast with Alberti's great church! It is built

in the form of a Latin cross, with a single nave and side chapels. The nave is barrel-vaulted; over the crossing is a dome (Juvara's, unfortunately, not Alberti's), the altar is placed in an apse. The chapels open on to the central nave by tall, and proportionately wide, round-headed arches. Between each of the chapels is a gigantic pier of masonry, as wide as the arches which they separate. A small door is pierced in each of these piers, giving access to subsidiary chapels hollowed out of their mass. But the doors are inconspicuous, and the general effect is one of void and solid equally alternating. Alberti's is essentially the architecture of masses, Brunelleschi's of lines. Even to the enormous dome of Santa Maria del Fiore, Brunelleschi contrives to impart an extraordinary lightness, as of lines with voids between them. The huge mass hangs aerially from its eight ribs of marble, A miracle is effortlessly consummated before our eyes. But a dome, however light you make it, is essentially an affair of masses. In designing his cupola for Santa Maria del Fiore, Brunelleschi found the plastic view of things imposed upon him. That is why, it may be, the dome is so incomparably the finest thing he ever made. He was not permitted by the nature of the architectural problem to be solved to give free play to his passion for lightness and the fine line. He was dealing here with masses; it could not be escaped. The result was that, treating the mass of the dome as far as was possible in terms of light, strong, leaping lines, he contrived to impart to his work an elegance and an aerial strength such as have never been equalled in any other dome. The rest of Brunelleschi's work, however charming and graceful, is, to my mind at any rate, far less satisfying, precisely because it is so definitely an affair of lines. Brunelleschi studied the architecture of the Romans; but he took from it only its details. What was essential in it—its majestic massiveness —did not appeal to him. He preferred, in all his church designs, to refine and refine on the work of the Romanesque architects, until at last he arrived at a slender and precarious elegance that was all vacuum and outline.

Alberti, on the other hand, took from the Romans their fundamental conception of an architecture of masses and developed it, with refinements, for modern Christian uses. To my mind, he was the better and truer architect of the two. For I personally like massiveness and an air of solidity. Others, I know, prefer lines and lightness and would put the interior of San Lorenzo above that of Sant' Andrea, the Pazzi chapel above San Francesco at Rimini. We shall never be reconciled. All who practice the visual arts, and, presumably, all who appreciate them must have some kind of feeling for form as such. But not all are interested in the same kind of forms. The lovers of pure line and the lovers of mass stand at opposite ends of an aesthetic scale. The aesthetic passion of one artist, or one art lover, is solidity; another is moved only by linear arabesques on a flat surface. Those formal passions may be misplaced. Painters may be led by their excessive love of three-dimensional solidity quite beyond the field of painting; Michelangelo is an obvious example. Sculptors with too great a fondness for mere linear effect cease to be sculptors, and their work is no more than a flat decoration in stone or metal, meant to be seen from only one point of view and having no depth; the famous Diana attributed to Goujon (but probably by Benvenuto Cellini) is one of these statues conceived in the flat. Just as painters must not be too fond of solidity, nor sculptors too much attached to flatness, so, it seems to me, no architect should be too exclusively interested in lines. Architecture in the hands of a linear enthusiast takes on the too slender, spidery elegance of Brunelleschi's work.

The psychoanalysts, who trace all interest in art back to an infantile love of excrement, would doubtless offer some simple fecal explanation for the varieties in our aesthetic passions. One man loves masses, another lines; the explanation in terms of coprophily is so obvious that I may be excused from giving it here. I will content myself by quoting from the works of Dr. Ernest Jones the reason why the worship of form should come to be connected in so many cases with the worship of a moral ideal; in a word, why art is so often religious. "Religion," says Dr. Jones, "has always used art in one form or another, and must do so, for the reason that incestuous desires invariably construct their phantasies out of the material provided by the unconscious memory of infantile coprophilic interests; that is the inner meaning of the phrase, 'Art is the handmaid of Religion.'" Illuminating and beautiful words! It is a pity they were not written thirty years ago. I should have liked to read Tolstoy's comments in *What is Art?* on this last and best of the aesthetic theories.

2

Sir Christopher Wren•

That an Englishman should be a very great plastic artist
is always rather surprising. Perhaps it is a matter of mere
chance; perhaps it has something to do with our national
character—if such a thing really exists. But, whatever may
be the cause, the fact remains that England has produced
very few artists of first-class importance. The Renaissance,
as it spread, like some marvellous infectious disease of the
spirit, across the face of Europe, manifested itself in
different countries by different symptoms. In Italy, the
country of its origin, the Renaissance was, more than anything, an outburst of painting, architecture, and sculpture.
Scholarship and religious reformation were, in Germany,
the typical manifestations of the disease. But when this
gorgeous spiritual measles crossed the Eglish Channel, its
symptoms were almost exclusively literary. The first pre-
monitory touch of the infection from Italy "brought out"
Chaucer. With the next bout of the disease England produced the Elizabethans. But among all these poets there
was not a single plastic artist whose name we so much as
remember.

And then, suddenly, the seventeenth century gave birth
to two English artists of genius. It produced Inigo
Jones and, a little later, Wren. Wren died, at the age of

• From *On the Margin*, 1923.

more than ninety, in the spring of 1723. We are celebrating today his bicentenary—celebrating it not merely by antiquarian talk and scholarly appreciations of his style but also (the signs are not wanting) in a more concrete and living way: by taking a renewed interest in the art of which he was so great a master and by reverting in our practice to that fine tradition which he, with his predecessor, Inigo, inaugurated.

An anniversary celebration is an act of what Wordsworth would have called "natural piety"; an act by which past is linked with present and of the vague, interminable series of the days a single, comprehensible, and logical unity is created in our minds. At the coming of the centenaries we like to remember the great men of the past, not so much by way of historical exercise, but that we may see precisely where, in relation to their achievement, we stand at the present time, that we may appraise the life still left in their spirit and apply to ourselves the moral of their example. I have no intention in this article of giving a biography of Wren, a list of his works, or a technical account of his style and methods. I propose to do no more than describe, in the most general terms, the nature of his achievement and its significance to ourselves.

Wren was a good architect. But since it is important to know precisely what we are talking about, let us begin by asking ourselves what good architecture is. Descending with majesty from his private Sinai, Mr. Ruskin dictated to a whole generation of Englishmen the aesthetic Law. On monolithic tables that were the Stones of Venice he wrote the great truths that had been revealed to him. Here is one of them:

> It is to be generally observed that the proportions of buildings have nothing to do with the style or general merit of their architecture. An architect trained in the worst schools and utterly devoid of all meaning or purpose in his work, may yet have such a natural gift of massing and grouping as will render his structure effective when seen at distance.

Now it is to be generally observed, as he himself would say, that in all matters connected with art, Ruskin is to be interpreted as we interpret dreams—that is to say, as signifying precisely the opposite of what he says. Thus, when we find him saying that good architecture has

nothing to do with proportion or the judicious disposition of masses and that the general effect counts for nothing at all, we may take it as more or less definitely proven that good architecture is, in fact, almost entirely a matter of proportion and massing, and that the general effect of the whole work counts for nearly everything. Interpreted according to this simple oneirocritical method, Ruskin's pontifical pronouncement may be taken as explaining briefly and clearly the secrets of good architecture. That is why I have chosen this quotation to be the text of my discourse on Wren.

For the qualities which most obviously distinguish Wren's work are precisely those whch Ruskin so contemptuously disparages and which we, by our process of interpretation, have singled out as the essentially architectural qualities. In all that Wren designed—I am speaking of the works of his maturity; for at the beginning of his career he was still an unpracticed amateur, and at the end, though still on occasion wonderfully successful, a very old man—we see a faultless proportion, a felicitous massing and contrasting of forms. He conceived his buildings as three-dimensional designs which should be seen, from every point of view, as harmoniously proportioned wholes. (With regard to the exteriors this, of course, is true only of those buildings which *can* be seen from all sides. Like all true architects, Wren preferred to build in positions where his work could be appreciated three-dimensionally. But he was also a wonderful maker of façades; witness his Middle Temple gateway and his houses in King's Bench Walk.) He possessed in the highest degree that instinctive sense of proportion and scale which enabled him to embody his conception in brick and stone. In his great masterpiece of St. Paul's every part of the building, seen from within or without, seems to stand in a certain satisfying and harmonious relation to every other part. The same is true even of the smallest works belonging to the period of Wren's maturity. On its smaller scale and different plane, such a building as Rochester Guildhall is as beautiful, because as harmonious in the relation of all its parts, as St. Paul's.

Of Wren's other purely architectural qualities I shall speak but briefly. He was, to begin with, an engineer of inexhaustible resource; one who could always be relied upon to find the best possible solution to any problem, from blowing up the ruins of old St. Paul's to providing the new with a dome that should be at once beautiful and thoroughly safe. As a designer he exhibited the same practical ingenuity. No architect has known how to make so much of a difficult site and cheap materials. The man who built the City churches was a practical genius of no common order. He was also an artist of profoundly original mind. This originality reveals itself in the way in which he combines the accepted features of classical Renaissance architecture into new designs that were entirely English and his own. The steeples of his City churches provide us with an obvious example of this originality. His domestic architecture—that wonderful application of classical principles to the best in the native tradition—is another.

But Wren's most characteristic quality—the quality which to his work, over and above its pure beauty, its own peculiar character and charm—is a quality rather moral than aesthetic. Of Chelsea Hospital, Carlyle once remarked that it was "obviously the work of a gentleman." The words are illuminating. Everything that Wren did was the work of a gentleman; that is the secret of its peculiar character. For Wren was a great gentleman: one who valued dignity and restraint and who, respecting himself, respected also humanity; one who desired that men and women should live with the dignity, even the grandeur, befitting their proud human title; one who despised meanness and oddity as much as vulgar ostentation; one who admired reason and order, who distrusted all extravagance and excess. A gentleman, the finished product of an old and ordered civilization.

Wren, the restrained and dignified gentleman, stands out most clearly when we compare him with his Italian contemporaries. The baroque artists of the seventeenth century were interested above everything in the new, the startling, the astonishing; they strained after impossible grandeurs, unheard-of violences. The architectural ideals of which they dreamed were more suitable for embodiment in theatrical cardboard than in stone. And indeed, the late seventeenth and early eighteenth century was the golden age of scene painting in Italy. The artists who painted the settings for the elder Scarlatti's operas, the later Bibienas and Piranesis, came nearer to reaching the wild Italian ideal than ever mere architects like Borromini or Bernini, their imaginations cramped by the stub-

bornness of stone and the unsleeping activities of gravitations, could hope to do.

How vastly different is the baroque theatricality from Wren's sober restraint! Wren was a master of the grand style; but he never dreamed of building for effect alone. He was never theatrical or showy, never pretentious or vulgar. St. Paul's is a monument of temperance and chastity. His great palace at Hampton Court is no gaudy stage setting for the farce of absolute monarchy. It is a country gentleman's house—more spacious, of course, and with statelier rooms and more impressive vistas—but still a house meant to be lived in by someone who was a man as well as a king. But if his palaces might have housed, without the least incongruity, a well-bred gentleman, conversely his common houses were always dignified enough, however small, to be palaces in miniature and the homes of kings.

In the course of the two hundred years which have elapsed since his death, Wren's successors have often departed, with melancholy results, from the tradition of which he was the founder. They have forgotten, in their architecture, the art of being gentlemen. Infected by a touch of the baroque *folie de grandeur,* the architects of the eighteenth century built houses in imitation of Versailles and Caserta—huge stage houses, all for show and magnificence and all but impossible to live in.

The architects of the nineteenth century sinned in a diametrically opposite way—towards meanness and a negation of art. Senselessly preoccupied with details, they created the nightmare architecture of "features." The sham Gothic of early Victorian times yielded at the end of the century to the nauseous affectation of "sham peasantry." Big houses were built with all the irregularity and more than the "quaintness" of cottages; suburban villas took the form of machine-made imitations of the Tudor peasant's hut. To all intents and purposes architecture ceased to exist; Ruskin had triumphed.

Today, however, there are signs that architecture is coming back to that sane and dignified tradition of which Wren was the great exponent. Architects are building houses for gentlemen to live in. Let us hope that they will continue to do so. There may be sublimer types of men than the gentleman: there are saints, for example, and the great enthusiasts whose thoughts and actions move the world. But for practical purposes and in a civilized, orderly society, the gentleman remains, after all, the ideal man. The most profound religious emotions have been expressed in Gothic architecture. Human ambitions and aspirations have been most colossally reflected by the Romans and the Italians of the baroque. But it is in England that the golden mean of reasonableness and decency—the practical philosophy of the civilized man—has received its most elegant and dignified expression. The old gentleman who died two hundred years ago preached on the subject of civilization a number of sermons in stone. St. Paul's and Greenwich, Trinity Library and Hampton Court, Chelsea, Kilmainham, Blackheath and Rochester, St. Stephen's Wallbrook and St. Mary Abchurch, Kensington orangery and Middle Temple gateway—these are the titles of a few of them. They have much, if we will but study them, to teach us.

3

The Taj Mahal[•]

I am always a little uncomfortable when I find myself unable to admire something which all the rest of the world admires—or at least is reputed to admire. Am I, or is the world the fool? Is it the world's taste that is bad, or is mine? I am reluctant to condemn myself, and almost equally reluctant to believe that I alone am right. Thus, when all men (and not the professors of English literature only, but Milton too, and Wordsworth and Keats) assure me that Spenser is a great poet, I wonder what to do. For to me Spenser seems only a virtuoso, a man with the conjuror's trick of extracting perfectly rhymed stanzas by the hundred, out of an empty mind. Perhaps I am unduly prejudiced in favor of sense; but it has always seemed to me that poets should have something to say. Spenser's is the art of saying nothing, at length, in rhyme and rumbling meter. The world admires; but I cannot. I wish I could.

Here at Agra I find myself afflicted by the same sense of discomfort. The Taj Mahal is one of the seven wonders. My guide assures me that it is "perhaps the most beautiful building in the world." Following its advice, we drove out to have our first look at the marvel by the light of the setting sun. Nature did its best for the Taj. The west was

• From *Jesting Pilate* ("Agra"), 1926.

duly red, and orange, and yellow, and, finally, emerald green, grading into pale and flawless blue towards the zenith. Two evening stars, Venus and Mercury, pursued the sunken sun. The sacred Jumna was like a sheet of silver between its banks. Beyond it the plains stretched grayly away into the vapors of distance. The gardens were rich with turf, with cypresses, palms, and peepul trees, with long shadows and rosy lights, with the noise of grasshoppers, the calling of enormous owls, the indefatigable hammering of a coppersmith bird. Nature, I repeat, did its best. But though it adorned, it could not improve the works of man. The Taj, even at sunset, even reverberated upside down from tanks and river, even in conjunction with melancholy cypresses—the Taj was a disappointment.

My failure to appreciate the Taj is due, I think, to the fact that, while I am very fond of architecture and the decorative arts, I am very little interested in the expensive or the picturesque, as such and by themselves. Now the great qualities of the Taj are precisely those of expensiveness and picturesqueness. Milk-white amongst it dark cypresses, flawlessly mirrored, it is positively the *"Toteninsel"* of Arnold Böcklin come true. And its costliness is fabulous. Its marbles are carved and filigreed, are patterned with an inlay of precious stones. The smallest rose or poppy on the royal tombs is an affair of twenty or thirty cornelian onyxes, agates, chrysolites. The New Jerusalem was not more rich in variety of precious pebbles. If the Viceroy took it into his head to build another Taj identical with the first, he would have to spend as much as a fifteenth, or even perhaps a twelfth or tenth of what he spends each year on the Indian Army. Imagination staggers. . . .

This inordinate costliness is what most people seem to like about the Taj. And if they are disappointed with it (I have met several who were, and always for the same reason) it is because the building is not quite so expensive as they thought it was. Clambering among the roofs they have found evidence to show that the marble is only a veneer over cheaper masonry, not solid. It is a swindle! Meanwhile the guides and guardians are earning their money by insisting on the Taj's costliness. "All marble," they say, "all precious stones." They want you to touch as well as look, to realize the richness not with eyes alone, but intimately with the fingers. I have seen guides in Europe doing the same. Expensiveness is everywhere admired. The average tourist is moved to greater raptures by St. Peter's than by his own St. Paul's. The interior of the Roman basilica ia all of marble. St. Paul's is only Portland stone. The relative architectural merits of the two churches are not for a moment considered.

Architecturally, the worst features of the Taj are its minarets. These four thin tapering towers standing at the four corners of the platform on which the Taj is built are among the ugliest structures ever erected by human hands. True, the architect might offer a number of excuses for his minarets. He would begin by pointing out that, the dimensions of the main building and the platform being what they are, it was impossible to give the four subsidiary structures more than a certain limited mass between them, a mass small in proportion to the Taj itself. Architecturally, no doubt, it would have been best to put this definitely limited mass into four low buildings of comparatively large plan. But, unfortunately, the exigencies of religion made it necessary to put the available mass into minarets. This mass being small, it was necessary that the minarets should be very thin for their height.

These excuses, so far as they go, are perfectly valid. By the laws of religion there had to be minarets, and by the laws of proportion the minarets had to be unconscionably slender. But there was no need to make them feebly taper, there was no need to pick out the component blocks of which they are built with edgings of black, and above all there was no need to surround the shaft of the minarets with thick clumsy balconies placed, moreover, at just the wrong intervals of distance from one another and from the ground.

The Taj itself is marred by none of the faults which characterize the minarets. But its elegance is at the best of a very dry and negative kind. Its "classicism" is the product not of intellectual restraint imposed on an exuberant fancy, but of an actual deficiency of fancy, a poverty of imagination. One is struck at once by the lack of variety in the architectural forms of which it is composed. There are, for all practical purposes, only two contrasting formal elements in the whole design—the onion dome, reproduced in two dimensions in the pointed arches of the recessed bays, and the flat wall surface with its sharply rectangular limits. When the Taj is compared with more or less contemporary European buildings in the neoclassic style of the High Renaissance and baroque periods, this poverty in the formal elements composing it becomes very apparent. Consider, for example, St. Paul's. The number of component forms in its design is very large. We have the hemispherical dome, the great colonnaded cylinder of the drum, the flat side walls relieved by square-faced pilasters and rounded niches; we have, at one end, the curved surfaces of the apse and, at the other, the West Front with its porch—a design of detached cylinders (the pillars), seen against a flat wall, and supporting yet another formal element, the triangular pediment. If it is argued that St. Paul's is a very much larger building than the Taj, and that we should therefore expect the number of contrasting elements in its design to be greater, we may take a smaller specimen of late Renaissance architecture as our standard of comparison. I suggest Palladio's Rotonda at Vicenza, a building somewhat smaller than the Taj and, like it, of regular design and domed. Analyzing the Rotonda we shall find that it consists of a far larger number of formal elements than does the Taj, and that its elegance, in consequence, is much richer, much more subtle and various than the poor, dry, negative elegance characteristic of the Indian building.

But it is not necessary to go as far as Europe to find specimens of a more varied and imaginative elegance than that of the Taj. The Hindu architects produced buildings incomparably more rich and interesting as works of art. I have not visited Southern India, where, it is said, the finest specimens of Hindu architecture are to be found. But I have seen enough of the art in Rajputana to convince me of its enormous superiority to any work of the Mohammedans. The temples at Chitor, for example, are specimens of true classicism. They are the products of a prodigious, an almost excessive, fancy, held in check and directed by the most judicious intelligence. Their elegance —and in their way they are just as elegant as the Taj—is an opulent and subtle elegance, full of unexpected felicities. The formal elements of their design are numerous and pleasingly contrasted, and the detail—moldings and ornamental sculpture—is always, however copious, subordinated to the architectural scheme and of the highest decorative quality.

In this last respect Hindu ornament is decidedly superior to that employed by the later Moguls. The *pietra dura* work at the Taj and the Shahdara tombs at Lahore is marvelously neat in execution and of extravagant costliness. These qualities are admirable enough in their way; but they have nothing to do with the decorative value of the work considered as art. As works of art, the *pietra dura* decorations of the Taj are poor and uninteresting. Arabesques of far finer design are to be seen in the carved and painted ornamentation of Rajput palaces and temples. As for the *bas reliefs* of flowers which adorn the gateway of the Taj—these are frankly bad. The design of them vacillates uncertainly between realism and conventionalism. They are neither lifelike portraits of flowers nor good pieces of free floral decoration. How anyone who has ever seen a fine specimen of decorative flower painting or flower carving, whether Hindu or European, can possibly admire these feebly laborious reliefs passes my understanding. Indeed, it seems to me that anyone who professes an ardent admiration for the Taj must look at it without having any standards of excellence in his mind—as though the thing existed uniquely, in a vacuum. But the Taj exists in a world well sprinkled with masterpieces of architecture and decoration. Compare it with these, and the Imperial Mausoleum at once takes its proper place in the hierarchy of art—well down below the best. But it is made of marble. Marble, I perceive, covers a multitude of sins.

4

A Note on Architecture in India[•]

The fort of Chitor is larger than that of Jodhpur and therefore less spectacular. The Jodhpur fort is perched on the summit of what is almost a crag. The hill on which Chitor is built is probably as high, but it seems much lower, owing to its great length; it is a ridge, not a pinnacle of rock. And the buildings, which, at Jodhpur, are crowded into a single imposing pile, are scattered at wide intervals over the space enclosed within the circuit of the walls of Chitor. Jodhpur is wildly picturesque, like something out of a Doré picture book. Examined at close quarters, however, it is not particularly interesting. From a distance, Chitor is less imposing; but climb up to it, and you will find it full of magnificent buildings—temples among the finest in Upper India, great ruined palaces, towers fantastically carved from base to summit. None of these buildings is much more than five hundred years old; but time has dealt hardly with them. The soft stone of which they are built has crumbled away under the rain and sun and wind. The sharp edges have become blunt, the innumerable sculptures are blurred and defaced. The splendors of Hindu art are only dimly seen, as though through an intervening mist, or with myopic and unspectacled eyes.

• From *Jesting Pilate* ("Chitor"), 1926.

Decoration is costly nowadays and money scarce. Making a virtue of economic necessity, we have proclaimed the beauty of unadorned simplicity in art. In architecture, for example, we mistrust all "fussy details," and can admire only the fundamental solid geometry of a building. We like our furniture plain, our silver unchased, our stage scenery flat and unconventional. Our tastes will change, no doubt, when our purses grow longer. Meanwhile, simplicity is regarded as an almost necessary quality of good art.

But the facts are against us. The best art has not been always and necessarily the simplest. Profusion of decorative detail need not obscure the main lines of the composition considered as a whole. Those who require a more convincing proof of these statements than can be found at home, should come to India. They will find in the best specimens of Hindu architecture an unparalleled extravagance of decorative details, entirely subordinated to the main architectural design. It would be difficult to find on the walls of the Chitor temples a single blank square foot. But so far from distracting the attention from the architectural composition, the sculpture and the ornament serve to emphasize the characteristic forms and movements of the strange design. If the sculpture at Chitor is unsatisfactory, that is due, not to its elaborateness and profusion, but to its poor intrinsic quality. It is all fairly good, but none of it is first-rate. The innumerable carvings at Chitor are the product of a great anonymous labor. No great original artist stands out from among the craftsmen. It is all nameless, unindividual.

1

Gesualdo: Variations on a Musical Theme●

Space has been explored, systematically and scientifically, for more than five centuries; time, for less than
five generations. Modern geography began in the four-
teen-hundreds with the voyages of Prince Henry the
Navigator. Modern history and modern archaeology came
in with Queen Victoria. Except in the Antartic there
is today no such thing as a *terra incognita;* all the corners
of all the other continents have now been visited. In
contrast, how vast are the reaches of history which still
remain obscure! And how recently acquired is most of
our knowledge of the past! Almost everything we know
about paleolithic and neolithic man, about the Sumerian,
Hittite, and Minoan civilizations, about pre-Buddhist
India and pre-Columbian America, about the origins of
such fundamental human arts as agriculture, metallurgy,
and writing, was discovered within the last sixty or
seventy years. And there are still new worlds of history
to conquer. Even in such well-dug regions as the Near
and Middle East literally thousands of sites await the
burrowing archaeologist, and thousands more are scattered far and wide over Asia, Africa, and the Americas.
Moreover, there is work for the explorer in times and
cultures much nearer home. For, strange as it may seem, it

● From *Tomorrow and Tomorrow and Tomorrow,* 1956.

is only within the last generation that certain aspects of quite recent European history have come to be critically investigated. A very striking example of this failure to explore our own back yard is supplied by the history of music. Practically everybody likes music; but practically nobody has heard any music composed before 1680. Renaissance poetry, painting, and sculpture have been studied in minutest detail, and the labors of five generations of scholars have been made available to the public in hundreds of monographs, general histories, critical appreciations, and guidebooks. But Renaissance music —an art which was fully the equal of Renaissance poetry, painting, and sculpture—has received relatively little attention from scholars and is almost unknown to the concert-going public. Donatello and Piero della Francesca, Titian and Michelangelo—their names are household words and, in the original or in reproduction, their works are familiar to everyone. But how few people have heard, or even heard of, the music of Dufay and Josquin, of Okeghem and Obrecht, of Ysaac and Wert and Marenzio, of Dunstable, Byrd and Victoria! All that can be said is that, twenty years ago, the number was still smaller than it is today. And a couple of generations earlier the ignorance was almost total. Even so great a historian as Burckhardt— the man who wrote with such insight, such a wealth of erudition, about every other aspect of the Renaissance in Italy—knew next to nothing about the music of his chosen period. It was not his fault; there were no modern editions of the music and nobody ever played or sang it. Consider, by way of example, the *"Vespers,"* composed in 1610 by one of the most famous, one of the most historically important of Italian musicians, Claudio Monteverdi. After the middle of the seventeenth century this extraordinary masterpiece was never again performed until the year 1935. One can say without any exaggeration that, until very recent times, more was known about the Fourth Dynasty Egyptians, who built the pyramids, than about the Flemish and Italian contemporaries of Shakespeare who wrote the madrigals.

This sort of thing, let us remember, has happened before. From the time of the composer's death in 1750 to the performance under Mendelssohn, in 1829, of the *Passion According to St. Matthew,* no European audience had ever heard a choral work by John Sebastian Bach.

What Mendelssohn and the nineteenth-century musicologists, critics and virtuosi did for Bach another generation of scholars and performers has begun to do for Bach's predecessors, whose works have been rediscovered, published in critical editions, performed here and there, and even occasionally recorded. It is gradually dawning upon us that the three centuries before Bach are just as interesting musically speaking, as the two centuries after Bach.

There exists in Los Angeles a laudable institution called the Southern California Chamber Music Society. This society sponsors a series of Monday evening concerts, at which, besides much fine and seldom-heard classical and contemporary music, many pre-Bach compositions are performed. Among these earlier compositions one group stands out in my memory as uniquely interesting—a group of madrigals and motets by an almost exact contemporary of Shakespeare, Carlo Gesualdo. Another English poet, John Milton, was an admirer of Gesualdo and, while in Italy, bought a volume of his madrigals which, with a number of other books, he sent home by ship from Venice. Milton's admiration is understandable; for Gesualdo's music is so strange and, in its strangeness, so beautiful that it haunts the memory and fires the imagination. Listening to it, one is filled with questioning wonder. What sort of a man was it who wrote such music? Where does it fit into the general musical scheme, and what is its relevance for us? In the paragraphs that follow I shall try, in the light of my sadly limited knowledge of Gesualdo's time and of Gesualdo's art, to answer, or at least to speculate about, these questions.

Let us begin, then, with the biographical facts. Carlo Gesualdo was born in or about 1560, either at Naples or in one of his father's numerous castles in the neighborhood of Naples. The Gesualdi were of ancient and noble lineage, had been barons for fifteen generations, counts for eight, dukes for four or five, and, for the past three generations, hereditary Princes of Venosa. Carlo's mother hailed from northern Italy and was a sister of the great Cardinal Carlo Borromeo, who died in 1584 and was canonized in 1610. In his later years Gesualdo could speak not only of my father, the Prince, but even (going one better) of my uncle, the Saint. Of the boy's education we know nothing and can only infer, from his later achievements, that he must have had a very thorough grounding in music.

Every age has its own characteristic horrors. In ours there are the Communists and nuclear weapons, there are nationalism and the threat of overpopulation. The violence in which we indulge is truly monstrous; but it is, so to say, official violence, ordered by the proper authorities, sanctioned by law, ideologically justified, and confined to periodical world wars, between which we enjoy the blessings of law, order, and internal peace. In the Naples of Gesualdo's day, violence was ruggedly individualistic, unorganized, and chronic. There was little nationalism and world wars were unknown; but dynastic squabbles were frequent and the Barbary Corsairs were incessantly active, raiding the coasts of Italy in search of slaves and booty. But the citizen's worst enemies were not the pirates and the foreign princes; they were his own neighbors. Between the wars and the forays of the infidels there were no lucid intervals, such as we enjoy between our wholesale massacres, of civic decency, but an almost lawless and policeless free-for-all in a society composed of a class of nobles, utterly corrupted by Spanish ideas of honor (Naples was then a Spanish colony), a small and insignificant middle class, and a vast mob of plebeians living in bestial squalor and savagery, and sunk, head over ears, in the most degrading superstition. It was in this monstrous environment that Carlo grew up, an immensely talented and profoundly neurotic member of the overprivileged minority.

In 1586 he married Maria d'Avalos, a girl of twenty, but already a widow. (Her previous husband, it was whispered, had died of too much connubial bliss.) Gesualdo had two children by this lady, one of his own begetting, the other almost certainly not; for after two years of marriage, the lovely and lively Donna Maria had taken a lover, Don Fabrizio Carafa, Duke of Andria. On the night of October 16, 1590, accompanied by three of his retainers, armed with swords, halberds, and harquebuses, Gesualdo broke into his wife's room, found the lovers in bed, and had them killed. After which he took horse and galloped off to one of his castles where, after liquidating his second child (the one of doubtful paternity), he remained for several months—not to escape the law (for he was never prosecuted and, if he had been, would certainly have been acquitted as having done only what any injured husband had the right and even the duty to do), but to avoid the private vengence of the

Avalos and Carafa families. These last were outraged, not so much by the murder (which was entirely in order) as by the fact that the killing had been done by lackeys and not by Gesualdo himself. According to the code of honor, blue blood might be spilled only by the possessor of blue blood, never by a member of the lower classes.

Time passed and the storm, as all storms finally do, blew over. From his feudal keep in the hills Gesualdo was able to return to Naples and the cultivated society of madrigal-singing amateurs and professional musicians. He began composing, he even published. Second and third editions of his madrigals were called for. He was almost a best seller.

The Prince of Venosa, the *Serenissimo* as he was called by his respectful contemporaries, was now an eligible widower, and sometime in 1592 or 1593 his paternal uncle, the Archbishop of Naples, entered into negotiations with Alfonso II, Duke of Ferrara, with a view to securing for his nephew a princess of the great house of Este. Suitable financial arrangements were made, and in February 1594, the nuptials of Carlo Gesualdo and Donna Leonora d'Este were celebrated at Ferrara with all the usual pomp. After a short stay in the south, Gesualdo returned to Ferrara with his bride, now pregnant, rented a palace, and settled down for a long stay.

Ferrara in 1594 was a setting sun, still dazzling, but on the brink of darkness. Three years later, on the death of Duke Alfonso without a male heir, the city, which was a papal fief, reverted to its overlord, the Pope, and was incorporated into the States of the Church. The glory that was Ferrara vanished overnight, forever.

That Ferrara should ever have become a glory is one of the unlikeliest facts in that long succession of actualized improbabilities which make up human history. The ducal territory was small and, in those malarious days, unhealthy. Its material resources were scanty, and the most important local industry was the smoking of eels, caught in the winding channels of the delta of the Po. Militarily, the state was feeble in the extreme. Powerful and not always friendly neighbors surrounded it and, to make matters worse, it lay on the invasion route from Germany and Austria. In spite of which Ferrara became and for a hundred and fifty years—from the middle of the fifteenth to the end of the sixteenth century—remained not only a sovereign state of considerable political importance, but also one of the most brilliant intellectual centers of Western Europe. This position the city owed entirely to the extraordinary ability and good taste of its rulers, the dukes of the house of Este. In the game of international and interdynastic politics, the Estensi were consummately skillful players. At home they were not too tyrannical, and had a happy knack, when discontent ran high, of blaming their ministers for everything and so maintaining their own popularity.

Their domestic life was relatively harmonious. Unlike many of the ruling families of Italy, the Estensi seldom murdered one another. True, a few years before Carlo's marriage to Leonora, the Duke had had his sister's lover strangled. But this was an exceptional act—and anyhow he refrained from strangling the lady; the integrity of the clan was preserved. But from our present point of view the most remarkable thing about the Dukes of Ferrara was their steady patronage of talent, especially in the fields of literature and music. The greatest Italian poets of the sixteenth century—from Ariosto at the beginning to Guarini and Tasso at the end—were summoned to Ferrara, where the dukes either gave them jobs in the administration of the state, or else paid them a pension, so that they might devote the whole of their time to literature. Musicians were no less welcome than poets. From 1450 to 1600 most of the greatest composers of the time visited Ferrara, and many of them stayed at the court for long periods. They came from Burgundy and Flanders, the most productive centers of early Renaissance music; they came from France; they came even from faraway England. And later, when the Italians had learned their lesson from the North and had become, in their turn, the undisputed leaders in the field, they came from all over the peninsula. The huge square *castello* at the heart of the city, the ducal hunting lodges, the summer palaces by the sea, the mansions of the nobles and the foreign ambassadors—all of them resounded with music: Learned polyphonic music and popular songs and dances. Music for lutes (there was a functionary at the ducal court whose sole duty it was to keep the lutes perpetually in tune) and music for the organ, for viols, for wind instruments, for the earliest forms of harpsichord and clavichord. Music performed by amateurs sitting around the fire or at a table, and music rendered by professional virtuosi. Music in church, music at home, and (this was a novelty) music in the concert hall. For there were daily concerts in the various ducal palaces, concerts in which as many as sixty players and singers would take part. On grand occasions—and at Ferrara there seems to have been a grand occasion at least twice a week—there were masques with choral interludes, there were plays with overtures and incidental music, there were performances, in those sunset years of decline, of the first rudimentary operas. And what wonderful voices could be heard at Alfonso's court! Ferrara's Three Singing Ladies were world famous. There was Lucrezia Bendidio, there was Laura Peperara, and, most remarkable of the trio, there was the beautiful, learned, and many-talented Tarquinia Molza. But every Eden, alas, has its serpent, and, in Tarquinia's musical paradise, there was not merely a reptile to rear its ugly head; there were several Adams as well.

Tarquinia married and was widowed; then, in her middle thirties she fell under the spell of that most charming and romantic of men, Torquato Tasso. The poet, who wrote a great deal about love, but very seldom made it, was alarmed, and, putting up a barrage of Platonic verse, beat a hasty retreat. Tarquinia had to be content, for several years, with lovers of less exalted intellectual rank. Then, in her forties, she found another man of genius, the great Flemish composer, Giaches Wert, who was in the employ of the Duke of Mantua. Their passion was reciprocal and so violent that it created a scandal. The unhappy Tarquinia was exiled to Modena, and Wert returned, alone, to the court of the Gonzagas.

For a man of Gesualdo's gifts and sensibilities, Ferrara combined the advantages of a seat of higher education with those of a heaven on earth. It was a place where he could simultaneously enjoy himself and learn. And learn he certainly did. The madrigals he composed before 1594 are admirable in their workmanship; but their style, though his own, is still within the bounds of sixteenth-century music. The madrigals and motets written after his stay at Ferrara are beyond those bounds—far out in a kind of no man's land.

Gesualdo left no memoirs and, in spite of his high contemporary reputation and his exalted position in the world, very little is known of his later life, except that he was unhappy and dogged by misfortune. His son by his second wife died in childhood. His son by the murdered Donna Maria, the heir to all the family titles and estates, grew up to loathe his father and long for his death; but it was he who died first. One of Gesualdo's daughters went to the bad and presented him with several illegitimate grandchildren. Meanwhile he was constantly tormented, says a contemporary gossip writer, by a host of demons. His lifelong neurosis had deepened, evidently into something like insanity. Apart from music, which he went on composing with undiminished powers, his only pleasure seems to have been physical pain. He would, we are told, submit ecstatically to frequent whippings. These at last became a physiological necessity. According to that much persecuted philosopher, Tommaso Campanella, the Prince of Venosa could never go to the bathroom (*cacare non poterat*) unless he had first been flogged by a servant specially trained to perform this duty. Remorse for the crimes of his youth weighed heavily on Gesualdo's conscience. The law might excuse, public opinion might even approve; but Holy Writ was explicit: *Thou shalt not kill.* A few years before his death in 1613 he endowed a Capuchin friary in his native town of Gesualdo and built a handsome church. Over the altar hung a huge penitential picture, painted to the prince's order and under his personal direction. This picture, which still survives, represents Christ the Judge seated on high and flanked by the Blessed Virgin and the Archangel Michael. Below Him, arranged symmetrically, in descending tiers, to right and left, are Saint Francis and Saint Mary Magdalen, Saint Dominic and Saint Catherine of Siena, all of them, to judge by their gestures, emphatically interceding with the Savior on behalf of Carlo Gesualdo, who kneels in the lower left-hand corner, dressed in black velvet and an enormous ruff, while, splendid in the scarlet robes of a Prince of the Church, his uncle, the Saint, stands beside him, with one hand resting protectively on the sinner's shoulder. Opposite them kneels Carlo's aunt, Isabella Borromeo, in the costume of a nun, and at the center of this family group is the murdered child, as a heavenly cherub. Below, at the very bottom of the composition, Donna Maria and the Duke of Andria are seen roasting everlastingly in those flames from which the man who had them butchered still hopes against hope to be delivered.

So much for the facts of our composer's life—facts which confirm an old and slightly disquieting truth: namely, that between an artist's work and his personal behavior there is no very obvious correspondence. The work may be sublime, the behavior anything from silly to insane and criminal. Conversely the behavior may be blameless and the work uninteresting or downright bad. Artistic merit has nothing to do with any other kind of merit. In the language of theology, talent is a gratuitous grace, completely unconnected with saving grace or even with ordinary virtue or sanity.

From the man we now pass to his strange music. Like most of the great composers of his day, Gesualdo wrote exclusively for the human voice—to be more precise, for groups of five or six soloists singing contrapuntally. All his five- or six-part compositions belong to one or other of two closely related musical forms, the madrigal and the motet. The motet is the older of the two forms and consists of a setting, for any number of voices from three to twelve, of a short passage, in Latin, from the Bible or some other sacred text. Madrigals may be defined as nonreligious motets. They are settings, not of sacred Latin texts, but of short poems in the vernacular. In most cases, these settings were for five voices; but the composer was free to write for any number of parts from three to eight or more.

The madrigal came into existence in the thirties of the sixteenth century and, for seventy or eighty years, remained the favorite art form of all composers of secular music. Contrapuntal writing in five parts is never likely to be popular, and the madrigal made its appeal, not to the general public, but to a select audience of professional musicians and highly educated amateurs, largely aristocratic and connected for the most part with one or other of the princely or ecclesiastical courts of the day. (One is amazed, when one reads the history of Renaissance music, by the good taste of Europe's earlier rulers. Popes and emperors, kings, princes, and cardinals—they never make a mistake. Invariably, one might almost say infallibly, they choose for their chapel masters and court composers the men whose reputation has stood the test of time and whom we now recognize as the most gifted musicians of their day. Left to themselves, what sort of musicians would our twentieth-century monarchs and presidents choose to patronize? One shudders to think.)

Gesualdo wrote madrigals, and a madrigal, as we have seen, is a nonreligious motet. But what else is it? Let us begin by saying what it is not. First and foremost, the madrigal, though sung, is not a song. It does not, that is to say, consist of a tune, repeated stanza after stanza. Nor has it anything to do with the art form known to later musicians as the aria. An aria is a piece of music for a solo voice, accompanied by instruments or by other voices. It begins, in most cases, with an introduction, states a melodic theme in one key, states a second theme in another key goes into a series of modulations, and ends with a recapitulation of one or both themes in the original key. Nothing of all this to be found in the madrigal. In the madrigal there is no solo singing. All the five or more voices are of equal importance, and they move, so to speak, straight ahead, whereas the aria and the song move in the equivalent of circles or spirals. In other words, there are, in the madrigal, no returns to a starting point, no systematic recapitulations. Its form bears no resemblance to the sonata form or even to the suite form. It might be described as a choral tone poem, written in counterpoint. When counterpoint is written within a structural pattern, such as the fugue or canon, the listener can follow the intricacies of the music almost indefinitely. But where the counterpoint has no structural pattern imposed upon it, where it moves forward freely, without any returns to a starting point, the ear finds it very hard to follow it, attentively and understandingly, for more than a few minutes at a stretch. Hence the brevity of the typical madrigal, the extraordinary succinctness of its style.

During the three quarters of a century of its existence, the madrigal underwent a steady development in the direction of completer, ever intenser expressiveness. At the beginning of the period it is a piece of emotionally neutral polyphony, whose whole beauty consists in the richness and complexity of its many-voiced texture. At the end, in the work of such masters as Marenzio, Monteverdi, and, above all, Gesualdo, it has become a kind of musical miracle, in which seemingly incompatible elements are reconciled in a higher synthesis. The intricacies of polyphony are made to yield the most powerfully expressive effects, and this polyphony has become so flexible that it can, at any moment, transmute itself into blocks of chords or a passage of dramatic declamation.

During his stay at Ferrara, Gesualdo was in contact with the most "advanced" musicians of his day. A few miles away, at Mantua, the great Giaches Wert, sick and prematurely old, was still composing; and at the same court lived a much younger musician, Claudio Monteverdi, who was to carry to completion the revolution in music begun by Wert. That revolution was the supersession of polyphony by monody, the substitution of the solo voice, with instrumental or vocal accompaniment, for the madrigalist's five or six voices of equal importance. Gesualdo did not follow the Mantuans into monody; but he was certainly influenced by Wert's essays in musical expressionism. Those strange cries of grief, pain, and despair, which occur so frequently in his later madrigals, were echoes of the cries introduced by Wert into his dramatic cantatas.

At Ferrara itself Gesualdo's closest musical friends were Count Fontanelli and a professional composer and virtuoso, Luzzasco Luzzaschi. Like Gesualdo, Fontanelli was an aristocrat and had murdered an unfaithful wife; unlike Gesualdo, he was not a man of genius, merely a good musician passionately interested in the latest developments of the art. Luzzaschi was a writer of madrigals, and had invented a number of expressive devices, which Gesualdo employed in his own later productions. More important, he was the only man who knew how to play on, and even compose for, an extraordinary machine, which was the greatest curiosity in Duke Alfonso's collection of musical instruments. This was the archicembalo, a large keyboard instrument belonging to the harpsichord family, but so designed that a player could distinguish, for example, between B-flat and A-sharp, could descend chromatically from E, through E-flat, D-sharp, D, D-flat, C-sharp to a final C major chord. The archicembalo required thirty-one keys to cover each octave and must have been fantastically difficult to play and still harder, one would imagine, to compose for. The followers of Schönberg are far behind Luzzaschi; *their* scale has only twelve tones, *his*, thirty-one. Luzzaschi's thirty-one tone compositions (none of which, unfortunately, survive) and his own experiments on the archicembalo profoundly influenced the style of Gesualdo's later madrigals. Forty years ago, the

Oxford musicologist, Ernest Walker, remarked that Gesualdo's most famous madrigal, *"Moro lasso,"* sounded like "Wagner gone wrong." Hardly an adequate criticism of Gesualdo, but not without significance.

The mention of Wagner is fully justified; for the incessant chromaticisms of Gesualdo's later writing found no parallel in music until the time of *Tristan*. As for the "gone-wrongness"—this is due to Gesualdo's unprecedented and, until recent times, almost unimitated treatment of harmonic progression. In his madrigals successive chords are related in ways which conform neither to the rules of sixteenth-century polyphony, nor to the rules of harmony which hold good from the middle of the seventeenth century to the beginning of the twentieth. An infallible ear is all that, in most cases, preserves these strange and beautiful progressions from seeming altogether arbitrary and chaotic. Thanks to that infallible ear of his, Gesualdo's harmonies move, always astonishingly, but always with a logic of their own, from one impossible, but perfectly satisfying, beauty to another And the harmonic strangeness is never allowed to continue for too long at a stretch. With consummate art, Gesualdo alternates these extraordinary passages of Wagner-gone-wrong with passages of pure traditional polyphony. To be fully effective, every elaboration must be shown in a setting of simplicity, every revolutionary novelty should emerge from a background of the familiar. For the composers of arias, the simple and familiar background for their floridly expressive melodies was a steady, rhythmically constant accompaniment. For Gesualdo, simplicity and familiarity meant the rich, many-voiced texture of contrapuntal writing. The setting for Wagner-gone-wrong is Palestrina.

Every madrigal is the setting of a short poem in the vernacular, just as every motet is the setting of a short passage from the Vulgate or some other piece of sacred Latin literature. The texts of the motets were generally in prose, and the early polyphonists saw no obvious reason for imposing upon this essentially rectilinear material a circular musical form. After the invention of the aria, the composers of music for prose texts habitually distorted the sense and rhythm of their words in order to force them into the circular, verselike patterns of their new art form. From Alessandro Scarlatti, through Bach and Handel, Mozart,

Haydn, and Mendelssohn—all the great composers from 1650 to 1850 provide examples, in their musical settings, of what may be called the versification of prose. To do this, they were compelled to repeat phrases and individual words again and again, to prolong single syllables to inordinate length, to recapitulate, note for note, or with variations, entire paragraphs. How different was the procedure of the madrigalists! Instead of versifying prose, they found it necessary, because of the nature of their art form, to prosify verse. The regular recurrences of lines and stanzas—these have no place in the madrigal, just as they have no place in the motet. Like good prose, the madrigal is rectilinear, not circular. Its movement is straight ahead, irreversible, asymmetrical. When they set a piece of poetry to music, the madrigalists set it phrase by phrase, giving to each phrase, even each word, its suitable expression, and linking the successive moods by a constant adaptation of the polyphonic writing, not by the imposition from outside of a structural pattern. Every madrigal, as I have said, is a choral tone poem. But instead of lasting for a whole hour, like the huge, spectacular machines of Liszt and Richard Strauss, it concentrates its changing moods into three or four minutes of elaborate and yet intensely expressive counterpoint.

The Italian madrigalists chose their texts, for the most part, from the best poets. Dante was considered too harsh and old-fashioned; but his great fourteenth-century successor, Petrarch, remained a perennial favorite. Among more recent poets, Ariosto, though set fairly frequently, was much less popular than Guarini and Tasso, whose emotional tone was more emphatic and who took pleasure in just those violent contrasts of feeling which lent themselves most perfectly to the purposes of the madrigalist. In their shorter pieces (pieces written expressly to be set to music) Tasso and his contemporaries made use of a kind of epigrammatic style, in which antithesis, paradox, and oxymoron played a major part and were turned into a literary convention, so that every versifier now talked of dolorous joy, sweet agony, loathing love, and living death—to the immense delight of the musicians, for whom these emotional ambiguities, these abrupt changes of feeling offered golden opportunities.

Gesualdo was a personal friend of Torquato Tasso and, during the last, mad, wandering years of the poet's life, helped him with money and letters of introduction. As we should expect, he set a number of Tasso's poems to music. For the rest he made use of anything that came to hand. Many of his finest madrigals are based on snatches of verse having no literary merit whatsoever. That they served his purpose was due to the fact that they were written in the current idiom and contained plenty of emphatically contrasting words, which he could set to appropriately expressive music. Gesualdo's indifference to the poetical quality of his texts, and his methods of setting words to music, are very clearly illustrated in one of the most astonishing of his madrigals, "*Ardita zanzaretta*"—a work, incidentally, whose performance at Los Angeles in the autumn of 1955 was probably the first in more than three hundred years. This extraordinary little masterpiece compresses into less than three minutes every mood from the cheerfully indifferent to the perversely voluptuous, from the gay to the tragic, and in the process employs every musical resource, from traditional polyphony to Wagner-gone-wrong chromaticism and the strangest harmonic progressions, from galloping rhythms to passages of long, suspended notes. Then we look at the text and discover that this amazing music is the setting of half-a-dozen lines of doggerel. The theme of "*Ardita zanzaretta*" is the same as the theme of a tiny poem by Tasso, tasteless enough in all conscience, but written with a certain elegance of style. A little mosquito (*zanzaretta*) settles on the bosom of the beloved, bites, and gets swatted by the exasperated lady. What a delicious fate, muses Tasso, to die in a place where it is such bliss to swoon away!

Felice te felice,
piú che nel rogo orientale Fenice!

(Oh happy, happy bug—more happy than the Phoenix on its oriental pyre!)

Gesualdo's nameless librettist takes the same subject, robs it of whatever charm Tasso was able to lend it, and emphasizes the bloodiness of the mosquito's fate by introducing—twice over in the space of only six lines—the word *stringere*, meaning to squeeze, squash, squelch. Another improvement on Tasso is the addition of a playful sally by the lover. Since he longs to share the mosquito's fate, he too will take a bite in the hope of being squashed to death on the lady's bosom. What follows is a literal translation of this nonsense, accompanied by a description of the music accompanying each phrase. "A bold little mosquito bites the fair breast of her who consumes my heart." This is set to a piece of pure neutral polyphony, very rapid and, despite its textural richness, very light. But the lady is not content with consuming the lover's heart; she also "keeps it in cruel pain." Here the dancing polyphony of the first bars gives place to a series of chords moving slowly from dissonance to unprepared dissonance. The pain, however unreal in the text, becomes in the music genuinely excruciating. Now the mosquito "makes its escape, but rashly flies back to that fair breast which steals my heart away. Whereupon she catches it." All this is rendered in the same kind of rapid, emotionally neutral polyphony as was heard in the opening bars. But now comes another change. The lady not only catches the insect, "she squeezes it and gives it death." The word *morte*, death, occurs in almost all Gesualdo's madrigals. Sometimes it carries its literal meaning; more often, however, it is used figuratively, to signify sensual ecstasy, the swoon of love. But this makes no difference to Gesualdo. Whatever its real significance, and whoever it is that may be dying (the lover metaphorically or, in a literal sense, a friend, a mosquito, the crucified Savior), he gives to the word, *morte*, a musical expression of the most tragic and excruciating kind. For the remorseful assassin, death was evidently the most terrifying of prospects.

From the insect's long-drawn musical martyrdom, we return to cheerfulness and pure polyphony. "To share its happy fate, I too will bite you." Gesualdo was a pain-loving masochist and this playful suggestion of sadism left him unmoved. The counterpoint glides along in a state of emotional neutrality. Then comes a passage of chromatic yearning on the words "my beloved, my precious one." Then polyphony again. "And if you catch and squeeze me. . . ." After this, the music becomes unadulterated Gesualdo. There is a cry of pain—*ahi!*—and then "I will swoon away and, upon that fair breast, taste delicious poison." The musical setting of these final words is a concentrated version of the love-potion scene in *Tristan*—the chief difference being that Gesualdo's harmonic progressions are far bolder than any attempted, two and a half centuries later, by Richard Wagner.

Should pictures tell stories? Should music have a connection with literature? In the past the answer would have been, unanimously, yes. Every great painter was a raconteur of Biblical or mythological anecdotes; every great composer was a setter-to-music of sacred or profane texts. Today the intrusion of literature into the plastic arts is regarded almost as a crime. In the field of music, this antiliterary reign of terror has been less savage. Program music is deplored (not without reason, considering the horrors bequeathed to us by the Victorian era); but in spite of much talk about "pure music," good composers still write songs, masses, operas, and cantatas. Good painters would do well to follow their example and permit themselves to be inspired to still better painting by the promptings of a literary theme. In the hands of a bad painter, pictorial storytelling, however sublime the subject matter, is merely comic-strip art on a large scale. But when a good painter tells the same story, the case is entirely different. The exigencies of illustration—the fact that he has to show such-and-such personages, in such-and-such an environment, performing such-and-such actions— stimulates his imagination on every level, including the purely pictorial level, with the result that he produces a work which, though literary, is of the highest quality as a formal composition. Take any famous painting of the past—Botticelli's "Calumny of Apelles," for example, or Titian's "Bacchus and Ariadne." Both of these are admirable illustrations; but both are much more than illustrations—they are very complex and yet perfectly harmonious and unified arrangements of forms and colors. Moreover the richness of their formal material is a direct consequence of their literary subject matter. Left to itself, the pictorial imagination even of a painter of genius could never conjure up such a subtle and complicated pattern of shapes and hues as we find in these illustrations of texts by Lucian and Ovid. To achieve their purely plastic triumphs, Botticelli and Titian required to be stimulated by a literary theme. It is a highly significant fact that, in no abstract or nonrepresentational painting of today, do we find a purely formal composition having anything like the richness, the harmonious complexity, created in the process of telling a story, by the masters of earlier periods. The traditional distinction between the crafts and the fine arts is based, among other things, on degrees of complexity. A good picture is a greater work of art than a good bowl or a good vase. Why? Because it unifies in one harmonious whole more, and more diverse, elements of human experience than are or can be unified and harmonized in the pot. Some of the nonrepresentational pictures painted in the course of the last fifty years are very beautiful; but even the best of them are minor works, inasmuch as the number of elements of human experience which they combine and harmonize is pitifully small. In them we look in vain for that ordered profusion, that lavish and yet perfectly controlled display of intellectual wealth, which we discover in the best works of the "literary" painters of the past.

In this respect the composer is more fortunate than the painter. It is psychologically possible to write "pure music" that shall be just as harmoniously complex, just as rich in unified diversities, as music inspired by a literary text. But even in music the intrusion of literature has often been beneficent. But for the challenge presented by a rather absurd anecdote couched in very feeble language, Beethoven would never have produced the astonishing "pure music" of the second act of *Fidelio*. And it was Da Ponte, with his rhymed versions of the stories of Figaro and Don Giovanni, who stimulated Mozart to reveal himself in the fullness of his genius. Where music is a matter of monody and harmony, with a structural pattern (the sonata form or the suite form) imposed, so to speak, from the outside, it is easy to write "pure music," in which the successive moods shall be expressed, at some length, in successive movements. But where there is no structural pattern, where the style is polyphonic and the movement of the music is not circular, but straight ahead, irreversible and rectilinear, the case is different. Such a style demands extreme brevity and the utmost succinctness of expression. To meet these demands for brevity and succinctness, the musical imagination requires a text—and a text, moreover, of the kind favored by the madrigalists, paradoxical, antithetical, full of

All things counter, original, spare, strange
Whatever is fickle, freckled (who knows how?)
With swift, slow; sweet, sour; adazzle, dim.

Contemporary musicians, who aspire to write "pure music" in forms as rich, subtle, and compact as those devised by Gesualdo and his contemporaries, would do well to turn once more to the poets.

2

Music in India and Japan*

By the kindness of our hospitable friends at Lahore, we were able to hear a good deal of Indian music, both classical and popular. Indian music is innocent of any harmony more subtle than that with which the bagpipe has made us familiar—the drone on the dominant. It knows of no form more highly organized than that of the air with variations. It is played on but few instruments (two kinds of lute and a kind of wire-stringed viola are the commonest), and these few are, alas, rapidly being ousted by a form of miniature American harmonium, pumped with one hand and played with one finger of the other. Yet, in spite of these limitations, Indian music is surprisingly rich and various. How rich and how various depends entirely upon the individual player. For in India, where music has never been committed to writing, but is an affair of tradition tempered by personal inspiration, the part of the interpreter is more important even than with us. Of European music even a bad player can give us some idea; and those who have acquired the art of reading a score can get their musical pleasure through the eye alone. Not so in India. Here the performer is all-important. He is everything; not only the interpreter, but also the repository and publisher of music—Breitkopf and Här-

* From *Jesting Pilate* ("Lahore," "Japan"), 1926.

tel as well as Paganini; not only the guardian of ancient tradition, but also the inspired improvisator. The bad performer can give you nothing of Indian music.

At Lahore, we were fortunate in hearing a most accomplished performer on the sitar or Indian lute. He was a middle-aged man with a walrus moustache and an explosion of most musical long hair, in the center of which he wore a red plush cap embroidered with gold. He looked, I thought, like a reproduction in brown of an old-fashioned German pianist. But how humble, in comparison with the lordly artists of Europe, how very definitely an inferior the poor man was! He sat on the floor awaiting our good pleasure, played when he was told, stopped at a word in the middle of a musical phrase, played on uncomplainingly through our conversation. Music in India has strangely come down in the world. From being, it is said, the accomplishment of princesses, it has come to be the monopoly of prostitutes. Courtesans are the only professional female musicians in India, and very many of the male professionals are only the hereditary teachers of courtesans. Our musician had climbed a little way above his congenital station in life; he gave lessons to amateurs.

The sitar is a long-necked guitar, bellied with the half of a bisected pumpkin (and having, sometimes, the second half attached like a goiter to its neck), wire-strung, and played with a plectrum. From this lute a skilled musician can draw an extraordinary variety of sounds—from sharp staccato to notes long-drawn, as though produced by a bow; from clear, full, ringing sounds to a whining slither through fractions of a tone; from loudly martial to sweet and tender. The melody is played only on the first string, the remaining wires (tuned to sound the dominant, in various octaves, of the key to whose tonic the first string is tuned) being used to produce the accompanying drone.

Our lutanist's repertory was large, and he was prepared to play anything we asked for. Folk songs in the pentatonic black-note scale—first cousins, these, to what we are accustomed to regard as characteristically Scottish airs—were followed by classical pieces, in which the most elaborate variations were embroidered on themes that sounded now Gregorian, now like a rambling and, to our ears, rather tuneless Western folk song. We heard specimens of the music that is supposed to be played only in the morning, and specimens of that which is intended for the night. We heard the delightful song that is meant to be sung in cloudy weather. We heard the snake charmer's music, built up round a most snaky phrase of descending semitones, and the camel driver's song, wailing and romantic. Generally the instrument sounded alone. But sometimes the minstrel lifted his shaggy head and gave vent to shrill tenor notes, neighed out from somewhere between the nose and the upper gullet. Strange sounds, and to our ears somewhat ludicrous, particularly when taken in conjunction with certain nods and vibrations of the head, certain almost girlishly coquettish gestures made with a hand that was lifted for the purpose from the sounding strings.

I was able to understand and appreciate the music tolerably well. All of it, that is, except the music played, traditionally, when a man gives up the world for the life of meditation. One of these renunciatory pieces—a most elaborate, classical affair—was played for our benefit. But I must confess that, listen as I might, I was unable to hear anything particularly mournful or serious, anything specially suggestive of self-sacrifice in the piece. To my Western ears it sounded much more cheerful than the dance which followed it.

Emotions are everywhere the same; but the artistic expression of them varies from age to age and from one country to another. We are brought up to accept the conventions current in the society into which we are born. This sort of art, we learn in childhood, is meant to excite laughter, that to evoke our tears. Such conventions vary with great rapidity, even in the same country. There are Elizabethan dances that sound as melancholy to our ears as little funeral marches. Conversely, we are made to laugh by the "Anglo-Saxon attitudes" of the holiest personages in the drawings and miniatures of earlier centuries. Only with the aid of a historically trained imagination can we see or hear as our ancestors heard or saw. Remoteness in space divides no less than remoteness in time, and to the untrained auditor or spectator the artistic conventions of strangers are as little comprehensible as those of his own fathers.

It is in the visual arts that the conventions for the expression of emotions vary most widely. This is due, I suppose, to two main causes, of a character respectively physiological and intellectual. Form and color have very little direct physiological effect upon the perceiving organism. Sounds, on the other hand, act directly on the nerves and can stimulate, exasperate, daze, bemuse, as forms and colors can never do. Certain types of rhythmical sounds produce certain almost specific effects upon the nervous system. It is obvious that in forming his conventions of expressions the musician must take into account these specific physiological effects of sound. Drumbeats and loud brassy notes sounded in regular, even time are specifically exciting; it therefore follows that the convention for expressing the martial emotions can never involve slow croonings of violins in an undulating three-four time, or elaborate birdlike warblings on the flute. Thus it comes about that there is a certain family likeness common to the conventions of expression of every system of music—a family likeness which does not exist among the conventions of the various systems of pictorial art. But even in music the differences between the conventions of expression are very great. Music affects us physiologically through rhythm and the volume and quality of sounds. Conventions, which we have come to regard as fundamental, but which do not involve these particular factors, are found, when we compare them with the conventions of other systems, to be purely arbitrary. Thus, what we regard as the fundamental difference between major and minor keys—the minor being for us essentially melancholy—is not fundamental at all, but the result of a recent and arbitrary convention of Western musicians. Before the seventeenth century the convention did not exist even in European music, and in Oriental music it is not thought of, the most cheerful, jolly, and martial music being pitched in the minor.

So much for physiology. There are other and purely intellectual reasons why the conventions of expression should vary more widely in the different systems of visual art than they do in the systems of music. The visual arts lend themselves to storytelling and the symbolical exposition of philosophical theories and religious dogmas. Music does not. Thus, to Western eyes, the picture of a man with four arms, an elephant's head, and a lotus growing out of his navel seems grotesque. But an orthodox Hindu would see nothing comical in it. To us pictures of monsters and impossible hybrids are by convention, funny. To him they are symbolical of the highest truths.

JAPAN

It was gray when we landed at Kobe, and the air was cold and smelled of soot. There was deep mud in the streets. A little while after we had stepped on shore, it began to rain. We might have been landing at Leith in the height of a Scotch November.

Lifted above the mud on stiltlike clogs, little men paddled about the streets; they were dressed in Inverness capes of gray or brown silk and cheap felt hats. Women in dressing gowns, with high-piled, elaborately architectured hair, like the coiffure of an old-fashioned barmaid, dyed black, toddled beside them, leading or carrying on their backs gaudily dressed children, whose round expressionless button-faces were like the faces of little Eskimos. It seemed, certainly, an odd sort of population to be inhabiting Leith. Reluctantly we had to admit that we were indeed in the Extreme Orient, and the flowers in the shops had to be accepted as a sufficient proof that this funereal wintry day was really a day in the month of Cherry Blossom.

We got into the train and for two hours rolled through a gray country, bounded by dim hills and bristling with factory chimneys. Every few miles the sparse chimneys would thicken to a grove, with, round their feet—like toadstools about the roots of trees—a sprawling collection of wooden shanties: a Japanese town. The largest of these fungus beds was Osaka.

It was late in the afternoon when we arrived at Kyoto, the ancient capital, "the Art City of Japan" (we had been well primed before starting with touristic literature). Declining the proffered taxi, we climbed into rickshaws, the better to observe the town. It was only feebly drizzling. Dressed like Anglo-Saxon messengers in blue jerkins and tights, our coolies drew us splashing through the mud. Kyoto is like one of those mining camps one sees in the movies, but two or three hundred times as large as any possible Wild Western original. Little wooden shack succeeds little wooden shack interminably, mile after mile; and the recession of the straight untidy roads is emphasized by the long lines of posts, the sagging electric wires that flank each street, like the trees of an avenue. All the cowboys in the world could live in Kyoto, all the forty-niners. Street leads into identical street, district merges indistinguishably into district. In this dreary ocean of log cabins almost the only White Houses are the hotels.

For a few hours that evening it ceased to rain. We took the opportunity to explore the city on foot. The streets were well lighted, the shops—and almost every one of the hundred thousand shacks in Kyoto is a shop—were mostly open. We walked through the city, seeing the commercial life steadily and seeing it almost whole. It was like walking, ankle-deep in mud, through an enormous Woolworth's bazaar. Such a collection of the cheap and shoddy, of the quasi-genuine and the imitation-solid, of the vulgar and the tawdry, I have never seen. And the strange thing was that, in Kyoto, even the real, the sound, the thoroughly *pukka* had an air of flimsiness and falsity. Looking at the most expensive kimonos with a lifetime of wear woven into their thick silk, you would swear that they were things of wood pulp. The ivories resemble celluloid; the hand embroideries have the appearance of the machine-made article. The genuine antiques—the ones you see in the museums, for there are none elsewhere—look as though they had been fabricated yesterday. This is due partly to the fact that in recent years we have become so familiar with the conventional forms of Japanese art turned out on machines by the million for the penny bazaar market, that we cannot associate them with anything but cheapness and falsity; partly too, I think, to a certain intrinsic feebleness and vulgarity in the forms themselves. That sobriety, that strength, that faultless refinement which are the characteristics of Chinese art, and which give to the cheapest piece of Chinese earthenware, the most ordinary embroidery or carving or lettering, a magistral air of artistic importance and significance, are totally lacking, so it seems to me, in the art of Japan. The designs of Japanese fabrics are garish and pretentious; the sculpture even of the best periods is baroque; the pottery which in China is so irreproachable both in hue and shape is always in Japan just not "right." It is as though there were some inherent vice in Japanese art which made the genuine seem false and the expensive shoddy.

Factories, smoke, innumerable Woolworths, mud—were

these Japan? We were assured they were not. The "real" Japan (all countries have a "real" self, which no stranger can ever hope to see) was something different, was somewhere else. Looking at the celebrated Cherry Dances in Kyoto, we were almost ready to believe it. The costumes, it is true, were extraordinarily vulgar and garish. The scenery in Western style—the Western style of the prewar provincial pantomime—was deplorable. Any self-respecting producer of revues in London or New York could have staged a far more adequate Old Japan. But he could not have got the dancing. That was an enchantment. A chorus of thirty or forty geishas, drilled to a pitch of almost Prussian efficiency, their farded faces impassive as white masks, performed a ballet that was the formalization of the gestures of courtesy, that was polite conversation made more gracefully polite, that was the apotheosis of good manners at the tea table. And hardly less lovely were the movements of the orchestra. In Europe one pays to listen to music; in Japan one pays to see it played. When European performers make their appearance upon the platform, one generally wants to shut one's eyes; in a Japanese concert room, on the other hand, one desires to keep one's eyes wide open and to close one's ears. Not that the music is unpleasant. What I heard at Kyoto might have been the remote and geological ancestor of Russian music. It stood in relation to Rimsky-Korsakov as pithecanthropus stands to man; it was a kind of *ur*-Stravinsky, a fossil and primitive form of the genus Moussorgsky. Not unpleasing, I repeat, but after a while a little boring. The guitars, on which twenty geishas played with plectrums that looked like ivory combs, were singularly poor in tone. And the tambourines, the cymbals, and the drums, which were being played by twenty of their sisters on the opposite side of the hall, beat out only the simplest and most obvious rhythms. No, the orchestra was not much to listen to. But what a ravishment to behold! They were as well drilled as the ballerinas. The twenty guitar players sat in identically the same position, and when they combed the strings of their instruments their hands performed the same movements simultaneously, as though they were the synchronously moving parts of one machine. Similar machines actuated the eight hourglass-shaped tambourines, the eight small kettledrums, the two sets of cymbals, the two little gongs. Most exquisite of all were the drummers. They knelt in front of their instruments as though before a row of little gods. Each held a pair of enormous white drumsticks, so thick that the tiny hands could hardly grasp them. With these, in unison, they tapped the little gods before whom they knelt; and the little drum gods answered them, boom boom—a response, it must be admitted, rather more clear and comprehensible than that which deities are accustomed to vouchsafe to their worshippers. But then the ritual of these Japanese adorers was so beautiful that it could hardly fail to be magically compelling. Their arms, prolonged by the enormous white drumsticks, were held out before them almost at full stretch. And when they beat, they beat from the shoulder, lifting and letting fall the whole arm. But "letting fall" is not the right expression; it connotes a loose and undeliberate movement, and the drummers did nothing undeliberately. On the contrary, each stroke was applied with a perfectly controlled precision. Tap, tap, tap-a-tap, tap; they touched the drum face as though they were fitting into position, one by one, the tesserae, now large, now small, of an elaborate mosaic.

Perhaps these dancers, these exquisitely disciplined musicians, were the "real" Japan. Perhaps, too, it existed in the country which we saw on our way to Yokohama. The sun had come out at last. The sky was palely blue and alive with clouds that trailed great indigo shadows across the earth beneath them. It was an almost Italian country of abrupt hills and lakes and mountain-encircled plains. A paler variety of our mustard was blooming in the fields. Great expanses of primrose yellow covered the plains to the edge of the blue lakes, to the feet of the dim blue mountains. The mustard seemed to me far more impressively beautiful than the cherry blossom. The near hills were brown, steep, almost bare, their crests fringed with a growth, not of the Tuscan umbrella pine, but of the trees which figure so largely in the native woodcuts, the ragged, yet strangely elegant, pine trees, whose silhouette against the sky is like a Chinese ideograph. To one familiar with the Celestial symbols, the whole landscape, I liked to fancy, would be an open book. Wisdom and poetry would sprout for him on every hill. Or perhaps, who knows? the trees might just be saying, "Foreign Devil, Foreign Devil," and repeating it monotonously, mile after mile. The second, I am afraid, is the more probable hypothesis.

We rolled on, through miles of innumerable little rice fields laboriously embanked to hold the water with which they were being flooded; among sloping plantations of tea shrubs, round and shinily green, like bushes of clipped box; through luminous plains of mustard and young green corn; past villages of thatched houses beautifully set among the trees. And every twenty miles or so, we would catch glimpses of a thing which seemed, at first, only a white cloud among the clouds of the horizon, a pale small ghost, but a ghost which, at every glimpse, became more definite, clearer, larger, until—hours after we had had our earliest sight of it—it stood shining high above us, a huge white cone, girdled with clouds, a miracle of regular and geometrical form among the chaotic hills which it overtopped, the sacred mountain of Japan, Fujiyama. We saw it first at noon, a tiny cloud melting into the clouds; and at sunset we were looking back on it, an enormous mass rising clear of all vapors, naked and perfect, into the colored sky. Was this the "real" Japan? I suppose so.

But a little later, at Yokohama, we were plunged again, head over ears, into the unreal. If Kyoto looks like a mining camp, Yokohama after the earthquake looks like a mining camp that has not yet been finished. There are dust heaps among the shanties, there are holes in the roadways, there are unbuilt bridges. But in a little while, when the mass is all cleared up and the damage repaired, it will be just like Kyoto—miles of dreary ill-kept roads, hundreds of thousands of ugly little wooden shanties, and every shanty a shop and every shop a Woolworth. But there are differences of quality, there is a higher and a lower, even among Woolworths. At Kyoto the shops had looked like threepenny bazaars. At Yokohama they were only penny ones.

We boarded our ship with thankfulness. "Real" Japan had been delightful. But there had been more of the unreal than of the real, and the unreal, moreover, was obviously so much the more significant and important that it had quite eclipsed the real. In every country the places, the people, the institutions which are said by lovers of that country to constitute its "real" self are the least characteristic and significant. Cornwall and county families and the Anglican Church may be the esoterically "real" England. But the England that matters, that makes history, that impresses itself on the world and casts its shadow into the future, is represented by Lancashire, Trade Unions, and

Big Business Men. It is the same, I suppppose, with Japan. Fuji and village life, traditional dances and cultured gentlemen of leisure, are what the lovers of Japan would have us believe to be the "real" thing. But it is the unreal Japan, the wholesale producer of shoddy, which is at present projecting itself on history. Not the dancers, not the cultured and religious gentlemen, but the manufacturers of shoddy direct the country's policy. And in the enormous mining-camp cities more and more of the Japanese are being transformed, for good or for evil, from peasants and craftsmen into proletarian factory hands, the brothers of all the other proletarian workers of the world. The future of Japan, as of every other country, depends on its "unreal" self. Someday, in the Utopian future, when things are very different from what they are now, English and Japanese patriots, desirous of exalting their respective countries, will point, not to Cornwall or Fuji, not to the county families or the descendants of the Tea Masters, but to Manchester and Osaka, to the cotton spinners and the weavers of silk. "Here," they will say, "here is the real England, the real Japan." Progress may be defined in this connection as the gradual transformation of what we now call "unreal" into something sufficiently noble and decent to be styled "real." Meanwhile we have the misfortune to live in a world in which all that is historically significant is so repulsive that we are compelled, if we have any pride in our country or our human species, to practice a wholesale Christian Science on it and deny it reality.

3

Music at Night●

Moonless, this June night is all the more alive with stars. Its darkness is perfumed with faint gusts from the blossoming lime trees, with the smell of wetted earth and the invisible greenness of the vines. There is silence; but a silence that breathes with the soft breathing of the sea and, in the thin shrill noise of a cricket, insistently, incessantly harps on the fact of its own deep perfection. Far away, the passage of a train is like a long caress, moving gently, with an inexorable gentleness, across the warm living body of the night.

Music, you say; it would be a good night for music. But I have music here in a box, shut up, like one of those bottled djinns in the *Arabian Nights*, and ready at a touch to break out of its prison. I make the necessary mechanical magic, and suddenly, by some miraculously appropriate coincidence (for I had selected the record in the dark, without knowing what music the machine would play), suddenly the introduction to the "Benedictus" in Beethoven's *Missa Solemnis* begins to trace its patterns on the moonless sky.

The "Benedictus." Blessed and blessing, this music is in some sort the equivalent of the night, of the deep and living darkness, into which, now in a single jet, now in a fine interweaving of melodies, now in pulsing and almost

● From *Music at Night,* 1931.

solid clots of harmonious sound, it pours itself, stanch-lessly pours itself, like time, like the rising and falling, fall-ing trajectories of a life. It is the equivalent of the night in another mode of being, as an essence is the equivalent of the flowers from which it is distilled.

There is, at least there sometimes seems to be, a certain blessedness lying at the heart of things, a mysterious bless-edness, of whose existence occasional accidents or provi-dences (for me, this night is one of them) make us ob-scurely, or it may be intensely, but always fleetingly, alas, always only for a few brief moments aware. In the "Bene-dictus" Beethoven gives expression to this awareness of blessedness. His music is the equivalent of this Mediter-rean night, or rather of the blessedness at the heart of the night, of the blessedness as it would be if it could be sifted clear of irrelevance and accident, refined and separated out into its quintessential purity.

"Benedictus, benedictus . . ." One after another the voices take up the theme propounded by the orchestra and lovingly meditated through a long and exquisite solo (for the blessedness reveals itself most often to the soli-tary spirit) by a single violin. "Benedictus, benedictus . . ." And then, suddenly, the music dies; the flying djinn has been rebottled. With a stupid insectlike insistence, a steel point rasps and rasps the silence.

At school, when they taught us what was technically known as English, they used to tell us to "express in our own words" some passage from whatever play of Shake-speare was at the moment being rammed, with all its annotations—particularly the annotations—down our re-luctant throats. So there we would sit, a row of inky urchins, laboriously translating "now silken dalliance in the wardrobe lies" into "now smart silk clothes lie in the wardrobe," or "To be or not to be" into "I wonder whether I ought to commit suicide or not." When we had finished, we would hand in our papers, and the presiding peda-gogue would give us marks, more or less, according to the accuracy with which "our own words" had "expressed" the meaning of the Bard.

He ought, of course, to have given us naught all round with a hundred lines to himself for ever having set us the silly exercise. Nobody's "own words," except those of Shakespeare himself, can possibly "express" what Shakespeare meant. The substance of a work of art is inseparable from its form; its truth and its beauty are two and yet, mysteriously, one. The verbal expression of even a metaphysic of a system of ethics is very nearly as much of a work of art as a love poem. The philosophy of Plato expressed in the "own words" of Jowett is not the philosophy of Plato; nor in the "own words" of, say, Billy Sunday, is the teaching of St. Paul St. Paul's teaching.

"Our own words" are inadequate even to express the meaning of other words; how much more inadequate, when it is a matter of rendering meanings which have their original expression in terms of music or one of the visual arts! What, for example, does music "say"? You can buy at almost any concert an analytical program that will tell you exactly. Much too exactly; that is the trouble. Every analyst has his own version. Imagine Pharaoh's dream interpreted successively by Joseph, by the Egyptian soothsayers, by Freud, by Rivers, by Adler, by Jung, by Wohlgemuth: it would "say" a great many different things. Not nearly so many, however, as the Fifth Symphony has been made to say in the verbiage of its analysts. Not nearly so many as the "Virgin of the Rocks" and the "Sistine Madonna" have no less lyrically said.

Annoyed by the verbiage and this absurd multiplicity of attributed "meanings," some critics have protested that music and painting signify nothing but themselves; that the only things they "say" are things, for example, about modulations and fugues, about color values and three-dimensional forms. That they say anything about human destiny or the universe at large is a notion which these purists dismiss as merely nonsensical.

If the purists were right, then we should have to regard painters and musicians as monsters. For it is strictly impossible to be a human being and not to have views of some kind about the universe at large, very difficult to be a human being and not to express those views, at any rate by implication. Now, it is a matter of observation that painters and musicians are *not* monsters. Therefore . . . The conclusion follows, unescapably.

It is not only in program music and problem pictures that composers and painters express their views about the universe. The purest and most abstract artistic creations can be, in their own peculiar language, as eloquent in this respect as the most deliberately tendencious.

Compare, for example, a Virgin by Piero della Francesca with a Virgin by Tura. Two Madonnas—and the current symbolical conventions are observed by both artists. The difference, the enormous difference between the two pictures is a purely pictorial difference, a difference in the forms and their arrangement, in the disposition of the lines and planes and masses. To any one in the least sensitive to the eloquence of pure form, the two Madonnas say utterly different things about the world.

Piero's composition is a welding together of smooth and beautifully balanced solidities. Everything in his universe is endowed with a kind of supernatural substantiality, is much more "there" than any object of the actual world could possibly be. And how sublimely rational, in the noblest, the most humane acceptation of the word, how orderedly philosophical is the landscape, are all the inhabitants of this world! It is the creation of a god who "ever plays the geometer."

What does she say, this Madonna from San Sepolcro? If I have not wholly mistranslated the eloquence of Piero's forms, she is telling us of the greatness of the human spirit, of its power to rise above circumstance and dominate fate. If you were to ask her, "How shall I be saved?" "By Reason," she would probably answer. And, anticipating Milton, "Not only, not mainly upon the Cross," she would say, "is Paradise regained, but in those deserts of utter solitude where man puts forth the strength of his reason to resist the Fiend." This particular mother of Christ is probably not a Christian.

Turn now to Tura's picture. It is fashioned out of a substance that is like the living embodiment of flame—flame-flesh, alive and sensitive and suffering. His surfaces writhe away from the eye, as though shrinking, as though in pain. The lines flow intricately with something of that disquieting and, you feel, magical calligraphy, which characterizes certain Tibetan paintings. Look closely; feel your way into the picture, into the painter's thoughts and intuitions and emotions. This man was naked and at the mercy of destiny. To be able to proclaim the spirit's stoical independence, you must be able to raise your head above the flux of things; this man was sunk in it, overwhelmed. He could introduce no order into his world; it remained for him a mysterious chaos, fantastically marbled with patches, now of purest heaven, now of the most excruciating hell. A beautiful and terrifying world, is this Madonna's verdict; a world like the incarnation, the material projection, of Ophelia's madness. There are no certainties in it but suffering and occasional happiness. And as for salvation, who knows the way of salvation? There may perhaps be miracles, and there is always hope.

The limits of criticism are very quickly reached. When he has said "in his own words" as much, or rather as little, as "own words" can say, the critic can only refer his readers to the original work of art: let them go and see for themselves. Those who overstep the limit are either rather stupid, vain people, who love their "own words" and imagine that they can say in them more than "own words" are able in the nature of things to express. Or else they are intelligent people who happen to be philosophers or literary artists and who find it convenient to make the criticism of other men's work a jumping-off place for their own creativity.

What is true of painting is equally true of music. Music "says" things about the world, but in specifically musical terms. Any attempt to reproduce these musical statements "in our own words" is necessarily doomed to failure. We cannot isolate the truth contained in a piece of music; for it is a beauty-truth and inseparable from its partner. The best we can do is to indicate in the most general terms the nature of the musical beauty-truth under consideration and to refer curious truth-seekers to the original. Thus, the introduction to the "Benedictus" in the *Missa Solemnis* is a statement about the blessedness that is at the heart of things. But this is about as far as "own words" will take us. If we were to start describing in our "own words" exactly what Beethoven felt about this blessedness, how he conceived it, what he thought its nature to be, we should very soon find ourselves writing lyrical nonsense in the style of the analytical program makers. Only music, and only Beethoven's music, and only this particular music of Beethoven, can tell us with any precision what Beethoven's conception of the blessedness at the heart of things actually was. If we want to know, we must listen—on a still June night, by preference, with the breathing of the invisible sea for background to the music and the scent of lime trees drifting through the darkness, like some exquisite soft harmony apprehended by another sense.

4

The Rest Is Silence[*]

From pure sensation to the intuition of beauty, from pleasure and pain to love and the mystical ecstasy and death—all the things that are fundamental, all the things that, to the human spirit, are most profoundly significant, can only be experienced, not expressed. The rest is always and everywhere silence.

After silence that which comes nearest to expressing the inexpressible is music. (And, significantly, silence is an integral part of all good music. Compared with Beethoven's or Mozart's, the ceaseless torrent of Wagner's music is very poor is silence. Perhaps that is one of the reasons why it seems so much less significant than theirs. It "says" less because it is always speaking.)

In a different mode, on another plane of being, music is the equivalent of some of man's most significant and most inexpressible experiences. By mysterious analogy it evokes in the mind of the listener, sometimes the phantom of these experiences, sometimes even the experiences themselves in their full force of life—it is a question of intensity; the phantom is dim, the reality, near and burning. Music may call up either; it is chance or providence which decides. The intermittences of the heart are subject to no known law. Another peculiarity of music is its capacity

[*] From *Music at Night,* 1931.

(shared to some extent by all the other arts) to evoke experiences as perfect wholes (perfect and whole, that is to say, in respect to each listener's capacity to have any given experience), however partial, however obscurely confused may have been the originals thus recalled. We are grateful to the artist, especially the musician, for "saying clearly what we have always felt, but never been able to express." Listening to expressive music, we have, not of course the artist's original experience (which is quite beyond us, for grapes do not grow on thistles), but the best experience in its kind of which our nature is capable —a better and completer experience than in fact we ever had before listening to the music.

Music's ability to express the inexpressible was recognized by the greatest of all verbal artists. The man who wrote *Othello* and *The Winter's Tale* was capable of uttering in words whatever words can possibly be made to signify. And yet (I am indebted here to a very interesting essay by Mr. Wilson Knight), and yet whenever something in the nature of a mystical emotion or intuition had to be communicated, Shakespeare regularly called upon music to help him to "put it across." My own infinitesimally small experience of theatrical production convinces me that, if he chose his music well, he need never have called upon it in vain.

In the last act of the play which was drawn from my novel, *Point Counter Point,* selections from the slow movement of the Beethoven A minor Quartet take their place as an integral part of the drama. Neither the play nor the music is mine; so that I am at liberty to say that the effect of the *"Heilige Dankgesang,"* when actually played during the performance, was to my mind, at least, prodigious.

"Had we but world enough and time . . . " But those are precisely the things that the theater cannot give us. From the abbreviated play it was necessary to omit almost all the implied or specified "counter" which, in the novel, tempered, or at least was intended to temper, the harshness of the "points." The play, as a whole, was curiously hard and brutal. Bursting suddenly into this world of almost unmitigated harshness, the *"Heilige Dankgesang"* seemed like the manifestation of something supernatural. It was as though a god had really and visibly descended, awful and yet reassuring, mysteriously wrapped in the peace that passes all understanding, divinely beautiful.

My novel might have been the Book of Job, and its adapter, Mr. Campbell Dixon, the author of *Macbeth;* but whatever our capacities, whatever pains we might have taken, we should have found it absolutely impossible to express by means of words or dramatic action what those three or four minutes of violin playing made somehow so luminously manifest to any sensitive listener.

When the inexpressible had to be expressed, Shakespeare laid down his pen and called for music. And if the music should also fail? Well, there was always silence to fall back on. For always, always and everywhere, the rest is silence.